ˈEDSA COLLEGE

ːHESTER

before the day marked
ɔw :-

THE AUTHOR

Ph.D. is Associate Professor of
ɾsity of Iceland and is currently a
University of Virginia School of
blished a number of research papers
ˈchology and is author of *At the Hour*
(Hastings House, New York) which
ɪrteen languages.

RIDER

KA 0070495 4

'MIRACLES ARE MY VISITING CARDS'

An Investigative Report on the Psychic Phenomena Associated with Sathya Sai Baba

Erlendur Haraldsson, Ph.D

CENTURY

LONDON   MELBOURNE   AUCKLAND   JOHANNESBURG

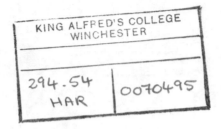

KING ALFRED'S COLLEGE
WINCHESTER

294.54
HAR
0070495

© Erlendur Haraldsson 1987

All rights reserved

A Rider Book published in the
Century Paperback Series in 1987 by Century Hutchinson Ltd,
Brookmount House, 62-65 Chandos Place, Covent Garden,
London WC2N 4NW

Century Hutchinson Australia Pty Ltd,
PO Box 496, 16-22 Church Street, Hawthorn, Victoria 3122,
Australia

Century Hutchinson New Zealand Ltd,
PO Box 40-086, Glenfield, Auckland 10,
New Zealand

Century Hutchinson South Africa Pty Ltd,
PO Box 337 Bergvlei, 2012 South Africa

Photoset in North Wales by
Derek Doyle & Associates, Mold, Clywd.
Printed and bound in Great Britain by
Richard Clay plc, Bungay, Suffolk

British Library Cataloguing in Publication Data

Haraldsson, Erlendur
    Miracles are my visiting cards : an
    investigative report on the psychic
    phenomena associated with Sathya Sai Baba.
    1. Sathya Sai Baba   2. Gurus—Biography
    I. Title
    294.5'61   BL1175.S385

ISBN 0-7126-1514-8

Contents

6　　　　　　　　　　　　　　*Contents*

Acknowledgements

First I would like to thank the many people in India, many of whom I now count among my friends, who allowed me to interview them concerning their experiences with Sai Baba. In addition I owe many thanks to the following people:

Dr Karlis Osis, with whom I made my first two visits to Sai Baba, for stimulating discussions and suggestions in the preparation of this book.

Dr Ian Stevenson and the staff of the Division of Parapsychology, University of Virginia, Charlottesville; Dr Stevenson for the use of office and library facilities while part of this book was written, Mrs Emily Williams Cook for precious editorial help, and Mr Carlos Alvarado for bibliographical assistance.

My colleagues in the Faculty of Social Science, University of Iceland, for twice supporting my request for leave to work on this project.

Dr Michael Thalbourne, Washington University, St Louis, who spent several months with me in India interviewing many witnesses.

Dr M. Narasimhachary, Department of Sanskrit, University of Madras, for translations of Telugu texts and other information.

For helping me in various ways, I would also like to thank Dr S. Roerich of Bangalore; M. Sherif of Nandi International Travels in Bangalore; Prof Vinoda Murthy, Department of Psychology, University of Bangalore; V. Srinivasan and N. S. Sethuramon of Madras; and D. K. Hirlekar, Honorary Consul for Iceland in Bombay.

E. H.

Announcement to Readers

The author would welcome correspondence from any reader who has relevant facts or observations concerning the contents of this book. Write to Dr Erlendur Haraldsson, Department of Psychology, University of Iceland, 101 Reykjavik, Iceland.

Foreword

'Miracles are my visiting cards' has merits of unique proportions. Although miraculous phenomena occurring in connection with religious leaders have been reported throughout history, Haraldsson's presentation is a first of its kind. The study is based upon the firsthand observation of a scientist and is supported by his careful interrogation of witnesses. It describes paranormal phenomena of extraordinary variety and strength attributed to one of the most remarkable men of the century.

India, the land of guru worship, abounds with holy men who are often called 'babas'. Sathya Sai Baba is a unique individual – a kind of genius towering over the whole landscape. He sees his mission as primarily devoted to the spiritual and moral renewal of India – extricating his country from its present confusions. Baba's powerful influence, however, touches the whole fabric of Indian life, be it social justice, political problems, or the educational system. The meek and the downtrodden, as well as the powerful and the mighty, flock around him in never-ending crowds streaming through his *ashram*. I was present when a person holding one of the highest elected offices in India, escorted by a three-star general, approached him. They both got down on the floor and touched Baba's feet with their bare foreheads.

Most Westerners visiting India's ashrams desire spiritual guidance and enlightenment, but Haraldsson was attracted by something else: the stories of Baba's paranormal phenomena describe powers of a magnitude, variety and sustained frequency not encountered anywhere else in the modern world. I have seen violent storms of controversy about them on the front pages of publications all over India. Indian journalists are as aggressive as their counterparts anywhere in the world, but no one has been able to find tricks behind his reported phenomena.

Is there some truth behind the said phenomena? This book is a record of ten years' work of a highly qualified European psychology professor trying hard to find reliable answers. It was not easy for him. Legends grow fast on the fertile soil of India, and observations are often couched in religious terms; for example ESP (extrasensory perception) becomes 'Baba's omniscience'. Sleight of hand and other arts of the magician are well developed in India, and some famous swamis don't mind resorting to them, as I have personally observed. Haraldsson is acutely aware of these 'other explanations'. Readers will see with what vigour he cuts through the jungle of storytelling and candidly reports the outcome of his quest.

Neither Haraldsson nor I were able to persuade Baba to participate in experiments. Nothing would have clinched the matter so well as, say, a week or two spent in the best parapsychological laboratories in the world, and that we offered. Nevertheless I could understand the reluctance of a religious leader of millions to submit to experimental protocol designed by people of different beliefs and cultures. After all no one asked the Pope to go to the laboratory, before his holiness could be trusted.

In the absence of laboratory evidence Haraldsson states his reservations. In the Western tradition of experimental sciences, nothing that has not withstood the controlled experiment is considered certain. Many social scientists, however, including myself, have later put more trust in observations of real-life events, which often reveal what the lab distorts. Haraldsson wisely presents all sides and asks intelligent readers to judge for themselves.

Millions of Baba's followers – East and West – call him an *avatar*, that is, an incarnation of a deity. This is by no means universally accepted in India, just as Jesus, who is also said to be an incarnation of God, is not universally accepted in the West. These matters of belief and theological reasoning are clearly not within the domain of parapsychology, and Haraldsson wisely avoids evaluation of the religious side of the issues. The paranormal is what Haraldsson is trying to document and understand; and even that – as the reader will see – is not easy. Although some of the phenomena go hand in hand with the Western concepts of telepathy, clairvoyance, foresight of future and mind over matter (psychokinesis), there are other phenomena for which we are not prepared.

Translocations of objects and liquid substances, which at times are said to have materialized, are not in the books of modern parapsychology. Some of Baba's out-of-the-body experiences seem to be similar to what we observe in our experiments, and to what many Western people report; others are much more substantial such as claims of the translocation or bilocation of his body – flesh and bones.

Conceptualizations in scientific parapsychology do not go that far. For something so mind-shattering and unique we need stronger evidence than is usually required. Haraldsson wisely reports what he has found so far and keeps the matter open for further research developments. It would have been cowardly simply to ignore what so many witnesses have said and what our own eyes have observed, just because it is so out of the ordinary. I hope the research will go on, impartially, wherever it leads. Some observations may be explained away, others may lead to a deeper understanding of the reality of the human mind, the real miracle behind miracles.

Most open-minded readers, I feel, will be stimulated by his kind of knocking at the very doors of the unknown. Even those whose minds are not receptive to these possibilities of the unexplored – be it paranormal or be it spiritual – will not go away empty-handed: they at least will find something exciting to scoff at.

So daring a book as *'Miracles are my visiting cards'* will mean many things to many people because it presents carefully collected data, rather than opinions, on one of the most remarkable men of our times. For some it will be an unforgettable treat for the heart, for others food for thought. I personally felt vibrant excitement when reading this book – so pregnant with untold potentialities.

Karlis Osis Ph.D.
Chester F. Carlson Research Fellow
American Society for Psychical Research
New York, NY, USA

Introduction

In the Western world, India has acquired a reputation as a country of mysteries and seemingly miraculous feats of yogis. These phenomena are generally associated with holy men or religious groups, of which a great diversity are found in India. During the last 100 years, some of these movements have become established in the West, and most of them have made claims that paranormal phenomena occurred among their leaders or founders (such as Paramahansa Yogananda's Self-Realization Fellowship, Vivekananda's Ramakrishna Order, to some extent the Theosophical Movement, and in recent times Maharishi Mahesh Yogi's TM Siddhi programme). This is probably one reason for India's reputation. Travellers' accounts may be another reason (Jacolliot 1884, Oman 1903, Brunton 1935).

In Western investigations of psychics the main purpose and difficulty has always been to separate genuine phenomena from exaggerations and fraudulent imitations, for example those performed with magicians' techniques. Great psychics in Europe, such as Daniel Dunglas Home (Crookes 1874), Indridi Indridason (Hannesson 1924), Eusapia Palladino (Carrington 1909; Feilding, Baggally and Carrington 1909), and Rudi Schneider (Schrenck-Notzing 1920; Gregory 1985), were extensively and carefully investigated by experienced researchers. A reasonable judgment can therefore be formed about them. But research on such claims from India has been scanty (Chari 1960, 1982).

During the last two or three decades, some investigations by reputable scientists have been conducted on yogis; however these have been exclusively physiological, dealing with the astonishing control of breath, heartbeat, blood flow or brain waves (Anand, Chhina, and Singh 1961; Wenger and Bagchi 1961; Kolhari, Bordia and Gupta 1973; Green and Green 1977). It remains true that in-depth extensive studies of

13

individual psychics in India are still missing. In fact, despite India's legendary reputation, very few attempts have been made to investigate the supposed abilities of individual psychics.

One of the reasons may be that the paranormal and the divine, miracles and religion, are closely interwoven in India. Seemingly paranormal phenomena are often considered a sign of a swami's or yogi's godliness. Because of the religious setting, investigations of a swami's alleged psychic feats border on the sacriligious for many Indians, and this greatly complicates research efforts. In addition, both such an attitude and the religious setting can serve as a cloak of protection for fraudulent individuals against 'doubting Thomases'.

We were therefore very aware of the difficulties involved in the investigation of claims of paranormal phenomena when we first heard about Sai Baba during a scientific project in India in 1972-73.

My colleague, Dr Osis, and I were frequently told that astounding miracles abounded around a certain Sri Sathya Sai Baba whom I later learnt to be the most colourful religious personality living in India today, noted for gathering crowds that only the late Indira Gandhi could match. Many of these alleged miracles, we were told, resembled those we read about in the New Testament, such as multiplication of food, 'changing of water into wine', wondrous healings, and the reading of a person's innermost thoughts at a first meeting.

Enthusiastic, highly educated Indians informed us that these were not just occasional occurrences, but rather were taking place several times every day year in and year out. Our dealings were mostly with physicians and high university officials. Some of them reported personal observations and how they had become fascinated with Sai Baba. I should add that they frequently became devoted to him after one short personal encounter. Myths – unchecked rumours – are a solid part of the swami-scene in India, that I was keenly aware of through my previous acquaintance with the country. But the rumours and personal stories about Sai Baba far exceeded in magnitude and frequency all that I had known before.

We were at that time working on a project in Northern India for the American Society for Psychical Research. Sai Baba was living in a remote village in Southern India. As our work in Northern India was coming to completion we decided to try to meet the alleged miracle-maker, though we were warned that his movements were unpredictable and the crowds around him were such that he might be very difficult to reach.

We had good luck. We met the swami, and the phenomena that we had been told about were apparently also there. Some we had a chance to observe, and a number of witnesses were ready to attest to others. However, these were informal observations, impressive – yes, but for us as scientists only controlled experiments and extensive observations would constitute satisfactory evidence. Alternative explanations had to be ruled out with reasonable certainty. Sleight of hand and trickery have been constant companions in the history of psychical research (or parapsychology, to use a more modern term).

On this short visit we had several long interviews with Sai Baba. We did not fail to notice the charisma that had fascinated so many, and we learnt that he was not only a reputed man of miracles and religious leader but also an activist very much aware of social issues.

The first visit led to another a year later. This time we were equipped for laboratory experiments. We had long discussions on the importance of science and research, but the swami's final words were that his powers were not for display. He continued to be generous in allowing us to observe him 'in action' and also gave us freedom and help in contacting people who had frequently observed his alleged miracles.

The anecdotal evidence was impressive and our observations had intrigued us, but could that justify further efforts to come to grips with Baba's phenomena and discern their true nature? After our second trip to Sai Baba in 1975 the American Society for Psychical Research withdrew its support. In due course, after much thought on the pros and cons, I decided to continue the investigation alone. I had some support for this from the University of Iceland, where I had recently begun to teach. With Baba's refusal to participate in experiments, the only way open was to embark upon extensive enquiries by interviewing a number of witnesses. These would be not only his followers and close associates, but also his critics and those who had left him for whatever reason.

I made six further journeys to India, the first in 1976 and the last in 1983, each lasting one to four months. In four of these eight journeys I was accompanied by fellow researchers, twice by Dr Osis, once for three months by Dr Michael Thalbourne of Washington University, St Louis, and once for a month by Dr Joop Houtkooper of the University of Amsterdam.

I interviewed dozens of people who had known Sai Baba and observed his feats, people who had known him in the various periods of his life, especially in his younger days when those around him used to stay with him practically day and night. I tried to corroborate evidence, I did my very best to trace critical rumours, in fact anything that I thought might throw some light on the nature of the perplexing phenomena that have made Sai Baba boldly affirm that 'miracles are my visiting cards'.

This book is the result. It is in two parts. In the first part I have described my encounters with Sai Baba and supplied the transcript of detailed interviews with followers, ex-devotees and critics. Among the interviewees are a succession of Baba's personal attendants from the late 1940s to the mid-1970s. They drew a highly revealing picture of his life and activities.

In nearly all cases I interviewed these people several times, usually with a year or more between each interview, which was tape recorded. I did this primarily to check the accuracy of the statements given to me, but also to come to know my interviewees better. In the final text practically every statement made by the interviewees has been checked and rechecked with them. I tried as well to find contemporary documents, diaries or letters to support the testimony.

I make little attempt in Part I to evaluate the various statements made in the interviews. That is done in Part II, where several of the major kinds of phenomena reported about Sai Baba are discussed at length.

The primary purpose of this book has been to report basic data and to supply the testimony of various witnesses.

Part One

1
We Are Intrigued

'If you want to see miracles, then go and visit Sai Baba.'

Dr Karlis Osis and I heard this on several occasions during a visit to India in 1972. Our dealings were mainly with professional people – doctors, hospital staff and university officials – most of whom spoke excellent English; and many of the older and middle-aged men had studied in either Great Britain or the United States. Their scientific background was as rejecting of the existence of psychic phenomena as it tends to be among Western scientists. The cultural background, however, was much more accepting of the possibility of *psi* (psychic abilities), and we often found ourselves in interesting conversations.

It is an age-old and accepted view in India that psychic powers can be acquired as a result of training, and also that they may be an inevitable product of following the path to spirituality and enlightenment taught by Hinduism. It is a traditional belief that Indian *yogis* (those who practise yoga) and *swamis* (religious teachers) may indeed possess such powers. Some people might even demand their occurrence as evidence of spirituality.

But was this, in fact, the case? Did any of those with whom we spoke know any swamis or yogis who were believed to perform miracles or to show any unusual capabilities of the mind beyond the endowment of the common man? Virtually none did, but a few had heard about such men. We came to know various names, such as Deoria Baba, Dadaji, Swami Rama, Aloyi Baba, Chandra Mohan, Mata Brahm Dyoti, Balyogi Premvarni, Angarika Munendra, and Sathya Sai Baba.

The name of Sathya Sai Baba came up repeatedly on such occasions and, eventually, more often than that of any other person. We would then hear fantastic stories about him that would often exceed anything we had read about in the history of psychical research in the more sober-minded West.

Our narrators related accounts of the experiences of friends, acquaintances or other people about which they had heard. They would tell of a miraculous healing, or an instance of prophecy or mind-reading, or the materialization of some small object that Sai Baba had then presented to someone. My amazement first concerned the storytellers themselves, but as we met more of them, and these extraordinary stories grew in number, the amazement began to spill over onto that man who was already becoming a legend in India, Sri Sathya Sai Baba.

In February 1973 we first met a person who had had a personal encounter with Sai Baba. This was the former chief medical officer of the state of Uttar Pradesh, which is the most populous state in India. He had met Sai Baba at a party given for the swami on one of his few visits to Delhi. The crowd was large, and the encounter with Baba was only brief. The doctor had recently retired from his post and he thought that his days of active employment were over. Casually, Sai Baba had remarked that the doctor would soon find himself busy in new and exciting work. Unemployment is a severe problem in India and it had never crossed the doctor's mind that he would ever take up another position of any kind. He did not believe that this prophecy would come true.

To the doctor's astonishment, he was soon afterwards asked by the Ministry of Education to become president of a new medical college to be built in the city of Meerut. He accepted. Unexpectedly, Baba's prophecy had come true within a few months. The doctor also told us that he had seen Baba produce out of his hand, as if they came from nowhere, small objects such as rings and pendants.

Later during this stay in India, in the congested, industrial city of Kanpur, we became acquainted with an active group of Sai devotees through a retired squadron leader in the air force, a Mr Kapur. He had met Sai Baba and had had several experiences which he related to us with great enthusiasm. I recall the details of one incident. The squadron leader had been driving in his car on an open road with nobody around when something suddenly appeared gently dangling on his windshield. It did not hit the windshield. He pulled over and stopped, and then the object slid down on the hood, as it had not been attached to the wiper. The piece was a *jappamala*, a necklace of small beads that some people carry as a sign of their religiousness, just as Christians might wear a cross.

Previously, Mr Kapur told us, he had insisted on receiving from Baba a particular type of jappamala, but Sai Baba had teased him by saying that he would give it to him, but then not doing so. As he took the jappamala in his hand, Mr Kapur realized that it was of the kind he had asked for. With evident pride and pleasure, he showed us his jappamala, which he treated as a great treasure.

Mr Kapur believed that Sai Baba had materialized the jappamala as a sign of his grace and blessing during a period of severe personal difficulties for the squadron leader.

The squadron leader also told us of a house in Kanpur where both *vibuti* (sacramental ash) and *amrith* (a honey-like substance) had mysteriously appeared on photos of Sai Baba. (Vibuti and amrith in Hinduism serve a purpose similar to holy water, the bread and the wine in Christianity.) They were, he said, still there. A family of devotees lived in the house. When we expressed a wish to visit the family, we were immediately taken there. We suggested that we should first telephone them or make an appointment, but that was rejected as unnecessary. 'All Sai devotees are one family', and off we went through the dirty and crowded roads of Kanpur until we stopped in front of a family house located in one of the suburbs. This was evidently a well-to-do family living in a house that was spacious by Indian standards.

We were received with great hospitality and taken to a special room, frequently found in Hindu homes, that was kept up for devotional ceremonies called *puja*. The puja room held a number of photos of Sai Baba on the walls which we were told we were welcome to look at and examine. The photos were of various sizes, some of them large, up to about two feet across. Some were covered with glass, others were not. Most, if not all, were glossy prints of Sai Baba – sitting, standing, stern or smiling, with his strong, round face and bushy Afro-style hair, and wearing his bright saffron-coloured robe. He certainly looked easily distinguishable from other men. That anyone could see.

Against one wall of the room was a rather fancy, decorated wooden armchair. This was a chair for the swami, always kept empty for him. Such a custom struck us as peculiar, but we later learned that it is common among devotees.

There were spots of that grey, dusty substance called vibuti on some of the photos. We were told that they had first appeared some time ago, but even if the photos were wiped clean the vibuti would soon start forming again. Small, narrow streams of a honey-like substance could also be seen on some of the photos, but they were not as clearly visible as the vibuti. There was no doubt, however, that some fluid had spilled onto the photos, and we were informed that it had a sweet taste. 'All Baba's grace', we were told.

For the devotees in Kanpur the phenomena were a sign of Sai Baba's presence, though members of this group and people I later came to know were usually quick to add that the physical phenomena were of no or only minor importance. Sai Baba's love and omnipresence and his message – these alone were important. They worshipped him as their Lord.

For various reasons, there arose no opportunity to examine these phenomena with the scrutiny that would be necessary to test their genuineness – nor in fact would we have expected a positive outcome. We left Kanpur without making any efforts at further examination.

Mr Kapur and his friends were eager to introduce us to some fellow devotees in Delhi. We were invited to a small party given by Mr Sohan Lal, a wealthy businessman who lived in a large apartment in one of the more fashionable suburbs of New Delhi. Not long before, Sai Baba had visited Delhi and stayed with the Sohan Lals. One of the guests at the party was Mr Nakul Sen, who had been the first Indian governor of Goa after the Portuguese colony had surrendered to the Indian army and Goa had become politically a part of India.

On one occasion, Sai Baba had visited Goa and stayed in the governor's palace for a few days. During that time, the governor told us, he witnessed a number of materializations. He showed us an extremely beautiful and precious-looking ring that Baba had presented to him. Both he and Sohan Lal were evidently convinced as a result of their personal encounters with Baba that he not only performed genuine miracles but also was a godly person, who at any time could know everything he wanted about anyone.

Evidently Baba found as ready an acceptance among some of the powerful and the rich as he did with many of the countless poor of India. He seemed to convince them, one after the other, of his genuineness and uniqueness.

No matter how Sai Baba managed to convince them, we thought, what an interesting man he would be to meet! If only a tiny fraction of the miraculous tales we were told were true, then a special trip to meet him would, in our view, be worth the expense.

Baba lived in the distant corner of the state of Andhra Pradesh in Southern India, north of Bangalore. When we arrived in that city we checked into what was then an old British-style hotel, the West End, located in a spacious lot with beautifully kept gardens. We soon learned that this was the place where many Westerners stayed before heading for a meeting with Sai Baba, who spends most of his time in Puttaparti, a small village some three hours' drive north of Bangalore. Only in recent years have roads been built for the last stretch to this village, which is situated in a sparsely populated area not far from the border between the states of Karnataka and Andhra Pradesh.

Fitted out with bedding and mosquito nets, some canned food, and other equipment for the trip, we left for Puttaparti the next morning, driving through dry but fertile flat land that gradually grew more rugged. The farther we went from Bangalore, the longer became the distances between the villages that we passed and the roads were unpaved as we came near our destination.

After almost four hours' drive, we were suddenly in Puttaparti, which lies in a valley between hills and mountains, near the banks of the Chitravati River. It was in this tiny, remote village, 'in the middle of nowhere', that Sai Baba was born in 1926, and where he still lives, making only occasional brief visits to other parts of India.

Sai Baba's ashram is only a few minutes' walk from the old village and has by now many more inhabitants than the village. Several three-storeyed concrete buildings, each containing a number of small apartments where devotees and visitors may stay, form a quadrangle around a huge assembly hall and a smaller hall of worship, called a *mandir*, where Sai Baba lives and receives visitors. It is a two-storeyed building with three beautiful domes on the roof. The mandir is the centre of the ashram, and twice a day hundreds of people assemble in front of it, sitting on the clean, soft sand. The men sit to the left of the building and the women to the right, in accordance with Indian custom. They wait and hope that Sai Baba may call them in for an interview. The place is meticulously clean and tidy, and devoted volunteer attendants and watchmen maintain a degree of order and discipline that is rarely seen in India.

We arrived in the late afternoon. Mr Kutum Rao, former High Court judge in Madras and now one of the Sai devotees led us to a one-room flat on the second floor of one of the three-storeyed buildings around the mandir. When we asked about an appointment with the swami, we were told that none were made. All we could do was to hand Sai Baba a letter when he walked his rounds in front of the mandir, which he did every morning and evening. Since there were a few hundred other people in the ashram waiting to meet the legendary swami, our chances did not look bright. Even so, we pushed our visiting cards and a short letter to Kutum Rao in the hope that he might show them to Sai Baba.

Our room was empty of furniture but had running water and a bathroom in an adjacent small room. We had brought with us from Bangalore thin mattresses and bedsheets. As we were preparing to go to bed, ruminating on our chances of a personal encounter with the swami we heard a knock on the door. It was Kutum Rao, bringing a message from the swami: 'He will see you around nine tomorrow morning'. 'Then' Mr Kutum Rao added, 'you shall move to a better apartment on the first floor'.

That sounded good. I still recall that I fell asleep in joyous anticipation of the coming day.

2
Face-To-Face With
The Miracle Worker

A crowd of people was already sitting in the open space in front of the mandir when we came out the next morning. Kept at a respectable distance from the mandir, the crowd formed a semicircle that Sai Baba would pass as he came out.

The volunteer attendants – of which there were several, all of whom could be recognized by saffron-coloured, boy-scout-like scarves around the neck – directed us to sit on a shaded veranda near the door to Sai Baba's interview room. A group of men sat on the spotless veranda. They looked as solemn and important as people in the waiting-room of a prime minister do.

A slight downward slope in front of the mandir permitted us to see over the crowd sitting there on the sand, which is meticulously swept twice a day. When Sai Baba appeared at the door, the crowd became dead silent. He was easily recognizable from the many photos we had seen of him. He wore a reddish-orange robe, had bushy hair reminiscent of the Afro-style, a rather dark complexion, a strong, thick neck and a round, forceful face. He was short but well-proportioned, and his hands and feet were small.

He said a few words to one or two men sitting on the veranda. His pace was slow and firm. One immediately got the impression of an exceptionally observant and powerful personality, a ruler. He generally starts his rounds on the men's side, picking up some letters that those in the front rows are eager to hand to him; he stops to have a few words with some of the men. Occasionally, with a wave of his right hand, he brings forth that greyish-white, fine-grained material called vibuti and gives it away to some of the men. They often rise to their knees to receive the vibuti, and they either swallow it, smear it on themselves or keep it.

Vibuti is the finest part of the ash that is left when cow-dung has been completely burnt. Its use is an ancient tradition in India. Even Marco Polo, who travelled in South India around 1300, describes it in his travelogue:

> They take cow-dung and burn it, and make a powder thereof; and make an ointment of it, and daub themselves withal, doing this with as great devotion as Christians do show in using Holy Water. (Polo 1929, p. 365)

Most of the few hundred people gathered were Indians, the men dressed according to tradition in white; but here and there one could spot a few Westerners. One of the watchmen-attendants followed Baba. When the swami had received a bundle of letters, he would give them to the watchman to hold, and after he had produced vibuti he would sometimes wipe his hand clean using a piece of cloth that served as a handkerchief and was carried by the attendant. The attendant also served as a bodyguard in case someone tried to snatch at Baba's clothes. Many Indians seemed eager to touch his feet, and some would bow their heads at the footprints he had left in the sand.

In India it is still the custom to kneel at the feet of a religious teacher and kiss them. In the West this habit has disappeared, though it still lives on in a ceremonial form around the Pope on certain occasions. For traditional Indians, this is an accepted way of showing respect and devotion, but mixed with it is the belief that a person may receive a special blessing or power by touching a holy man's feet. This belief, I later observed, would occasionally cause a minor problem for Baba, as some Indians were too eager to get at his feet – something that he obviously found a nuisance at times. It seemed wise to have attendants near.

He went over to the women's side and likewise spent ten to fifteen minutes with them. As he passed the rows, he would invite a few people for an interview, either verbally or by a gesture indicating that they should walk up to the veranda, where they were to wait until he called them in later. In this way, he would select some 20 to 40 people every morning and late afternoon and then receive them, in small groups, in the interview-room after he had finished his rounds.

The swami walked back up to the veranda, showed a few men sitting there into the house, and disappeared with them. After a while they came out, and he invited us into his interview room. He asked those around whether there was someone who could act as an interpreter. After some exchange of words among the men on the veranda, an elderly gentlemen, evidently a Northern Indian, rose from the veranda and came in with us. His name was Mr Khera, former Director of Prisons in Bengal, and originally from that part of Punjab now in Pakistan.

Sai Baba speaks some English and usually, I later learned, does not need to have an interpreter when meeting English-speaking people. As he greeted us, he immediately produced, with a wave of his hand, some vibuti, which he divided between us. After exchanging greetings, we all sat cross-legged on the bare stone floor. The room contained no furniture except for a wooden armchair in a corner. There were no carpets on the floor nor any decorations on the walls, except for a clock and a calendar. The room was relatively small. One door led to an inner room and another to a narrow staircase leading to Sai Baba's apartment on the upper floor. Instead of wooden doors, these openings were covered by a thin curtain on a string.

We told him we were researchers of psychic phenomena and had heard many accounts of miracles occurring in his presence. As we were talking, he again made with his right hand the typical small, circular movements that last for two or three seconds, and lo! – there was a large, shiny golden ring in his palm. He put it on Dr Osis' ring finger and said it was for him. It fitted. Set into the ring was a large coloured picture of Sai Baba on a stone (or some similar material) that was firmly encased by the ring. The picture was oval in shape and portrayed a good likeness of his face.

We expressed our admiration but told him we were primarily interested in a scientific investigation, which meant that we had to have some control over the situation. We wanted to have him participate in controlled experiments. We were, needless to say, well aware of what trained magicians may do by sleight of hand; hence, controlled experiments were essential. We were particularly interested in out-of-the-body experiments, and we had been told stories about his appearing to people at places distant from where he was reported to be physically.

There followed a long discussion concerning the value of science. He did not belittle science, but his point seemed to be that methods of science could never explain the miraculous phenomena – they were outside science. That, we tried to argue, was only because scientists had neglected to investigate them. He, with his extraordinary abilities, might provide new knowledge about these mysterious phenomena if some of the wonderful stories we had heard were true.

Thus we argued back and forth. He would say that he was not a showman and that he could use his paranormal powers only for the good of his devotees. Again and again his conversation would drift back to his favourite subject, spiritual and ethical issues. On one such occasion, he said that daily life and spiritual life should be 'grown together like a *double rudraksha*.' I did not even know what a rudraksha was, let alone a double rudraksha, so I asked him. He could not make this clear to me, nor could Mr Khera, whose assistance as an interpreter the swami used sparingly. He evidently understood us well enough, and his slightly broken English turned out to be sufficient for most purposes.

I was not satisfied, so I asked them again and again about the meaning of a double rudraksha. Perhaps my insistence was a bit of a tease – this thought occurred to me later – since I felt that we were not getting the cooperation from him that we wanted. Be my motives as they may, the fact was that my stubbornness and their inability to make their meaning clear, in spite of their efforts, was becoming embarrassing. Dr Osis was getting uncomfortable with my insistence on knowing the meaning of a rudraksha. Then suddenly, with a sign of impatience, Sai Baba closed his fist and waved his hand for a second or two. As he opened it, he turned to me and said: 'This is it'. In his palm was an acorn-like object about three centimetres at its widest point, brownish, and with a fine texture like an apricot stone. This was two rudrakshas grown together like a twin orange or a twin apple. His act seemed spontaneous, coming out of an embarrassing situation that did not look planned.

He gave it to us to touch and look at. It had the particular freshness and cleanness that I later observed to be characteristic of the objects he produces. Each of us took it in his hand and looked at it carefully and admired it. When it had gone around, he took it back, turned to me, and said: 'I want to give you a present'. He enclosed the rudraksha in both his hands, blew on it, and opened his hands towards me. In his palm we saw a beautiful piece. The double rudraksha was now covered, on the top and on the bottom, by two tiny, oval-shaped, golden shields that were held together around the rudraksha by a short golden chain at each side. On the top of the upper shield was a golden cross with a small ruby affixed to it, and behind it a tiny opening, so that it could hang on a chain and be worn around the neck.

Magicians cannot produce objects by sleight of hand without prior preparation. Could Baba have planned to give me the double rudraksha anyway and have staged the incident, having with him two double rudrakshas, with and without the golden shields? However, the incident seemed unprepared to both of us, arising out of an argument. We could not be sure either way. Later I learned from expert botanists that a double rudraksha is a rare anomaly in nature.[1] A goldsmith in London found the purity of the gold encasing the rudraksha to be at least 22 carats.

We asked him how he was able to produce such beautiful and precious things, apparently out of nothing. Why could he do it and not we? 'We are all like matches' he said, 'but the difference between you and me is that there is fire on mine'. He loved to speak in metaphors. Some of them were quite memorable, but were they true? How could we judge? It was dawning on us that the discourse of Sai Baba was in the realm of religion, not empirical science.

Our sympathetic swami was not a man of science. On the scientific and cultural level, there was a wide gap between us, and I soon wondered if it could ever be bridged. But on the personal level, this was not the case. It was easy to like him. There was an attractive and admirable freshness and spontaneity about him. When speaking about religion or philosophy, he did not do so with scholarly refinement; rather, his statements were short and direct and sometimes sounded like platitudes, though that impression may have been caused by his somewhat broken English.

He always spoke with the certainty of one who knows, not as one who has learned it from someone else. It also seemed to me that he was a man who would rule over the situation, wherever he might be. One did not have to be with him long to notice his charisma. He had a way of fascinating people. The ostensible miracles were undoubtedly a part of it, but that was not the whole story.

We had some hearty laughs with him. He was never sentimental and was sometimes jovial. Though we had not really gained anything except for some first-hand observations of his reputed materializations, we were in a refreshed and good mood when he showed us to the door at the end of the long interview. He told us that we would meet again next morning. Mr Khera, he said, would be our guide and interpreter, and he would take us to devotees we wanted to meet who had a number of psychical experiences concerning the swami.

The production of objects, such as the ring and the rudraksha, is common with Sai Baba. I noticed this in later interviews and also heard it from almost every person I have talked to who has had a personal encounter with the swami. Apparently these incidents occur many times every day. When I have described more observations of alleged materializations, I will discuss at length various explanatory hypotheses, pro and contra their genuineness.

The name of Sai Baba's ashram is Prashanti Nilayam, meaning Abode of Great Peace. It was in many ways different from other ashrams I had visited. The number of persons around was much greater, and probably around 95% were Indians. Most of the ashrams in Northern India I had visited so far had relatively few inhabitants. Usually most of them were Westerners – young Americans and Europeans who seemed to have lost faith in Western ways of living and thinking. Young Indians were seldom seen in these ashrams. They were not interested, we were told (sometimes not without some bitterness), by the gurus who complained about corruption and lack of morals in India. They were more interested in the good life, in Western ways or in science. Their dissatisfaction with their ancient culture was perhaps even deeper than the dissatisfaction felt by young Westerners with their occidental culture.

Most of the ashrams emphasized programmes of long meditation or hatha yoga, which required the greater part of the day. Members of these ashrams would stay for a long period, leaving their worldly duties and connections. In Prashanti Nilayam, the emphasis was on the singing of *bhajans* (ancient religious songs) for half an hour, morning and evening, and for the vigorous there was short, silent, early morning meditation at 4.30 in the hall of the mandir. Baba stressed purity of daily life, devotion and short meditation, and he urged devotees not only to fulfil their duties to family and community but also to serve enthusiastically through social and welfare work. Hence, people would come only for a while, and the residents were mostly retired people.

Many came for what the Indians termed *darshan*. This is the belief that a special blessing is conferred upon one simply by seeing a man who is considered holy. The two occasions every day when Baba came out of his mandir for all to see him were called darshans. These were the most important events of the day, and everyone attended.

The devotees seemed to come from all over India, though most were from the south. They had been drawn to the swami in various ways and for various reasons. Nearly all claimed some kind of paranormal experience concerning Baba. Practically all who had met Baba believed they had observed materializations, and most had a locket or a ring of some kind that they were proud to show us. Each treasure had reportedly appeared out of the swami's bare hand, and he had made a present of it to them. These objects were varied and made of a range of materials, including gold and precious stones, some of the pieces being jewellery of exquisite quality.

Many came with hopes of solving some personal or family problems, or of being healed of some ailment, and some were there as a result of some odd events in their lives which they explained as a mysterious intervention by the swami. Such was the case of an elderly wealthy gentleman, Mr D. D. Gupta, from the North Indian city of Meerut.

Two years prior to my meeting Mr Gupta, he had been suffering from lung cancer. He had been bedridden for three to four months, his cancer was in an advanced state and his weight was down to 38 kilograms. At the time of the event, he was suffering badly and was to be taken to a hospital in Kanpur the following morning. He did not expect to live much longer. Because of his poor condition his brother, B. D. Gupta, slept in the same room. After the lights had been switched off, he had difficulty falling asleep because of his discomfort. Then he suddenly heard a strange voice that seemed to whisper in English into his ear: 'Do not go for operation. Meet Radhey Shiam.'

He had never before had an hallucination of any kind, and he was baffled. He called his brother and told him about the incident. Mr Gupta was eager to do something, yet to

telephone Radhey Shiam was not an easy matter. It is a
common name, and even in Meerut there were three of them
listed in the telephone directory. It would be embarrassing to
call strangers and have to tell them about an hallucinated
voice. But his life would be over soon anyway, and he decided
to try the next morning as it was then about midnight. The
next morning they called the first Radhey Shiam listed in the
directory and told the man who answered what had taken
place. Radhey Shiam said that he knew nothing about the
incident but told Mr Gupta that he was a devotee of Sai Baba.
In fact, he was an important member of the Sai Baba group in
Meerut. He and another devotee came over immediately and
gave him vibuti. Already on hearing the voice, Mr Gupta had
started to feel better. Now his appetite came back, and the
same day he felt strong enough to attend bhajans at Radhey
Shiam's home. After one week he was almost back to normal.
He regained his health and was soon able to go about his daily
business.

Through Radhey Shiam and his small group of Sai devotees,
Mr Gupta learned more about Sai Baba, and some months
later he decided to visit the swami in Puttaparti. According to
Mr Gupta, the first words Sai Baba said to him were: 'I have
talked to you before.'

Mr Gupta was a wealthy man, and he was so impressed with
the unexpected miraculous healing of his deadly disease that
he donated to the Sathya Sai Educational Trust a large piece of
land near Meerut for a college that is to be built in the name of
Sai Baba.

When Mr Gupta told us his story in November 1973, two
years had passed since the incident, and the cancer had long
since disappeared. He believed that Sai Baba saved his life.

So far we have been able to verify the accuracy of Mr Gupta's
account only with his brother Mr B. D. Gupta. A colleague, Dr
Michael Thalbourne, visited Meerut for me in November 1981
and met Mr Gupta's brother, but during his one-day stay he
was unable to meet Mr Gupta's doctors, Dr Rashan Lal, now
Principal of Meerut Medical College, or Dr Pathak, who had
diagnosed Mr Gupta. One of the doctors was out of town and
the other could not be reached either at his home or office. Mr
D. D. Gupta appeared in good health. We did confirm with
people in Puttaparti that Mr Gupta had given a piece of land to
the Sathya Sai Educational Trust.[2]

That was the story of Mr Gupta. There were several people who shared with us various kinds of experiences that were no less impressive, if authentic and genuine.

Mr N. Kasturi, a former college professor and writer, had been close to the swami since the 1950s. He has written a eulogistic biography of Sai Baba that has run to four volumes (Kasturi 1971, 1972, 1973, 1980), and he has also edited ten volumes of Sai Baba's speeches and aphorisms.

We were warmly received by Prof. Kasturi, who seemed to have a better understanding of our need for verifiable cases. He told us a number of extraordinary incidents, some of which will be reported later in this book. Among these was a case occurring in Manjeri, a small town in the state of Kerala on the west coast of India, where one morning Sai Baba apparently knocked on the door of a small house and walked in. The Mohan Rao family who lived there were devotees of a deceased saint by the name of Sai Baba of Shirdi. They had never seen Sai Baba of Puttaparti in person but had only seen photos of him and heard him sing on the radio. The swami invited them to call in some neighbours, and he held a puja in their house, sang, accepted some refreshments, advised them on some difficult family problems, and as he typically does, gave them a few gifts before he went out of the door and disappeared.

The family later learned that Sai Baba had not in fact been in Kerala. He had actually been visiting the Venkatagiri District near the east coast of Southern India, which is some 350 miles northeast of Manjeri. There, as always, he had had a busy schedule, had been constantly surrounded by people, and had been living in the palace of the Raja of Venkatagiri.

The Manjeri case seemed worthy of a thorough investigation, since there were several witnesses and the date of the incident was reasonably well established. A detailed account of it is given in Chapter 28.

We had two further interviews with Sai Baba and continued to insist on experiments. He promised to give us a day for experiments in Bangalore, where he would be going in a few days. These would take place in the presence of Dr S. Bhagavantam, a distinguished Indian nuclear scientist and former head of the prestigious Indian Institute of Science in Bangalore. He had been a close associate of Sai Baba for a number of years. Sai Baba told us that Dr Bhagavantam would return from a trip abroad in a few days.

In the two further interviews in Puttaparti, Sai Baba gave us good doses of his teaching and philosophy though we constantly tried to bring the conversation back to our realm of interest. We observed him bring forth some objects on each of these occasions, among them a handful of a delicious, traditional Indian sweet. The means by which he produced these was as baffling as before.

Once we asked him if he would be coming to America. We thought he might perhaps be lured into some laboratory if he came. The answer was brisk: 'When I have cleaned up India'. Certainly not a small task he had set himself! As we left that interview, he waved his right hand once more. We saw two visiting cards in his hand. He gave one to each of us. They had a photo of him on the left side and his name and address on the right side. They looked fresh and clean as if they had come directly from the printer.

After a few days in Puttaparti we went to Bangalore as we were running out of time. Dr Bhagavantam did not return from his trip on the date Sai Baba had indicated. We managed to send a message to the swami through a close devotee and were told that our experimental session had to be cancelled as Dr Bhagavantam would not be returning in time for us. That was a real disappointment. We could understand that Sai Baba wanted to have an Indian scientist present. But was this a real excuse or a polite Indian way of saying no?

Notes

[1] Single rudrakshas can be bought in every marketplace, but a double rudraksha, I have been told by several Indian botanists, is a rare anomaly in nature, so rare, in fact, that none of them had ever seen a specimen, though they had heard that such pieces exist. Rudrakshas are of considerable religious significance in India, since Lord Shiva, one of the principal deities of Hinduism, is always pictured with a chain of rudrakshas around his neck.

In 1980 a Dutch physicist, Dr Joop Houtkooper, and I visited the Botanical Survey of India, near Calcutta, where there is a special division for plants that are of folkloristic or religious significance. We met its director, Dr Sathyanarayan Rao who called in the head of the special division in which is kept the largest collection in India of various species of rudrakshas. These two men were top experts on rudrakshas (the botanical name is *elaecarpus ganitrus*) and they had built up an excellent collection of them. Still, they had neither seen nor been able to acquire a double rudraksha for the Botanical Survey of India. They considered our piece a genuine rudraksha.

In 1983, after many further enquiries among botanists in India, I finally met a botanist who had seen double rudrakshas on sale in a shop in Madras. There they were: in Khadi Granodygog Bhavan on Mount Road; available for 272 rupees, for the average Indian buyer probably equivalent to 272 dollars. According to the shopkeeper a swami had collected them in Nepal and sold several pieces to this shop. They were small and malformed, some of them barely touching one another. Compared to my beautiful one they were ugly and poor examples, perhaps forced to grow together. Were the expert botanists wrong about the rarity of double rudrakshas?

[2] Education of the young has long been a great concern of Sai Baba's. By 1973 he had already founded three colleges, which were run under his supervision. As of 1986, the Sathya Sai Educational Trust runs five colleges in various parts of India and a university in Puttaparti headed by Dr V. K. Gokak, former Vice-Chancellor of Bangalore University.

3
'Look At Your Ring'

We found it difficult to get across to our colleagues in the West the impressions we took home with us from India. The reports about Sai Baba were too extraordinary for even our colleagues in parapsychology to consider seriously. The board of the American Society for Psychical Research, where Dr Osis was director of research, rejected a proposal for further research, but after some difficulty Dr Osis and I were able to return to India under joint sponsorship of the ASPR and the University of Iceland.

This would be our second attempt to engage Sai Baba in experiments. But we questioned his willingness to participate in any project requiring the tight experimental controls that we would find necessary. This was our dilemma.

Kutum Rao had evidently noticed the attention that Baba had given to us during our last visit to Puttaparti for we were given the best available accommodation, a two-room flat equipped even with beds. When Baba saw us at bhajan time late that afternoon in a hall full of people, he gave us a warm smile and a handshake, which with him is a sign of special attention.

The following morning Baba showed the two of us unaccompanied into his interview room. By a wave of hand he immediately brought forth a sizable piece of white rock candy. He then broke it into two and handed a portion to each of us. It looked spotlessly fresh and clean. We both broke off a piece and ate it, but kept the rest. When we asked: 'How do you do this?' his answer was: 'Mental creation. I think, imagine, and then it is there.' Then he was off into his philosophy: 'Spiritual love is central, miracles are small items. Love is giving and forgiving.'

The interview was short. He would be going to Bangalore in

a day or two, where Dr Bhagavantam was expected in a day or two. There all four of us could have plenty of time together.

When Sai Baba left the mandir for Bangalore the following morning just after sunrise, the devotees gave him a warm regal farewell. As a traditional Indian sign of good luck, a Brahmin *pujari*[1] broke a coconut on Baba's white Mercedes as Baba was driven off towards Brindavan, his estate in Whitefield some 15 miles southeast of Bangalore. Since the legendary Krishna had lived in a place called Brindavan, Baba had probably chosen this name for his ashram in Whitefield. In Brindavan, Baba's second residence, he runs a boys' college, and he also receives visitors and gives interviews, but to a much lesser degree than in Puttaparti. The beautiful Mercedes was given to Baba by a wealthy Bombay family of industrialists, the Kamanis. One member of that family was reported to have been miraculously healed of a serious disease by the swami. The same family (one of the richest in India, we have been told) had erected the enormous Poonachandra lecture hall in the middle of Baba's ashram. There Baba gives his darshan and lectures, and invited speakers, musicians and theatre groups give their performances during festival times, such as Dasara, Sivaratri and Baba's birthday, when thousands of visitors flock to Puttaparti. It is often estimated that more than 100,000 people are present at Prashanti Nilayam for some of these festivals.

When Baba leaves Puttaparti, almost everyone leaves and so did we. That same afternoon we took a taxi to Whitefield from our hotel in Bangalore, hoping for a word on our next meeting with the swami. We arrived just in time for the afternoon darshan. We took a seat on the ground in a long line of people. After a while Baba appeared and walked past the line. As he passed us, he clapped me on the shoulder and muttered 'Good boys', and then was off to the men on our left, Dr D. K. Banerjee of the Indian Institute of Science, with whom we were already acquainted, and his friend Mr G. D. Hazra, a pharmaceutical chemist. He stopped in front of Mr Hazra and waved his hand with that quick circular movement that always indicates that something will appear in his hand. Since we were sitting on the ground and he was standing, his hand was slightly above the level of our eyes.

His palm was open and turned downwards, and his fingers were stretched out as he waved his hand in a few quick, small circles. As he did this, we observed a grey substance appearing close to his palm. This substance appeared in the air just below his palm, and Sai Baba seemed to grasp it into his fist with a quick downward movement of his hand, as if to prevent it from falling to the ground. Dr Osis, who sat slightly closer to Sai Baba than I did, observed that this material first appeared entirely in the form of granules, like rough-grained sand. Sai Baba then poured the granules into the palms of Mr Hazra and Dr Banerjee, where most of them disintegrated into amorphous ash, which they then smeared on their foreheads. The granules seemed to be fragile to the touch and might have disintegrated earlier if Baba had produced them by a sleight of hand that was undetectable by us. I have observed such incidents numerous times but only rarely at so short a distance and from such a favourable angle.to

Not until two days later did Baba address us again, to tell us that Dr Bhagavantam would be in Bangalore the next afternoon. In the meantime we had visited several people in Bangalore who had been drawn into the swami's fold.

All of the people we interviewed described observations and experiences of ostensible paranormal phenomena that concerned Sathya Sai Baba. But the most wonderful thing, they usually hastened to say, was Baba's beneficial effect on their lives and way of living, often causing a dramatic change. Most of these people, often several members of the same family, carried some object, such as a talisman, ring, necklace, pendant, or a small statuette, that the swami had presented to them. Of the apparently paranormal phenomena the materializations were most often reported. They happened many times each day, frequently arising spontaneously out of a particular situation. One could probably fill a book with such descriptions. Most of these incidents provide little or no weight as evidence or proof of the reality or paranormality of these phenomena. But something important would be missing in a description of the Sai phenomena if some of them were not presented to the reader.

Dr V. K. Gokak, former vice chancellor of Bangalore University, described one incident to us. It took place in April 1971 at the Krishna temple in Dwarka on the west coast of Gujarat. Sai Baba was there to inaugurate a gate to another temple there. Dr Gokak:

It is not necessary for him to wave his hand. Do you know how.

the Krishna figure came ...? After the inauguration some of us went to see the Krishna temple, but thousands of people were inside the temple area wanting to see Bhagavan (that is, Sai Baba), as the word had spread that he would be coming to the temple. As we entered the temple it was impossible to walk because of the crowd. So we could not even go to the shrine and came back without seeing the famous Krishna statue that is kept in the temple. After lunch and rest we drove back in six cars towards Jamnagar, some 20 miles out of Dwarka, where we were put up.

As we drove near the coast, Swami stopped the cars and we went down to the seashore. We sat down in a crescent on the fresh sandy beach only a few yards from the sea with Sai Baba sitting in the middle. Many of us had come to this area from afar, and we were disappointed because we had not been able to see the Krishna in the temple. 'Never mind' Swami said, 'I will show it to you.' Then he drew with his hand a figure on the sand in front of him, a very sketchy figure of a man. And then he put his hand into the sand and kept it there for a minute and a half or two. 'Aha, it is ready now,' he said in English, as this was a multilingual group. Then he pulled out of the sand this huge statue of Krishna.

It was so heavy that he had to lift it with both hands. It was a golden statue. You can see it with the Rajamata (former queen) of Nawanagar in Bombay. The statue was passed around, and we all had to hold it with both hands. Finally he handed the statue to the Rajamata of Nawanagar for worship as we were her guests.

Then I asked him: 'How does this happen? You sort of draw a figure on the sand, but it is a most beautiful figure that you get, Krishna playing on the flute, standing cross-legged, all the folds of his garment one can see coming out beautifully, and what a fine expression on his face and such marvellous workmanship?' I put the question to him. He said there is nothing in his hand. 'Everything happens here' he said and pointed to his head.

The statue was of the traditional kind, and he told us that if he showed us how Krishna had really looked we would not recognize him at all. 'I said to myself,' Baba said, 'let that image of Krishna which is traditionally present in the minds of all these people appear in the form of a golden statue.' That was his command and then the statue is there. The thing is done. Sai Baba's word is that it was created, materialized there in the sand. When objects are teleported by him, he says they are teleported.

Dr Gokak gave me the names of several people who had been present on this occasion, among them the Rajamata of Nawanagar, her sister-in-law, her daughter, Mr and Mrs Ratan

Lal, Prof. Kasturi, Mr Raja Reddy, and Mrs Gokak. I have since interviewed two, the Rajamata of Nawanagar and Prof. Kasturi, and in essence their descriptions were the same as Dr Gokak's. Prof. Kasturi told me that Baba always likes the sea and likes to walk on the seashore and play with the waves: 'He jumps and escapes the waves and makes others also do it.... He is then just like a rollicking kind of a happy, young man.'

Prof. Kasturi continued:

> Then we sat on the sand, and, of course you know, whenever we sit on the sand Baba is usually creating out of the sand. He will make people pile up sand in front of him, so that you won't be of the impression that he has put something in. When the heap has come about a foot high, he will level the top with his hand and make a drawing or sign on the sand. By looking at the design you may be able to find out what he is creating. Then just after finishing the design he will immediately say: 'Oh, it is ready already' and put his hand into the heap of sand and take out the thing he has created, more or less according to the sign he has drawn on the levelled top of the sand.

The statue, about 18 inches high, was made of gold, beautiful, fresh and finely polished. Mr Ratan Lal took a photograph that day of Baba sitting on the beach and holding the statue. The police learned about this incident and said the statue was a treasure-trove because it had been taken from inside the soil. According to Indian law such finds must be given to the authorities. The Rajamata managed to solve that problem and convince the police that the statue had been created. The Rajamata of Nawanagar told me at her Bombay residence in February 1975, that she remembered the incident particularly well and the statue was in her shrine room in Jamnagar.

At last Dr Bhagavantam arrived in Bangalore, a week later than Baba had originally expected him. We went to the residence of Dr Bhagavantam's son, a new two-storey house in one of the suburbs of Bangalore. We waited for a while, sitting on the floor in a group of 16 men and women. Baba arrived, sat on an armchair and started to give a general talk about scientists, which Dr Bhagavantam translated. The theme was the difference between the spiritual approach (that is, Baba's) and the scientific approach. We felt that it was aimed at us. In his

view science is concerned with the physical realities, whereas
the spiritual approach deals with the higher reaches of the
mind. Control of mind is essential in the spiritual approach,
since mind can potentially create anything. He was quite hard
on scientists. According to him, they tend to lose common
sense and are materialistic. He complained that there is too
much freedom and laxness in education, with the result that
students pass through college 70% wrong and just 30% right;
consequently they go 200% wrong when later in life they have
to shoulder responsibilities. Here, he said, the spiritual
approach could provide some controls. The mind must be
cultivated to be pure and uncluttered with everyday needs. The
scientific and spiritual approaches are basically different. The
spiritual is learned through personal experience and discipline,
not, as science is, through information or knowledge about
physical phenomena. He went on for ten or fifteen minutes. I
had the impression that he was implying that we were not quite
in the right camp, not the 'good boys' he had called us earlier.

Afterwards we were called into a small room. Again he gave
us a short talk on his philosophy. Then he allowed us to ask
some questions and to talk about our research. He would give
us opportunities to observe him as he worked, but he would
not participate in experiments. When Dr Osis told him about
our project on out-of-the-body experiences, he stated that he
often had such experiences but would not demonstrate them
for us.

As he frequently does, he illustrated his point by an allegory.
He explained that a prime minister has great powers. Under
some circumstances he can order the arrest of people, but he
cannot do that just to demonstrate his power. It is the same
with him. He cannot use his power for demonstrations. 'Divine
powers can only be used for the good and protection of
devotees.'

We tried to convey to him the need to advance knowledge of
the phenomena that he produces. He then said that only
purification and sublimation of the mind can give true
knowledge that will help mankind. He told us a little story.
When fire (the spiritual force) burns wood (the unpurified
mind), the wood becomes charcoal, and as it burns further it
becomes white and light as ash. So the mind, through spiritual
wisdom, becomes white and light, and then it can create
anything. When he produces things, Baba explained, he does

not have to think about the chemical composition. If he
produces a sweet, he does not think about what is in it; he
simply gets it.

He rose from his chair, indicating that the interview was
over. Although he was expecting other visitors, he did not let
us leave the room. We were taken by surprise when we learned
that the visitor was no other than the Vice President of India,
with an entourage of eight or ten people that included a
three-star general, a chief minister or governor, some ladies
and bodyguards. They were immediately shown into the small
room. One or two of the men looked slightly askance at the
presence of two foreigners, but they accepted us. Baba was
standing while talking to them. He was evidently the boss of
the situation. The Vice President and the general prostrated
and touched his feet, and then the rest of them did so and
seemed to enjoy it.

We did not understand what they said since they spoke in
Hindi. Apparently they were asking something of him. He
treated them warmly and gave animated answers. He produced
vibuti with the usual wave of his right hand and gave it
generously, starting with the ladies. When he had given it all
away, one of the party who accidentally had not received any
vibuti asked for some. Baba produced more in his quick and
effortless way.

The interview lasted for only about five minutes. It was
a cordial meeting, and everyone seemed in a happy mood as
they left. 'All is one' Sai Baba said when we were left with him
alone.

He took me aside for a little while and wanted to talk about
my private life, as I understand he often does with his visitors.
His statements dealt with my marital history but revealed no
specific details that impressed me as particularly good evidence
of mind-reading or clairvoyance. What he said, however, was
correct. He said that I had been married more than once, but
this is true for many Westerners. I tried not to give him any
clues about my personal life. His statements were interesting
and correct but not compellingly impressive, since they would
probably apply equally well to many Western men around
forty. He further said that my wife had been unhappy about
my going away on this trip to India and that we had had an
argument about it. That was also true, but I wondered how
many men who go to a far-off, underdeveloped country for

several weeks would not have had an argument with their good wives about such a trip. It was, however, interesting that both the points that he raised were correct.

He was quite cordial with us. He repeated that he would allow us to observe him in action, that is, when he was meeting people. He seemed more willing to cooperate in this way with us than he had been previously. Finally he invited us to join him in his car on a trip from Whitefield to Puttaparti two days later, on January 29, leaving at 9.00 a.m. In some ways we were pleased with this interview. We had been given promising assurances, and he had been quite cordial with us. But we had still not obtained what we most wanted – experiments. We looked forward to accompanying him in his car, since this meant that we could spend several hours with him.

Our friends among the devotees were both happy and impressed when we told them of our meeting with Baba. They suggested, though, that we take our own taxi with us to Puttaparti in case he might invite someone else to sit in his car for a part of the way. Dr. Bhagavantam advised us not to pester Baba further with requests for experiments, since that might spoil our relationship with him.

On 29 January at 8.30 in the morning, we arrived in a taxi at Whitefield and drove into Brindavan. We had arrived half an hour before Baba had told us to go to join him on his tour to Puttaparti, but the place looked deserted. We were told that the swami had left at 8:00 a.m. That came as a blow to our pleasant expectations. In India we were used to a lack of strict punctuality even among medical personnel. But this was quite different and something we had not expected from a self-proclaimed apostle of truth. It resembled the treatment he is said to give his disciples when he wants to teach them a lesson, 'to test their faith and detachment'. We were not devotees, so why did he treat us in this manner? Could there have been a misunderstanding? Was he a spontaneous and therefore unpredictable personality in whom the dictates and needs of the moment would overrule all past commitments? Had something unexpected come up? Or was he simply a capricious and whimsical personality spoiled by the constant adoration and subservience of his hordes of devotees? We found no answers to the enigmas of Sai Baba's personality.

In Puttaparti Sai Baba did not look at us when he passed us that afternoon in the long rows of people waiting for him at darshan-time. This meant little, however, since he rarely smiled or nodded to people as he walked among them. Our feelings then were mixed, but we reserved judgment about him. At times we thought we saw a primadonna, fiercely independent and somewhat boyish and playful. But he more frequently expressed the captivating charm, sweetness and genuine cordiality that could make almost anyone he talked to leave in a joyful mood. We could see that he fascinated people and could command their instant respect; many people have described to me uprushes of awe and devotion that they have felt in his presence. I wondered if some of the relief and joy many people experienced, whether in an interview or just by a kind word from him, was not at least partially built up by the suspense in which everyone was kept by never knowing if they would succeed in meeting him. Hundreds or thousands of people were always waiting for him, some desperately. We tried to count them once when the crowd was relatively small. Our estimate was around eight hundred.

Sai Baba called us in the next morning along with a few other people: a Los Angeles lawyer and his wife, Mr and Mrs Sydney D. Krystal; a young doctor from Bombay; an engineer from Varanasi, Mr Roy, who served as an interpreter for us when needed; Dr D. Sabnani, a medical doctor from Hong Kong and Mrs L. Hirdaramani, a lady from Sri Lanka.

First he quickly produced vibuti for the Sri Lankan lady, and then he turned his attention to the Los Angeles couple, who had been married for several decades and had their wedding anniversary around that time. Sai Baba seemed to have known about this beforehand and he appeared to be happy about the occasion. He decided to marry them again according to an old Indian custom that arranges a second marriage as soon as one of the partners has reached sixty. He waved his hand, and as he opened his fist we saw a golden ring. He handed it to Mrs Krystal, telling her to put it on one of her husband's fingers, as is customary for the bride to do at a traditional Indian wedding. Sai Baba's open hand was still stretched out in the air without having touched his clothing or any other object. We watched closely.

Immediately thereafter Sai Baba waved his hand again for two or three seconds, the palm turned down, and then quickly closed it. His arm was approximately horizontal to the ground, which was not a position favourable for allowing an object to fall from his sleeve. We observed at close range as Sai Baba loosened the grip of his fist so that he could hold the large, bulky necklace that appeared in his hand. It was a *mangalasutra*, a traditional piece of jewellery for a woman given at her wedding. It was 32 inches long, 16 inches each side, and it contained nine kinds of stones, arranged in nine groups, each group interspaced by a gold bead. Attached to it was a picture of Sai Baba set in a golden rosette frame an inch and a half in diameter. This necklace was presented to Mrs Krystal. The necklace was too large to be hidden in a man's fist, particularly Baba's small hand. Its sudden appearance left those present amazed.

Baba went into a spirited discourse, aimed at us, attacking scientists. He said that scientists could not understand the spiritual, and he insisted that the spiritual starts where science ends. We found ourselves back to our earlier discourse on the need for experimentation and empirical research on paranormal phenomena, of which he was allegedly a master.

When we showed Baba the few things that we had brought with us to test the paranormality of his materializations experimentally, he politely put them aside. It would be black magic to exhibit his powers that way, he stated.

In the midst of our rather heated discussion, Sai Baba impatiently said to Dr Osis: 'Look at your ring.' We did. The enamel picture on the ring had disappeared. The large golden ring that Sai Baba had presented to Dr Osis during our first visit was on the ring finger of his left hand. The stone encased in it had on the top a large enamel coloured picture of Sai Baba. The stone with picture had been oval, about 2 centimetres long and 1½ centimetres wide, and it had been framed by the ring. The edges of the ring above and below the picture, together with four little prongs that protruded over it from the circular golden frame, kept it fixed in the ring. Thus the picture was set as firmly in the ring as if it and the ring were one solid article.

Now the stone with the picture was missing from the ring and we could see the bare skin of Dr Osis's finger through the hole. We looked for the picture on the floor, but no trace of it could be found. For the picture to have fallen out of the frame, it would have to be broken, or it would have been necessary to bend at least one of the prongs and probably also to bend the frame at some point, but the frame and the prongs were undamaged.

When the picture could not be found, Sai Baba somewhat teasingly remarked: 'Well, this was my experiment.' Later he implied that this was a joke, and then he added: 'You asked for a miracle and I just gave it to you.'

When Sai Baba made us aware of the picture's absence, we were sitting on the floor about five or six feet away from him. We had not shaken hands when we entered the room, and he did not reach out to us or touch us. As we sat cross-legged on the floor, Dr Osis had his hands on his thighs, and I had noticed the picture in the ring during the interview before this incident occurred. My first reaction was that the picture had suddenly become transparent. Two people, Dr Sabnani and Mrs Hirdaramani, whom we had met for the first time during this interview, certified that they had seen the large golden ring with Sai Baba's picture in Dr Osis's left hand before the picture disappeared. I also clearly remembered seeing them admiring the beautiful ring. Two days earlier Dr Osis had been wondering if the setting was strong enough. He had taken out his nail clippers and with the file end of it had tried hard to press the four prongs which held the enamel picture. He satisfied himself that they were as tight as possible. After the picture disappeared, we examined the prongs with a magnifying glass and found them unbent and fully intact. We found no reasonable normal explanation for the picture's disappearance. Later in this chapter I will discuss some arguments pro and contra a paranormal interpretation.

The interview lasted at least an hour, and most of that time was spent on us. Baba did not mention why he had left us behind in Brindavan, nor did we ask. He was rather tense in the beginning and put us on the defensive by pushing his point of view rather hard. As the interview went on, we had a chance to make our point. Our impression was that we parted on good terms. 'You work for the good of humanity' he remarked at one point. Evidently he was not used to people arguing and discussing with him as we did.

Then he told us that he would later grant us a personal experience that would bring us greater understanding. Finally he indicated he would see us again to talk further the same evening or the following morning.

Morning and evening at darshan we sat patiently in the sand outside the mandir, until finally he invited us in on the afternoon of the second day after the previous interview. Again

we were accompanied by the Krystals and Mr Roy. Also present
was a young American couple and a boy from Europe or
North America. Baba was friendly, affectionate and charming.

When we came in, he took Dr Osis's hands and asked about
the ring and the stone. 'Tell me the truth!' Then he asked for
the ring. It fitted tightly and it was difficult for Dr Osis to get it
off. Then Sai Baba asked: 'Did you like it?' 'Yes' was the
answer. 'Would you like the same stone or a different one?' Dr
Osis wanted the same. Sai Baba took the ring in his hand and
closed his fist. He held his hand still in front of him for about
10 or 15 seconds. He did not turn or move his hand, and he
did not bring the other hand near it. Then he opened his hand
and on his palm we saw a ring. As far as we could judge, it was
similar to the one he had just taken from Dr Osis, but not quite
the same. Again it was a beautiful golden ring. The stone and
its setting looked the same but the band seemed somewhat
altered.

He put the new ring on Dr Osis's finger, and it fitted well.
On his return to New York Dr Osis had the ring examined by a
jeweller. It was made of high carat gold and was valued at one
hundred dollars.

The ease with which Sai Baba does these things always baffles
observers, and he apparently enjoys this. Now Mr Krystal
mentioned that the beautiful golden ring Baba had presented
to him in our earlier interview was too loose, and he asked
Baba if he could change it. Mr Krystal gave it to him. Baba
took it between his forefinger and thumb, lifted his hand near
his mouth, and blew on it once. We saw the ring the whole
time. He gave it back to Mr Krystal, who said it was tighter.
One of us moved the ring on Mr Krystal's finger and it did
seem tighter. When he had removed it earlier, we had seen that
he had taken it off very easily.

After that we had a general discussion, the swami often
speaking in monologues as he tends to do. Unfortunately, we
were unable to tape-record our interviews. I think it was on the
first interview on this trip that I bought with me a bag with a
tape recorder and a camera. Baba told me not to take it into
the interview room. 'This is not a marketplace.'

His room was bare and spotlessly clean, with only one chair
in a corner of the room, on which Sai Baba often sat in
interviews. With us he always sat on the floor.

We asked him once more how he was able to produce these

objects. Now his answer was that the ability comes from the superconscious. He imagines the object he wants to create, and then it is there. 'It is so simple to imagine this', he said.

He continued talking about his philosophy, especially the necessity of worship, devotion and duty. He always stressed duty to fellow men and society, but devotion and worship were the key of his religion, strong devotion resembling what one may find in some charismatic churches. Control and discipline were other important aspects of his philosophy.

One odd item emerged from this interview. Baba told us that he would live to be 94 years of age (that would be the year 2020). Finally he indicated that he would see us again the following day.

Evening bhajan had started, and so we went right into the bhajan hall of the mandir. The hall was attractive and meticulously clean, and in it was a highly decorated altar made of silver. At the end of the hall, there was a life-size photo of Sai Baba of Puttaparti on one side and an equally large photo of Sai Baba of Shirdi on the other. To the right of the altar and the photos was a throne-like armchair on a podium where Baba sat during bhajans. The bhajan would last about half an hour, and Baba would usually come in during the latter half of it and take a seat on his chair.

We dutifully attended these bhajans while we were in Puttaparti. The music was sometimes quite pleasant, but we understood hardly a word of the singing. And sitting on the bare stone floor was an ordeal. Nevertheless, we attended because we wanted to do our best to gain his cooperation.

We were sitting side by side in the hall. On this occasion I happened to look at Dr Osis, and I noticed something unusual about the expression on his face. It changed, as if he were experiencing something most pleasant and enjoyable. The signs of the usual strain of having to sit uncomfortably on the hard floor were no longer there. Something on his face reminded me of an old Indian merchant from Singapore to whom I had talked a few days earlier. He had been called in by Baba. Inside Baba had asked him what he wanted. '*Anand*' (bliss), he answered. And on the spot he had experienced such ecstatic joy that tears started to roll down his cheeks.

In Dr Osis's case there were no tears as far as I could see, but later that evening when we reviewed the experiences of the day and spoke our impressions onto a tape recorder, he stated that he had fallen into an altered state of consciousness and felt that it might have been induced by Baba. 'It started by my feeling a very distinct source of radiating warmth to the left side of my forehead. At first it felt like it was some 10 centimetres away, but then it seemed to work closer and closer till I was in a quite altered state of consciousness. I closed my eyes and went with it. It was like what Baba calls the sweetness. It was really a feeling like that, not of world-shaking intensity, but a really serene, permeating, warm feeling.'

This experience was not what Dr Osis had expected. When Baba had remarked some days earlier and again that day that he would give us an experience, Dr Osis had paid little attention to it; if anything, he had expected a paranormal experience rather than an altered state of consciousness.

Dr Osis is well versed in the literature on meditation and mystical experiences. He was in fact one of the first psychologists to conduct experiments in that area, and his paper 'Dimensions of the Meditative Experience' (Osis, Bokert and Carlson, 1973) has become a classic in the psychology of meditation. He has also been personally acquainted with most of the researchers in this field, such as the late Aldous Huxley.

The next few days Baba came out dutifully morning and evening, and he called in a number of people, but not us. Our time was running out. On the fourth day after our last interview we managed to get Mr Surrya, an old attendant of Baba and a retired police officer in Venkatagiri, to give a note to Baba telling him that we were leaving at noon the following day. The next morning Baba went over to the women's side only.

We packed and left for Bangalore.

Note

[1] A pujari is normally a member of the Brahmin community, which in ancient India was the highest and most honored priestly class. In present times this term pujari denotes any one who conducts worship in a public place. Now he may even be a non-Brahmin.

4
How Real?

Before I report further findings and observations of the phenomena that have been associated with Sri Sathya Sai Baba, it seems appropriate to make a first tentative attempt at a critical evaluation. Are the phenomena real or not? Can that question be answered on the basis of the material that has so far been presented, and with what degree of certainty?

To limit that task to a more manageable size, let us for the time being consider only the materializations. They are certainly the most prominent feature of Sai Baba's repertoire. They, more than anything else, have given him national fame, and with them Sai Baba baffles practically everyone who has a personal encounter with him. The ostensible materializations will almost certainly be the most controversial among those persons interested in the scientific study of psychic phenomena as well as among members of the general public. If the phenomenon is genuinely paranormal, that is if he really creates the objects involved, then the theoretical implications are enormous, for physics and psychology alike.

Basically the phenomenon consists of an object appearing or disappearing in circumstances in which no physical cause of the event can be detected. This process is generally referred to as a 'materialization' whenever paranormal creation of the object is assumed, or as a 'teleportation' if it is assumed that an object has disappeared from one place and reappeared paranormally at another place. The object thus 'teleported' is called an 'apport'.

It should be kept in mind that enterprising showmen have for centuries played their tricks of making objects appear and disappear. With amazing dexterity, by clever diversion of attention, and in more recent times by sophisticated gadgetry, stage magicians have accomplished these illusions without being detected by their audiences. Such tricks also have a long history in religious or semireligious settings (Carrington 1920).

Reports of the allegedly paranormal appearance and disappearance of objects can be found in various times and cultures. They can be found, for example, in the New Testament, as well as in the heyday of the spiritualistic movement in the late 19th and early 20th centuries (Crookes 1874, Fodor 1966, Hannesson 1924, Richet 1923), and occasionally in recent times (Bender 1969, Hasted 1981).

The evidence supporting such reports is often of poor quality, and many claims for materializations and teleportations have been explained in quite natural – and sometimes quite entertaining – ways (Carrington 1920). Nevertheless, some studies have been conducted by outstanding scientists (for example, William Crookes's 1874 study of Daniel Dunglas Home, the most famous of all physical mediums). Some serious psychical researchers, such as Crookes and the French Nobel-prize winner in physiology, Charles Richet, spent much of their time and energy investigating and experimenting with physical mediums. Present-day researchers have generally frowned upon their work, apparently more because they themselves have not come across any such ostensible phenomena than because of the quality of the scientific reports of these highly qualified researchers. (Present-day researchers, however, have also felt the need for more detail than these reports provide.) A few cases of ostensible teleportation can be found in more recent studies of poltergeist phenomena, but none of them are supported by strong evidence (Bender 1969, Owen 1964, Roll 1972, Gauld and Cornell 1979).

However, if we assume for a moment that the phenomena that Crookes and Richet observed were genuine, then they differed from materializations allegedly produced by Sai Baba in that they were temporary, that is, the objects would vanish quickly after being visible and tangible for some minutes. In addition, these 'objects' were generally reported to be human bodies or parts of bodies. Sai Baba rejected our request that he participate in experiments where we could have imposed rigorous controls and made instrumental observations. Hence a decisive test of the paranormality of his phenomena was not possible.

Anyone who wished to was allowed to film him outdoors as much as he or she wanted. I filmed him extensively and managed to get a few shots of him waving his hand and producing vibuti, but these were either not close enough for decisive analysis or not from the optimal angle. For a film to have some evidential value, it would probably have to be taken both from close range and from more than one angle at the same time. A faster movie camera than I had would also be necessary. Therefore what we have for evaluation are primarily our own observations made under semispontaneous conditions, and the observations of witnesses, which at best can probably only lead to tentative conclusions.

Let us now state some hypothetical normal explanations for the appearance and disappearance of objects that we observed and discuss the problems of each one of them.

Could we have been hypnotized without our knowledge and thus been led to overlook actual observable events? Generally speaking, hypnosis has to be induced by verbal commands. During our observations of Sai Baba, nothing even vaguely resembling any hypnotic procedure was ever given.

Furthermore, numerous experiments have shown that susceptibility to hypnosis varies considerably between individuals, and almost never can everyone in an unselected group of people be even mildly hypnotized (Hilgard 1977), much less the fairly deep state required to cause an individual not to see something present in his or her visual field, namely a negative hallucination. In all our interviews with Sai Baba everyone present seems to have observed the same incidents. In addition, both Dr. Osis and myself were very much on our guard, and we feel confident that we experienced no altered states of consciousness during our interviews with Sai Baba. In most of the incidents about which we heard reports, everyone present seems to have observed the same phenomena.

Sai Baba has been filmed extensively while producing objects outdoors, and those present have reported seeing the same movements as were recorded on the film. Also, the objects that he produced for us in the interviews (the double rudraksha and the golden ring with the enamel picture) are still in our possession and were therefore not illusory. For these reasons we can reasonably reject the hypothesis of hypnosis as an explanation for the materializations.

Could the objects have been provided by an accomplice in the interview room? There are also problems with this explanation. In the course of our several interviews the people present varied widely. No single associate of Baba was present during all the interviews we had with him. If accomplices were involved there would have to have been several of them. This would increase Sai Baba's risk of being unveiled as fraudulent since he has produced objects in this fashion for forty years. Objects were also produced when we were alone with him in a room. This hypothesis can therefore be rejected for some incidents and seems unlikely for others.

Could the interview room have contained hidden devices that ejected the objects? The room was empty except for one armchair, which Baba did not use during our interviews. This armchair was not a heavy piece, but a slim French type of chair. The floor and the walls were made of concrete and painted, the walls with oilpaint. A small clock hung high on one of the walls, and a calendar hung on the only wall that contained a window. In India windows are generally without glass but have vertical iron bars a few inches apart. In our interviews Baba sat cross-legged on the floor and out of reach of the armchair or the clock or the window sill. He did not sit at any one particular place when he produced the objects in our presence. We also observed him produce objects outdoors and in a private room at the home of Dr Bhagavantam's son. It seems unlikely that the objects were somehow concealed in devices that ejected them to Sai Baba when he needed them.

Could Sai Baba have concealed the objects on his person and produced them by sleight of hand? This is the crucial normal hypothesis. Sai Baba wears a one-piece robe with sleeves that reach to his wrists and that are obviously potential hiding places for objects. There are rumours that he may hide things in his sleeves, in hidden pockets of his robe, or even in his bushy hair. However, Dr Osis and I found no one who had had or knew of any first-hand observations supporting the sleight of hand hypothesis.

By the time our second visit to India was over, Dr Osis and I had observed the ostensible paranormal appearance of objects in Baba's hand about 20 times. None of these events occurred under controlled conditions. Also, we were not able to examine Sai Baba physically either to confirm or to refute the hypothesis that he conceals objects on his body. At this stage, therefore, we have insufficient grounds for accepting the claims made about the genuineness (in terms of paranormal processes) of the reported phenomena. But it must also be stated that we detected no evidence of fraud.

There is no clear answer to the question of the genuineness of the phenomena we are discussing. There are however some puzzling facts that keep the question open and may lead to a paranormal interpretation of the phenomena. These are the points to be considered:

The first point in favour of the paranormality of the materialization phenomena is Sai Baba's lengthy history of producing objects apparently without being detected in fraud. According to a number of people who have had a long association with him, there has been a continuous flow of objects from him for over forty years, or since he was in his teens in the early 1940s. I felt this point needed closer examination by intensive interviewing of a large number of devotees and ex-devotees; my findings are reported and discussed in a later chapter.

The second point concerns the variety of circumstances in which objects appear. Magicians usually need a stage that separates them from their audience. They also sometimes need certain lighting conditions or other aids. Sai Baba is reported to produce objects in whatever situation he may find himself – during private interviews in his interview rooms, while travelling in a car or flying in an aeroplane, while greeting crowds outdoors, or while visiting private homes. In short, on almost every occasion, a number of times every day, in private or public, indoors or outdoors, he produces objects. Does he literally produce phenomena on all these occasions? This claim will also be further examined later.

The third point is that Sai Baba is reported to produce objects in response to specific situations or on demand. Stage magicians, in contrast, have a fixed, limited repertoire of objects that they can produce on each occasion. For example, our rudraksha incident apparently arose spontaneously out of a specific situation. As counterargument, one might say that a clever actor could stage such situations without the observers realizing it. Whatever the case might be, we encountered many witnesses who testified as to such occurrences, including the appearances of statuettes of a particular deity on request, a ring with a visitor's favourite deity, or specifically requested fruit and sweets. These claims also are examined in more detail in later chapters.

A fourth point may be mentioned. In India we met

prominent scientists who had become convinced of the genuineness of the phenomena after having had the opportunity to observe Sai Baba extensively. They stated that they had witnessed a number of phenomena that they considered unexplainable in normal terms, such as the materialization of objects in a variety of circumstances. These men included Dr S. Bhagavantam, a prominent nuclear scientist and former director of the Indian Institute of Science in Bangalore, which is one of the most prestigious scientific institutes in India; Dr D. K. Banerjee, former head of the Department of Chemistry in the same institute (an extensive interview with him is in the next chapter); and Dr P. K. Bhattacharya, the present head of the above-mentioned Department of Chemistry, who received his doctoral degree from the University of Illinois. We can also mention the physicist Dr K. Venkatessan of the same institute, who received his training at Oxford University and in Geneva, and Dr V. K. Gokak, a former president of Bangalore University. It should be emphasized, however, that none of these men has had any experience in investigating paranormal phenomena, nor did they seem to be familiar with the literature on such studies, except perhaps in a rudimentary way.

At least one magician has asserted that reputable scientists can be deceived by magicians' tricks just as easily as the general public can. Very likely scientists are no better qualified to discern how the tricks are done, especially if they observe them only once, twice or a few times. The situation may be different when scientists observe basically the same phenomena many times in different situations and over several years. In any case one would expect them as a group to require greater evidence or proof before they are convinced of the genuineness of the phenomena. Their whole educational background is bound to make them more suspicious of any paranormal claims, as these have no place in the textbooks of physical science. Scientists of high repute in their community are therefore bound to be more reluctant to express conviction about such phenomena until they feel that they have solid reasons for doing so.

Finally, one more point: in Bombay we met a British-trained dental surgeon, Dr Eruch Fanibunda. This Parsee gentleman is also an accomplished amateur magician and in his student days received the Linking Ring award from the International Brotherhood of Magicians (USA) for a series of articles on

'original methods and effects of conjuring, mind-reading, etc.'
(Fanibunda, 1976/1980, p. 6). Dr Fanibunda was fully aware
that 'There are scores of gurus and babas in this country
(India) who make a business of spirituality and use methods of
conjuring to beguile and trap gullible people for their selfish
ends' (ibid. p.6). He was therefore 'keen to find out whether
Baba was actually materializing the various objects from thin
air as claimed by His devotees, or He was producing them by
sleight of hand' (ibid. p. 6). He approached Baba as a sceptic
but became convinced of the paranormality of the phenomena.
He told us in an interview that he has had numerous
opportunities to observe Baba when producing objects, that he
has travelled with him and filmed him extensively, but that he
has found no evidence of fraud.

More points pro and contra could be discussed in this first
tentative evaluation but this will suffice until more material has
been presented[1]. In the following chapters, I present in-depth
interviews with people who have observed Sai Baba extensively
for a long period of time. These include scientists and laymen,
devotees, ex-devotees and non-devotees, both those who knew
him when he was unknown and those who know him now,
when his name has become a household word all over India
and is known to some people in most countries and major
cities in the West.

Note

[1] Dr Osis and I have written a few scholarly articles on our investigation of
Sai Baba (Haraldsson and Osis 1977; Osis and Haraldsson 1976, 1979). Dr
C. T. K. Chari (1978, 1982) of Madras University has responded to one of
them.

5
'No One Can Comprehend
My Glory'

Sathya Sai Baba, as he is now known, was born on 23 November 1926, in the tiny isolated village of Puttaparti as the son of a poor farmer and his wife. His father's name was Venkappa and his mother's Eswaramma. They carried the family name of Ratnakara and belonged to the Raju caste, a low caste whose duties in old India were to praise their king or raja by songs and poetry.

Sai Baba did not therefore belong to the priestly and learned Brahmin caste. Mr Gopal Krishna Yachendra, who has known him for over 30 years told me that this fact hindered him for a long time in his role as a religious leader which, in Hinduism, is traditionally held by the Brahmins only.

He was given the name Sathyanarayana, Sathya meaning truth and Narayana being a name for God. In India it is common for people to carry some name of God or of some other deity. His full name was therefore Sathyanarayana Ratnakara Raju. When he was born, his parents already had three children: two girls, Venka and Parvata (called, according to tradition, Venkamma and Parvatamma when they became mothers, 'amma' meaning mother), and one boy, Seshana. Another son born later was named Janaki Ramayya.

In due time Sathyanarayana attended elementary school in Puttaparti and later in Bukkapatnam, two and a half miles away. After that he attended high school in the more distant town of Uravakonda. According to Prof Kasturi, who has written a four-volume flowery biography of Baba (1971, 1972, 1973, 1980):

On 8 March 1940, the entire town was shocked to hear that a 'big black scorpion' had stung Sathya. It was at dusk, about

seven o'clock, when Sathya gave a shriek and leaped up
grasping his right toe as if he had been bitten! Although no
scorpion or snake was discovered, he fell as though
unconscious and became stiff. (Kasturi 1971, p. 37)

A doctor was brought in and gave him an injection, but Sathya
was apparently unconscious throughout the night. The next
morning the doctor declared that he was out of danger, and he
seemed back to normal. But he 'then began to behave in an
extraordinary manner' (ibid. p. 38). From that time onwards
he would intermittently fall into some kind of trance and
would not answer people who spoke to him, 'sometimes
bursting into song and poetry ... sometimes expounding the
philosophic wisdom of ancient India' (ibid. p. 39). He was
taken to another doctor who 'judged that the illness was allied
to fits, that it was a type of hysteria unconnected with the
alleged scorpion sting' (ibid. p. 40).

Further attempts to bring Sathyanarayana back to his old
normal self were of no avail. He left school. On 23 May 1940,
then aged 14 according to Kasturi[1], he called together all the
members of his home in Puttaparti and:

presented them with sugar-candy and flowers taken from
'nowhere'. At this the neighbors rushed in. He gave each a ball
of rice cooked in milk, also flowers and sugar candy, all
manifested by a mere wave of the hand. (ibid. p. 46).

On this occasion he stated that he was Sai Baba reborn. His
father was not impressed:

His father threatened to beat the alleged 'megalomania' out of
His head. He accosted Him, brandishing a heavy stick, 'Are you
God or a fraud?' When Baba replied, 'I am Sai Baba come
again; worship Me,' the stick dropped from his clasp. Miracles
soon convinced him that it was best to leave the Son alone.
(Kasturi 1980, p. 185)

'You have got nothing to do with me', he told his family,
when they complained about his extraordinary claims and his
independent ways at this early age, his sister Venkamma told
the author of this book. After that there was allegedly a steady
stream of miracles coming from him. According to Venkamma
his family was not aware of any miracles before this time.

Who was this Sai Baba that Sathyanarayana was talking about? Apparently not many people in Puttaparti knew that name.

In the year 1872 a young fakir had settled in a dilapidated mosque in the little town of Shirdi some 120 miles northeast of Bombay. According to Arthur Osborne, who has written a short biography of him in English, nothing is known of his early years except that 'It is fairly certain that he was born of a middle class Brahmin family in a small town in Hyderabad State' (Osborne 1958, pp. 15-16). His name was unknown, but he came to be called Sai Baba, Sai being a Persian (Moslem) word for saint, and Baba being a Hindi term of endearment and respect meaning father.

Sai Baba remained in Shirdi until his death in 1918. Shirdi, a village more than a town, was several miles from the nearest railway station and had not previously been a religious centre. About the turn of the century his fame began to spread among Hindus and Moslems alike. He remained unknown outside India, but according to Osborne, in India he came to have more devotees than any other religious personality of this time.

> That Sai Baba did exert a tremendously powerful influence over his devotees there is no doubt at all. Many have testified to the awakening and fostering of spiritual life in them .... He practiced the laying on of hands .... His touch conveyed certain impulses, forces, ideas .... Each such action had its own effect, causing a remarkable change in the sensations or feelings of the devotee. (ibid. p. 110)

Sai Baba trained his devotees to 'seek God through devotion to the Guru' (ibid. p. 110). He never wrote a book, nor did he read them, but his 'miracles were flamboyant' (ibid. p. 28). Whatever the truth may be about the miracles, there seem to be no reports that he produced objects such as Sai Baba from Puttaparti does, but he always kept a good stock of vibuti at hand. He was in many ways a strange man:

> Even apart from the miracles, there was something bizarre about Sai Baba. A strange figure, teaching Hindus and Moslems alike, keeping a sacred fire burning in a mosque, raging at his devotees, even beating them with sticks, answering unspoken thoughts, flinging stones and abuse at an unbelieving

visitor to drive him away or performing a miracle to attract him, openly asking for money and then giving it away to others .... He would fly into a towering rage for no reason that could be seen, pouring out abuse, but the storm would pass and he would suddenly speak graciously to someone who had just arrived or was taking leave. (ibid. p. 30)

What primarily seems to have attracted people to Sai Baba of Shirdi in ever greater numbers was his loving care for his devotees, the guidance he gave, and the spiritual development he brought about in his devotees.

Towards the end of his life annual celebrations were held for him, with pomp that probably only Indians can display, with processions, steeds and chariots, and decorated elephants as if he were a raja. It is stated that he disliked these celebrations but allowed them to please his devotees, who streamed into Shirdi in ever greater flocks. This was the man that Sathyanarayana Ratnakara Raju claimed to have been in his former life. He said he was back to attend to the welfare of his devotees.

The miracles, the charm of the young Sathya Sai Baba's personality, and his keen interest in religion and music led various people to be drawn to him like needles to a magnet. But not in his own village, Puttaparti – there he was widely rejected by all except for a family or two, his parents, and his elder sister.

Many of those who were drawn to him in the early days visited him again and again in spite of the long and difficult journey, the last part of which had to be done by bullock cart since there were no motor roads to the village.

His personality as well as the alleged miracles remained a riddle to most people, and his words did not reduce that mystery. His self-concept and confidence in himself seemed enormous right from the beginning. According to Prof Kasturi, the young swami announced in his 21st year: 'No one can comprehend My Glory, whoever he is, whatever his method of inquiry, however sustained his attempt' (1980, p. 185).

Puttaparti was in those days nothing more than a bunch of clay huts and a few small brick houses. There were no facilities to accommodate visitors and so these devotees, many of whom came from Bangalore, soon built for the young swami and his visitors a simple house in which some 40-50 people could sleep on the floor. This building became what we will refer to as the old mandir. In 1950, on Sai Baba's 24th birthday, a new mandir was inaugurated on a larger piece of land a short distance away from the village and the Chitravati River. It was given the name Prashanti Nilayam (abode of peace) and became an independent township.

With a steadily increasing number of visitors, the ashram has grown into many buildings, like a small town, including several large three-storey high apartment buildings with some 700 apartments, a number of sheds where thousands of people can be accommodated, a huge assembly hall, a hospital, a grade school, a high school, a college, and now a university that was founded there in 1981 and is staffed by fully qualified academics.

A brief digression into Hinduism, the religious background in which Sai Baba operates, is appropriate here. Traditionally in Hinduism, a close personal relationship between the guru and the disciple plays a very important, basic role[2]. Furthermore, disciples (chelas) or devotees are expected to exhibit unquestioning faith and complete subservience to their guru, which seems easily conducive to the formation of cults. Such blind faith in a religious leader is, however, a characteristic not only of religious movements in Hinduism. Many similarities can be found in Christianity, and as far back in time as in the life of Jesus.

On the one hand the powerful personality cults that develop around some gurus may, among other things, facilitate the occurrence of paranormal events. On the other hand the personality cults may promote the erratic, somewhat spoiled behaviour that some Indian gurus and god-men exhibit. This whole disciple-guru relationship and ashram atmosphere is utterly foreign to questioning and testing the guru or swami. It is the swami who is traditionally supposed to perform the testing of his disciple and not vice versa. Strange as it may seem to Western readers, this may from Sai Baba's point of view explain his refusal to partake in any experiments that we suggested to him or, as those more critical may think, have given him a welcome excuse.

Hinduism is probably the least known of the world's major religions, partly perhaps because it is so notably difficult to define and partly because it is primarily a national (Indian) religion. Its beliefs are of a confusing variety, and organizationally it is vastly different from, for example, the splintered but highly organized Christian religion. Organ (1974, p. 1) describes it aptly:

> Hinduism is a spectrum of beliefs and practices ranging from the veneration of trees, stones and snakes in villages scarcely out of the Stone Age to the abstract metaphysical speculations of sophisticated urban intellectuals whose attainments have been recognized by British knighthoods, Nobel prizes and entrance into international learned societies.

It falls outside the scope of this book to give any outline of the religious or philosophical aspects of modern Hinduism. The interested reader may be referred to such excellent sources as Organ's 'Hinduism' (1974) or Smart's highly readable and updated review of modern Hinduism in his book 'The Religious Experience of Mankind' (1976). Some characteristics of Hinduism, however, are particularly relevant to our under-standing of such movements as that of Sai Baba's. Basically Hinduism is a tolerant religion in the sense that it contains a variety of different, even contrasting, views although religious conflicts, particularly with Moslems, occasionally flare into violence. Secondly, it is probably more open to change and inclusion of new ideas than most religions since it is (or at least it can be argued that it is) not drastically bound to any basic dogmas. Thirdly, since it is for the most part so utterly disorganized and has nothing comparable to a Pope, an organized membership or church councils, it is particularly open to new religious leaders and movements.

In Hinduism religious personalities usually obtain promi-nence and popularity, not by advancing through an existing ecclesiastical hierarchy, but through popular acceptance and by the number and influence of their followers or devotees. One is tempted to say that Hinduism is an elastic, free-enterprise religion in spite of its strong, ancient historical roots. The widely accepted concept of *avatar* (reincarnation of God) also makes it easier for outstanding religious personalities to gain ground. Finally, an avatar is supposed to have exceptional powers and gifts, an expectation that favours a personality like Sai Baba.

Such aspects and elements of Hinduism form a background

and expectations that provide a right climate for growth of a personality like Sai Baba.

Notes

[1] Either the date of this incident is wrong or Sai Baba was 13 at this time. Being born on 23 November 1926, Baba was 13 years of age in May 1940.

[2] As religious movements of Hindu origin have become increasingly visible in Western countries a few books have been written for Western readers on the personalities of Indian gurus and god-men and their cults. The general approach of these books has ranged from the deeply reverential and uncritical, like Ram Dass' 'Miracle of Love' (1979), to Arthur Koestler's critical, almost cynical, 'The Lotus and the Robot' (1960).

Several books have already been written on Sai Baba besides Kasturi's official biography. Most noteworthy is Howard Murphet's 'Sai Baba – The Man of Miracles' (1971), 'Baba' by Arnold Schulman (1971), 'Sai Baba, the Holy Man and the Psychiatrist' (Sandweiss 1975), and Howard Murphet's second book, 'Sai Baba Avatar' (1977). These books are generally written from the devotees' points of view and reveal why the authors became so fascinated with the man. Since all of them quickly became convinced about the genuineness of the swami's paranormal abilities, none of them made a sustained critical effort to study the alleged paranormal phenomena. One book has been written against him by a religious enthusiast accusing him of homosexuality and of being Antichrist but not questioning the reality of his miracles (Brooke 1976).

6
No Experiments –
What Next?

When Dr Osis and I first visited Puttaparti in January 1973, several older followers told us that Baba had produced more miraculous feats in his twenties and early thirties than later in life, when preaching had become his main mission. In those early days, we were told, he had been more playful and jovial, and miracles of various kinds had been a part of his life every day, nay, almost every hour. I have, however, come to doubt if the number of the ostensible paranormal physical phenomena are any fewer now than they were earlier. From my third visit onwards I was particularly interested in meeting people who had been with him in the 1940s and 1950s. At that time most of the visitors lived under the same roof as the young swami, had their meals with him, and even slept with him in the hall of the old mandir (Baba in the middle, ladies on one side and men on the other). Thus these old devotees would be with Baba almost 24 hours of the day, some for weeks and months on end and many of them making several trips to Puttaparti each year. In this way they had come to know him rather intimately and in a way in which hardly anybody knows him today since his life has become more organized and his activities more compartmentalized.

After Sai Baba turned down our request to participate in experimental work, my main effort was directed towards finding and interviewing the old devotees who had had a chance to observe him extensively, both those who had remained in his fold and those who had left him, as well as critics who could offer any evidence that might throw some light on the man and his alleged paranormal abilities. Over the years I have interviewed a rather large number of people, usually visiting them in their homes in such cities as Madras, Bangalore, Hyderabad, Calcutta, Salem, Madurai, Kuppam, Kancheepuram and Coimbatore. Almost without exception, they were willing to relate their many and varied experiences and to put up with a lot of questions. In the chapters that follow, I will report their observations and experiences, as they were told to me. It would require too much space and repetition to mention all the interviews or all the incidents in each interview, and so I have chosen to report mostly on the experiences of a few individuals in a few families.

One of the reasons for choosing to report mainly on the experiences of several people within the same families rather than on those of isolated individuals is that this method usually gives a greater opportunity for corroborating the testimony of witnesses. Also, because I spent so much time with these families, I felt that I came to know them better and that they felt more comfortable in allowing me to probe into their past experiences.

It should be emphasized that most of my informants are now living in different localities; I interviewed them in their homes and, as a rule, individually, each person at least twice but more often, three or four times, usually with a year or more between the interviews. That gave me an impression as to the consistency of their reporting, or the lack of it. Nearly all of the interviews were tape-recorded[1].

Frequently I have been the only interviewer. In the early interviews I was with Dr Osis. On my trip in the latter part of 1981, when I had a sabbatical from my work at the University of Iceland, I was accompanied by Dr Thalbourne and I met once more nearly all of the informants whose experiences are reported in this book. In the summer of 1983 I met all of them again, with the exception of Mrs Radhakrishna.

In the following chapters, relevant parts of the interviews will be presented without an effort to evaluate these accounts. In later chapters (Part II), I will evaluate anew the evidence pertaining to the genuineness or paranormality of the various phenomena, this time also using the data of the critics and devotees who have left Baba.

Note

[1] The accuracy of all testimony quoted in this book has been checked by reading the relevant passages to each informant and obtaining his or her approval of the material. Secondhand accounts have generally been excluded for reasons obvious for anyone familiar with the psychology of rumour and the weakness of secondhand testimony. Courts, for example, do generally not accept such testimony and for good reasons.

7
Observations By Indian Scientists

As of this writing I have made a total of ten journeys to India over a period of ten years. Between my third visit in 1975-76 and my last in 1983, I have spent a total of eleven months there and almost two and a half years if visits prior to my study of Sai Baba are included.

On these journeys, I made considerable efforts to contact people who have had many encounters with the swami and have observed him over an extended period of time. I have become acquainted primarily with people who know English and who have therefore received some formal education.[1] Among those who have been able to observe Sai Baba closely on a number of occasions are several men with scientific training. Among them Dr D.K. Banerjee, Dr P.K. Bhattacharya, and Dr K. Venkatessan, all of whom work at the prestigious Indian Institute of Science in Bangalore.

These scientists were not close associates of the swami. They had not worked in his movement or held an official position in his ashram, but they had nevertheless known him over many years, had met him several times and the swami had even visited some in their homes. They all seemed to possess much common sense. Moreover, they probably had a better grasp than most people of what might constitute good evidence for the paranormality of the phenomena, since as scientists they were trained in careful observation and in the detailed reporting of whatever they study

How, then, did these men come to meet the swami? What did they observe? To what conclusions did they come?

Dr Banerjee and his wife were first interviewed by Dr Osis and myself in January 1975, and we found them forthright and articulate about their experiences with Baba. In early August 1981, I again interviewed them twice, my colleague on these occasions being Dr Thalbourne. It should be noted that we found the testimony they gave on the second and third occasions to be virtually identical with that of the first interview. When asked how he could retain such a clear memory of his experiences with Baba, Dr Banerjee's reply was: 'These were events of a lifetime!'

Dr Banerjee told us Mrs Banerjee met Baba first, when he came to the Indian Institute of Science in 1959. At that time Dr Banerjee was head of the department of organic chemistry. Baba stayed at the residence of the director, Prof Bhagavantam.

There was an occasion at that time, and that was the Thread Ceremony (roughly comparable to the confirmation ceremony in Christianity) of his son – that is, most probably, the third son, Radhakrishnan. I couldn't be there; we were invited to that ceremony, but I had an appointment in Calcutta. But my wife had gone. And when I came back, she told me that she had seen a *sadhu* (Hindu holy man) who had a hair style like that of a lady. That was the first time she saw him. And when he went to bless the boy – you know, that was the first time she saw him produce something – he moved his hand and there was a watch, which he produced and presented to the boy ....

I continued to hear a lot about his miracles. But I didn't believe in either God or ghosts or anything. And my friends used to say: 'Come on, let us go!' I used to hear and tell those stories to them, you know? It was nice telling those stories. And I said: 'Well, the magicians fool us; with Baba also I will not be able to follow what he is doing. It is just not possible for me to follow. Why should I go there?'

A friend, a squadron leader in the Air Force, one Chakravarty, came to our house in 1961, and I was telling him about all these experiences that I was hearing and all that. This squadron leader was of a different type – you know, he used to worship the goddess Kali and all that, and he was a great parachute jumper: at that time he was holding the record in India for jumping from the lowest height, and he had jumped some hundreds of times. He told me: 'Come on! Let us go!' At that, I agreed, and that was my first visit, on the 18th of November 1961.

After this first meeting, Dr Banerjee had numerous encounters with Baba; one of the more memorable was his second visit to Puttaparti, made on the 11th and 12th of January 1962. This visit was prompted by the chronic asthma of the son of Mr G. D. Hazra, a pharmaceutical manufacturer and a friend of Dr Banerjee's. Dr Thalbourne and I were able to interview Mr Hazra. He told us that from the time his youngest son was a month old, he had suffered from asthma attacks every 24 days.

> We had suggested various things, and we had done everything – whatever is possible, but nothing was of any use.
>
> Now Baba was coming to Professor Bhagavantam's house, and I never cared to go over there, at the meeting. (I was an atheist at that time.) Dr Banerjee once suggested I take my son to Baba because we had done everything – whatever is possible – to treat that boy. But we'd never cared to follow his instructions. In the month of December 1961, my boy got a very severe attack. And because it was such a painful thing he was having, it made it very difficult for us to stand. Next morning I went to Dr Banerjee and told him to make arrangements.

On the 11th of January, the Hazras and their son, along with his cousin, made the trip to Puttaparti with the Banerjees, Dr and Mrs Das Gupta and Professor B. H. Iyer. They reached Puttaparti in the afternoon.

Dr Banerjee takes up the story from there:

> I found Professor Bhagavantam, with his family there, and he asked me: 'Why are you here?' I told him: 'It is for the son of my friend, who is suffering from asthma.' In the evening, as usual, we took a seat on the veranda, and Professor Bhagavantam came out and told me: 'Banerjee, Baba will not call anyone this evening.' But I couldn't quite believe it, so I waited, but eventually I found out that it was true: he didn't call anyone to him.
>
> Next day we took our seat again in the morning, and I told my friends how Baba had received me, spoken to me, and so on. He was calling people, we were almost in the front, but then he stopped calling people, and we did not get an interview.
>
> So I was offended. I had told the people accompanying me how Baba had received me previously; now Baba did not pay any attention to me. I felt really offended! Then, after some time, Baba sent a man from the inside to Mrs Hazra: 'You tell them that Baba will call you in the evening at 7.00.' But I was not consoled. On the way back to our quarters, I said in my mind: 'Baba, if you don't talk to these people!' – You know how he gave me that golden thing on my first visit? – 'I'll throw it at your door! I'm going!'

Then, after some time, I calmed down. Then I thought to myself: 'These people can see what we cannot see – can perceive what we cannot perceive. Well, I should not try to judge them.' So in my mind, I told Baba: 'I beg your pardon for all that I have said. Will you please see this person? That's all I want; you need not talk to me.' Exactly, I'm telling you as it happened.

Now Professor Iyer had told his mother that he would get back by the next night, and therefore, since Baba said that he would call us at 7.00 in the evening, he (Professor Iyer) was anxious to know whether he would be going back the same evening. So he asked Hazra. He told us: 'No, the battery in the car is down.' They wouldn't travel at night ....

Then, about 4.00 in the afternoon, we went in front of the house in the hope that we would get a glimpse of Baba, but he didn't show up. So we thought of taking some tea when the second son of Bhagavantam came out of Baba's house and told us: 'Baba has told me to tell you that he would see you right now at 4.00.' So we took our seat on the veranda.

Now here I will tell you something which I came to know from Professor Bhagavantam. He told us that Baba had been talking to him and his family. While talking, suddenly he says: 'I told these people that I would see them at 7.00, but they'll have to be leaving around 7.00.' So Baba sent Bhagavantam's son to call me in! You see? He is inside the room talking with these people; we are far away outside, and all these things (our discussions about not being able to drive in darkness) happened outside! So we walked in.

We were sitting on the floor, and I was sitting next to Baba; he put his hand on my knees and shoulder. He called these kids close to him (three kids were there) and asked their names. Then he said in English: 'The kids must have some sweets.'

Baba then pulled up his sleeve, moved his hand, and opened it like this. And you see, there was just this grey-white ash – this vibuti – sprayed on his hand like powder. And then it passed through my mind, in my own language (Bengali), the thought: 'Is Baba going to give ash as a sweet?' And as I thought this, he put his fingers like this, and opened it. (Dr Banerjee extended his palm, fingers first outstretched, and then brought the index and middle fingers together down onto the palm, then raising them together again). And there was one large white sweet, sticky, a round solid ball. Then he gave it to one kid; then again, this; another to another kid; and again, another kid. Then he did it twice more and gave it to the two ladies. And it was not taking the time that I am spending in telling you! He told the two ladies to tie it up in their saris and take it home and then have it; to the kids he said: 'You finish it off here.' This was the first time I had seen anything of this kind in my life. My eyes were absolutely glued to the hand; he kept his hand open except for the movement of the two fingers. I was about half a metre from his hand. The vibuti had suddenly disappeared from his hand when the sweet appeared. I've never seen such a thing in my life.

Mr Hazra's recollection of this same incident, suggesting as it does Baba's telepathic ability as well as his shrewdness, is worth quoting here:

I thought that it was simply by the power of suggestion that he seemed to be able to create these things – that is, by mesmerism. As soon as this thought came to my mind, Baba looked at me. I was thinking to myself: 'If this sweet continued to exist for at least 24 hours, I would then say that matter had been created, that is, that matter could be created without using any other material.' Baba immediately said to my wife and to Dr Das Gupta's wife: 'Open your hand'; and once more he created this same sort of sweet. My wife and Dr Das Gupta's wife wanted to eat it immediately. But Baba said: 'No, take it back home to Bangalore and give it to all your relatives and guests in your house and then you can eat it.'

Dr Banerjee continues:

The name of the sweet? I learned it only when the ladies came back home and tasted it. They said it was kachagolla, which is a sweet preparation made of chaana (a milk product like cottage cheese) mixed with sugar syrup. You know, in those days, you couldn't get any chaana preparation in the south of India; it is characteristic of my part of India, that is, Calcutta. You know, you can't get kachagolla here at all; it is impossible. It is made in Bengal.

And then Baba kept his hand open like this (and my eyes were huge, as you can well expect), and there was a sticky white spot on his hand, and it got gradually dried up, and the white stuff became a white powder.

At that time there was a worn carpet on the floor, and I thought that this white powder would fall down onto it. Next moment, his hand was absolutely clean! There was nothing on it! Not a trace! It had completely disappeared! Yet when the ladies went back home they had to wash their saris because the sweet was sticky, and these kids had to wash their hands.

Then Sai Baba asked this boy's mother, Mrs Hazra: 'What do

you want to say?' She told about this boy's illness – she can
speak in the common language, that is, Kannada, because she
had lived here in Bangalore quite a long time. And Baba started
speaking in a very sympathetic manner, and this lady started
crying. Then, suddenly, he pulled out the boy's shirt, and
showed him the defect and told him: 'This is why you are
having the asthma.'

Mr Hazra explains:

My son's chest is what they call 'pigeon-breast' – a little
squeezed. And Baba said that it would be cured automatically
when he grows up. 'But now, as the boy is suffering, you will
take some *prasadam* (a blessed gift of food from a swami).' And
he created a gold locket and gave it to my wife and asked her to
put it around that boy's neck. And from that day onwards, up
until now, there is no trace of the disease. Doctors had attended
him previously – the family doctor and some specialists in
Calcutta and Madras. We had seen all the big doctors –
specialists in Calcutta, Bombay, Madras – they treated him, but
it was of no use; he was suffering for a few days every month.

Dr Banerjee has observed a large number of apparent
materializations and had come to accept them as genuine:

I tell you, I am a very sceptical person. I never blame anyone
for doubting Baba because I doubted for a very long time. Yes,
because even then on this occasion I was thinking: 'Does it
come out of some place?' and all these thoughts. Then one day
four of us were sitting – myself, Mrs Hazra, and two professors
from the Institute, Professor Iyer and Professor Krishna Rao.
Then this event ended my doubts, on that day, to tell you
frankly. What he did, he just closed his fist and opened it; there
was a soft paste, the color of cow dung – brown. Then he gave it
to us to eat. When I tasted it, it tasted of condensed milk mixed
with jaggery (sugar syrup) and scraped coconut – fresh coconut
– and superb ghee (clarified butter). If you mix all those things
up, it tasted like that. It had a wonderful smell – it was very
fresh. It tasted wonderful. Then, after he gave it to us, we ate it.
Then he scraped it in his hand and made a small round ball,
sticky, and told me to carry it home and give it to my wife, my
son and my nephew. That doubt had been there, somehow, but
this 'cow-dung' – you know, this pasty stuff – cannot come
from anywhere; it is impossible. He just closed his fist, and
opened it, and it was there! I took that ball. Yet this is
something so sticky that it is bound to leave traces, but next

moment his hand was clean! Absolutely nothing! No trace of anything! Yet this is something which does not go off!

Then my doubt vanished.

Another incident had impressed him greatly.

On New Year's Day, 1965, Baba invited us to lunch. He called us in at about 11:30 in the morning and gave us a talk in Telugu (that is, in his own language, which I can't understand) for two hours – from 11:30 till 1:30 – and I just listened to his voice. This was philosophy as you would call it, nothing else. Then suddenly he looked at everyone and said: 'Oh, it is late! You must be hungry.' So we all jumped up. Then he asked me: 'Have you got any prasadam?' I kept silent. Then he just closed his fist (his hands are small), and he moved towards me. As he moved, I automatically spread out my hands, cup-like, folded them with my palms turned upwards. He opened his hand, and this sweet – in small, broken bits, the size and consistency of broken-up plum cake – started falling into my hands. He was holding his hand flat, and it was falling. It filled my hands up and became a mound several inches high, and then overflowed onto the ground. At that point it stopped. He then started taking it out of my hand and giving everyone some, and it was enough for all present (about 12 to 15 people).

The ostensible materialization phenomena that Dr Banerjee associated with Sai Baba and adjudged to be genuinely paranormal would be described by modern parapsychologists as instances of apparent 'psychokinesis.' The following is a case that, at least for Dr Banerjee, demonstrated the swami's ability to know things happening at a distance – commonly termed 'extrasensory perception' or ESP.

In 1964 I was living inside the campus of the Indian Institute of Science. I had rented out my house in the city to a friend who was the director of an industrial museum. And this gentleman was going on a tour around the south of India in his car with his wife and two kids. My son was 12 years old at that time. They wanted to take him along with them, and so they did, and left. This friend of mine, I might add, is a very good driver; and he has won the trophy three times in long-distance driving competitions.

On the 23rd of December 1964, a tidal wave, coming in the wake of a cyclonic storm struck Rameswaram Island and Dhanushkodi, the southernmost point of India opposite Sri

Lanka. It destroyed the bridge connecting the island to the mainland. A train travelling in the area was smashed. More than 200 people had drowned, mostly passengers on the train. Dr Banerjee's friends had planned to be in that part of the country and, after leaving their car in the railway guest house, had intended to take that train.

He checked their schedule. They might well have been among the passengers. The area was cut off from all communication and was impossible to reach. Dr Banerjee and his wife were frantic with worry.

Then my wife told me that Baba was in Whitefield at that time. So I said: 'Let us go to Baba', because she was very disconsolate. She then told me that she had gone with my nephew in the morning but couldn't even get inside the gate – the gate was closed. So I said to her: 'That was in the morning. It's now five in the evening.' So we went. At the gate there was one person. I told him: 'Please send a slip saying that Banerjee would like to meet Baba.' We were immediately called in. Baba was talking to a few foreigners, and an Indian lady was translating for them. He was sitting in a chair; the other people were sitting on the floor. When we entered, Baba got up and gave us some refreshments. He then said: 'What has happened?' I told him. Then he said: 'Nothing can happen to Deepak (Dr Banerjee's son).' Then he forgot us and started talking to these people .... And then while he was talking, he suddenly turned to me and said: 'They are all safe.' Then another time he said: 'He is trying to communicate, but all communication has broken down.' Now I told him another thing: 'Baba, I found in the newspaper that the guest-house where they were to put their car has been washed away.' Immediately, he said: 'No, no, no. There are two guest-houses: one has been washed away, another is there!' I didn't know this but later found it to be true. Then after some time he said: 'He will get the news of their safety through to you tomorrow.' He was lecturing, but in between he talked to me like that. Next day, at 9.00 a.m., I got a telegram from my friend: 'All safe. Proceeding to Cape.'

Now, don't think that he had sent the telegram the day before, when Baba told us! He sent it early in the morning. But the system was not at all crowded, so the telegram reached us in three hours.

The Banerjees reported another type of experience, the mysterious occurrence of smells whose source is unexplained.

Dr Banerjee relates the story:

These smell experiences began on my first visit to Baba. I was smelling different sorts of things on the first day. Not just rose; it would also be sandalwood, then it would be something else, then something I couldn't even name, but always very fine smells.

My wife was very sceptical about these smells, because she had never experienced any. Now one day, what happened is this. My son was quite young (about 12½ years old), and the only language that was being taught at his school was English. But I was very keen on the boy learning my own language, Bengali. Anyway, before retiring to bed, I used to make him sit down and make him count from one to a hundred in Bengali (by the end of which he would almost be asleep!). So we were doing that.

Suddenly I got a strong smell of this rose. I said: 'Strong smell of rose!' My son also smelled it, saying: 'What a wonderful smell!' My wife came in, but by then the rose smell had gone, and she said: 'Oh, I put Ponds cold cream on his face. You must be smelling that.' I just said to myself: 'What are you talking about? The cream is still there, but its odour has gone.' But I didn't say anything more to her.

A week later his wife had cooked supper and the house was filled with the smell of frying meat.

... and nothing else. I went to bed, and my wife was putting out the lights in the pantry (where her stove was). She suddenly shouted: 'Smell!' and started running all around the house to find the source of the smell, which was of rose attar. I thought she had gotten an electric shock, the way she shouted! I was in the room next to the pantry, but all I could smell was the meat.

Once they were buying meat at a huge meatmarket.

Now on one occasion, the butcher was making some mincemeat, and my wife and I smelled this rose smell there. The man was sprinkling the meat with a little water, and I asked him: 'Are you sprinkling on rose attar?' He couldn't follow me at first. Then, when he had understood me, he said: 'What are you saying? Shall I put attar on the meat?' What he was using was just plain water! He couldn't smell any rose.

Other times we have smelled sandalwood. Sometimes these smells are in just one room, sometimes all over the house. And the smell comes suddenly. You can't get it simply by expecting it.

His friend, Mr Hazra, told of these incidents, simply did not believe it. Mr Banerjee:

> Now recall that Mr Hazra came with me on my second visit to Puttaparti, on the 11th of January 1962. On that visit I did not myself have any of these smells. But Mr Hazra, when we were all sitting in the interview room, suddenly started having the smell of *agarbathi* (incense). He looked around the room for the source of the smell (it is a small room) and, not finding any, thought: 'Banerjee told me that he had these smells, and so I am having it also, because of autosuggestion.' Next moment, he saw some smoke coming out of Baba's head – smoke, curling up. Then he was really flabbergasted! After we came out of the interview, he asked me: 'Did you see or smell anything?' 'No', we said, 'none of us saw or smelled anything. Why?' Then he told us about his experience.

Mr Hazra himself described this experience:

> I was very sceptical-minded at that time – always trying to find fault with Baba. When I entered the interview room, Baba was standing in a corner, and I immediately got the smell of the incense – very beautiful, very mild, extremely nice. But smell is such a subjective thing. I thought I was suffering from the obsession to see something special. I tried my level best to take my mind off the smell, but still it was going on. It continued during the whole interview – nearly three hours. Now you know how Baba's hair is very peculiar, very curly. From his hair was coming smoke, as if from an incense stick, from all over his head. I was dubious: 'What is it?' I thought. You see, I did not believe any of these things; I was all the time afraid that I was seeing all these things because of some peculiar mental condition. Many times our eyes create illusions – seem to see what is not there – so the best thing is to rub your eyes and look again. If you see the same thing again, you'll have to say the smoke is there. So I rubbed my eyes, and still I saw that smoke coming out. Three times I rubbed my eyes, and three times the experience was repeated. The smoke lasted for a pretty good time.

These experiences of Dr and Mrs Banerjee and Mr Hazra were in the end entirely convincing to them. But we, those who did not experience them, would probably have to have other explanations ruled out before these experiences could carry any substantial conviction with us. One must be able to exclude normal explanations such as misperception, faulty memory, mass hypnosis or fraud (on the part of either Baba or our informants). The additional evidence of the following chapters may permit the passing of a legitimate verdict.

Note

[1] As some readers might think this a serious limitation, it should be pointed out that English is widely spoken throughout India. Most people who have had some education know English, and indeed, it is the medium of instruction in almost all Indian universities and colleges. It is also the language of commerce and government. In the Indian parliament, most debates are conducted in English. Since there are many differing languages spoken in India – some as dissimilar as French and Chinese, at the extremes – frequently the only language with which Indians from different regions can communicate with one another is English.

8
The Mangoes Did It

The family of the late Raja of Venkatagiri first came into contact with Sathya Sai Baba in the late 1940s, when the latter was still in his twenties. At that time the Second World War had just ended, and India was gaining independence and freedom from British rule. Venkatagiri was then one of the many princely states of India. It was situated north of the city of Madras and covered a considerable area in the southernmost part of the present state of Andhra Pradesh. While the British ruled over India, they left considerable authority with the rajas (rulers) of the Indian kingdoms, but when India became independent in 1947, the rajas surrendered all their powers to the new federal state of India.

Mr Gopal Krishna Yachendra was the first person of the royal Venkatagiri family with whom I became acquainted. He was born in 1929 as the second son of the late Raja. His only and elder brother now holds the title of Raja and lives on the family's old estate in Venkatagiri. Dr Osis and I first met Gopal Krishna in 1975, and I have met him at least once on every trip to India thereafter. He was extremely helpful and introduced me to a number of the early devotees of Baba in Puttaparti and Madras. He has spent many years in active politics and was for some time the leader of the Congress Party in the Venkatagiri Province.

The Venkatagiri family was one of rulers and warriors who cherished a military tradition. In his younger years, Gopal Krishna's favourite sport was hunting tigers in the forests of Venkatagiri.

His father, the late Raja (who died in 1971), and his elder brother, the present Raja, had first met Sai Baba in 1948. Shortly after that Gopal Krishna met him briefly a few times in Bangalore and Madras. He describes the unusual way in which

76

he was led to visit Puttaparti for the first time:

In 1950 Sai Baba accepted an invitation to visit Venkatagiri for
the first time. My father had gone to the town of Bukkapatnam
to open a school there, naming it Sathya Sai High School. On
this occasion, a date was fixed for Sai Baba's visit. When my
father came back to Venkatagiri, he asked me to go to
Puttaparti and escort Sai Baba to Venkatagiri. It was a tradition
that when some great man comes on a visit then some member
of the family must accompany him from his home. My elder
brother was not present in Venkatagiri at that time, so my
father asked me to go. I said: 'Nothing doing. I will not go all
the 230 miles to Puttaparti. I am not interested in any babas,
gods or swamis. So, you can send someone else.'

Then my father asked some of our relatives to go and escort
him. The car was to start the following morning to Puttaparti. I
went to bed as usual. Not long after falling asleep, I had a vivid
dream of Sai Baba, who gave me two mango fruits to eat. I
relish mangoes more than anything else, and the mangoes in
the dream tasted delicious.

I woke up at 12.30 a.m. I still remember the time exactly. To
my surprise, I had a terrible urge to go immediately to
Puttaparti. I don't know what made me feel like that. I had a
great urge to set out for Puttaparti and could not stay in
Venkatagiri a minute longer. This was like a transformation. I
went to my father, woke him up, and said that I was leaving. I
did not tell anyone anything about the dream. Accompanying
me was one relative, Mr Darmo Rao, and a servant, Mr Venkat
Swami. We reached Puttaparti the next morning between 11.00
and 12.00. In those days, there was no proper road for the last
stretch of the journey. As we arrived, Sai Baba was just coming
out of the old mandir. He said to me: 'Bangaru (you know, he
calls everyone bangaru, which means very good gold), Bangaru,
when you thought of not coming to Puttaparti, these two
mangoes made you run, (did they) not?' he asked me jokingly.

What better proof can anybody have of (Baba's) omnipresence? I had this dream, which I had not told anyone, and then
this terrible urge to go there overcame me. And, to crown it all,
this was the first question he asked me.

We started our return to Venkatagiri straightaway that
evening. Now ours is a big estate, and so we were going to have
to receive Baba at the temple, with honours and elephants and
all these things. So Father had asked me to send telegrams from
every station we passed. I told Baba: 'Swami, Father asked me
to send him telegrams, so I must do so, from Madanapalli,
Kaderi and all the places on our route.' Baba said: 'Nothing

doing! Telegrams are due to your father, but don't bother.
Let's go straight there.'

We never stopped anywhere except at some place for lunch.
At that lunch, we brought Baba one or two empty vessels. He
just touched them, and there was food and there was curry.
And all of us ate.

We have a palace at Venkatagiri – it is a huge building. Baba
had never physically been there before. Yet on this journey to
Venkatagiri, Swami was describing to us some rooms in the
palace which I did not even know myself!

When we arrived at Venkatagiri, Father was ready with all the
paraphernalia. Well, I asked Father: 'What happened? I never
sent a telegram. How did you know so exactly what time we
would be arriving?' He said: 'We received your telegrams, just
as I asked you; I received one from every station.' They were all
on his bed. But none of them had a postmark on it. Yet there
they all were: telegrams from Kaderi, Madanapalli, Chittoor,
Tirupati. How can you explain this?

Father suffered from prostate trouble and used to have to go
to the bathroom frequently. On coming back from the
bathroom, he had found the telegrams on his bed, one at a
time. So he had thought that some postman had brought them.
But when we noticed that there was no postmark on them, we
sent for the postmaster. He said he had not received any
telegrams for us!

Another such incident occurred when the late Raja was on a
visit to London in 1952 or 1953. Sai Baba was then in Madras,
staying in the house of the Venkatagiri family (Osborne House
in Rajapettah). Both of the Raja's sons were there also. One
day Baba told them: 'Your father has lost his passport, and he
is praying to me for help.' And Baba described to them how
the Raja and his party were desperately searching his entire
luggage. The passport was not to be found.

The next day Baba told them that he would place the
passport back in the Raja's bag and that the Raja would find it.

On the Raja's return from England, he told his family that,
much to his distress, he had indeed lost his passport. He, his
party and the hotel staff had searched his bags most
thoroughly but had found no passport. He had prayed to Baba
for help. The next day something had told the Raja that the
passport was in one of his bags which had been turned inside
out several times the day before. There, much to his relief, he
had found his passport. Gopal Krishna and his family believed

that Baba had observed what was happening to his father in London, had taken note of his prayer for help, and had caused the passport to appear again where the Raja would find it.

Gopal Krishna recalled another instance of Sai Baba's apparent clairvoyance:

One day a *sanyasin* (a monk, one who has renounced the world), a saffron-robed fellow, was having some meeting in Venkatagiri. I was there. As a courtesy he and some others visited us at the palace and saw Baba's photo, and they began to criticize Baba. I could not answer some of the questions, like why should he travel only in a car, why is he wearing silks, why is he staying, for example, when he comes to Venkatagiri in Raja's house, why is he not staying in a poor man's house, and so on. I could not answer. After two days a letter came from Baba saying why should you feel bad about this, let people talk. But since you felt so bad about their questions, then these are the answers to the questions in the order they were given to you.

I showed that letter to that sanyasin. Immediately after reading the letter he went to Puttaparti and stayed there till he died. Unfortunately I no longer recall his name.

Another incident: one day I had spoken harshly to my father. I didn't do anything apart from talking rather harshly, as if we were fighting. That happened in Venkatagiri. Later I went to Puttaparti. Even there in Puttaparti I used to sleep by Baba's side. In fact all of us usually slept by his side – myself, my brother, and so on. But on this particular occasion I was there alone with him. We were taking our rest, and I was silent. Swami said to me: 'Gopal Krishna, why should you come here? You are wasting my time and your time. Hereafter, don't come here.' 'Swami,' I said, 'what have I done? If there is anything I have done, please excuse me!' And I began weeping. He said: 'When you can't respect your father, and when you talk to him so harshly (as you did that particular day in Venkatagiri), there arises the question of your coming and wasting my time and yours. If you do such things, don't come here. The most important people for you are your father and mother; they are the people who have given you this body. Yes, they are the people who matter for you. Be careful! If these things happen again, you will be prohibited from visiting me. This is the final warning!' This incident happened about four or five months after the harsh words with my father in Venkatagiri. I had almost forgotten about it and never thought of it, but it was a fact. Baba used the exact wording I had used to my father. He described the room, the day, the very minute – everything. And what more do I want than that for proof that Sai Baba is God omnipresent?

What can I say after seeing and hearing all these things? If someone comes and tells me that Baba is a fraud, I cannot believe him. I have experienced things which are just impossible for any ordinary man to do. Some people speak of conjuring. If you say he is a cheat, I won't believe it, not even if Indira Gandhi tells me. How can I?

There were other kinds of experiences as well.

I got an electric shock from touching him. In Venkatagiri my brother and I used to sleep in the same room as Baba, my brother on one side of him and myself on the other. I sometimes used to give Swami a massage as well. On this particular occasion, he asked me to touch his feet. So I touched them. You can't imagine what a shock I had! He was laughing. I have had some shocks from electricity, but never with that impact.

Sometimes, in fact many times, I observed his weight become different from his normal weight .... He used to ask me, jokingly: 'Lift me!' I never used to feel that I was carrying a human body; he was just like a paper, he was so easy to lift. But sometimes I couldn't even lift his little finger. That happened not once but many times. All these things took place in Venkatagiri.

People had told me of remarkable healing they believe they have received from Baba. I asked if Gopal Krishna knew of any such cases.

Personally I experienced a striking case of healing. I suffered from eczema for many years in my youth. It bothered me a lot, especially in winter, to the extent that I sometimes had to cover my face and throat with bandages as my skin was swollen and like an open wound. Baba produced vibuti and applied it over the eczema. It then healed in a matter of a few days and never came back.

This was a tremendous relief for me for I had been plagued by this for a long time and nothing we had tried had helped.

I have seen Sai Baba doing two or three operations on tonsils. In the case I remember best he first materialized vibuti and rubbed it on the man's throat – outside. Then he materialized a trident of metal (the trident is one of the insignia of Lord Shiva), removed the tonsils with the trident, cut them off, took them out, and showed them to everybody around. There was no bleeding, and the man apparently suffered no pain. This was in 1952 or 1953. This was, I think, in Sakamma's house in Bangalore. Many people were present, but I no longer remember who they were.

My brother has also seen such an operation, a different one. Generally, my brother and I were not with Baba at the same time in Puttaparti. When I was with Baba, he was in Venkatagiri and vice versa. We now much regret that we never kept any record of our experiences.

I asked about any changes that he might have noticed since the early days when he first met Baba.

Life with Baba was very interesting in those days. He was then very close and friendly, not in any spiritual way, just in a friendly way. He would sometimes tease me and I would tease him and we were playing pranks on one another. For example, he would say: 'What is the colour of the robe I am wearing?' I would answer blue or orange as the case might be. But within a second the colour would change. 'What are you saying, do you not see that the colour is – ?' And Baba would laugh and name the new colour of his robe. The robe would change colours in a split second. And later it might suddenly be back to its original colour.

Like this he might play. Then we would ask: 'Swami, give me this or that. I am hungry.' And he would produce something for us to eat. Nowadays this is not possible. Now we will talk about spirituality.

Today Swami is a different person, serious, frequently giving public speeches, talking in colleges, and so on. In the old days, we were having much more fun, joking, pulling each other's leg. He used to make a lot of fun, be very joyous.

If we were close to Baba in the old days, he would not allow us to go out, like going to the movies, move about with girls, or smoke or drink. Some of us would find it rather difficult. Some left Swami for this reason, or Baba pushed them out, like Varadu and Krishna. (Interviews with them follow in a later chapter.) At that time there was no work for the devotees. Now he more or less demands, encourages charity. Various kinds of social service to others is very important for him. If you are with him now, you can hardly have a minute's rest. But in those days it was not so. Then we were just sitting and talking and doing bhajans.

He commented on another change from the early days:

In the 1950s and 1960s, many people were against Swami even in the neighbouring villages. When we drove through with him, also when he was not with us, people would spit on our car as we drove through. They would make fun of us, abuse us, and use vulgar language that we could not repeat. You cannot imagine how anti-Baba the villages were. This lasted until the beginning of the 1970s. Now there is no hostility or criticism any more.

Baba himself had changed.

Yes, he underwent great changes. He did not preach then, there was little or no talk on *seva* (service to others) or *prema* (love). But gradually he expressed more philosophy and more religion. Before 1960 there was mostly just friendly talk, joking, teasing you like good friends might do. We were very young and playful in those days. And we used to laugh together.

At times he could be very moody; sometimes he might not speak to anybody for days. He was just thinking. But there was never anger unless one would do something bad. Then he used to send us fellows away from him. Then he was very cautious as far as women were concerned. He never used to see them alone. There might be scandals, you know.

... In the early 1960s Baba changed – for example, he stopped talking in a teasing manner, he virtually stopped telling jokes, did fewer materializations. For example, previously he used to give us dosas (similar to pancakes), and when they suddenly appeared, they were so hot that we simply could not hold them. How could he have hidden them anywhere? Besides, he might do a thing like that any place. Whatever we would want he would give us; it was not only on his initiative. Another person might ask for an idli (rice ball), still another might want a piece of fruit that might not be available in India because it was out of season. He would give all this, and he did this a large number of times. Like sometimes I would ask for a mango when it was out of season and no one could possibly get it anywhere in India. He would still produce it. Nowadays he is not doing as much of that and certainly not just for fun.

... In those days, there were plenty of miracles, sometimes every minute. He would give us to eat, if we were hungry, he would materialize things, change them, sometimes let them disappear again, and so on.

He could not have hidden these things on him. Sometimes he would give things on his own, but so often we would ask for something and he would give it. He could not have known that I was going to ask for these particular things, even I seldom knew till at the spur of the moment.

Did he sometimes make things disappear that were naturally there or that he had produced?

Yes, many times. Often he would also give a thing a different form. Suppose he had given me some ring, but I did not like it after some time. I would then give it to him and ask for a different one. He would take it in his hand, close his fist. As he opened it, the form of the ring had changed.

He recalled some really out of the ordinary incidents.

We always came by car to Puttaparti. Once in Puttaparti I jokingly said to him: 'Swami, you show me how to drive, you must drive.' He then sat himself in the driver's seat and drove off from the old mandir at the outskirts of the old village and towards the new mandir some 200-300 yards away, the last stretch being slightly uphill. Then he took his hands off the steering wheel, (and) cross-legged his feet in the seat, but the car drove, changing gears, etc., without him touching the wheel or pedals on the curvy road up to the new mandir. The new mandir was then, in 1950, under construction. We were two in the car. This I have only experienced once.

Concerning the new mandir, another incident comes to mind. In those days, there were at the most a few dozen people with him and only so during the big festivals. In those days he often used to fall down suddenly and go into trance. Once the following happened on Sri Rama's birthday in Venkatagiri on a very hot April day. I remember this very clearly; my brother, my cousin Madana and others were also present. As he was coming back to his senses, gushes of vibuti came shooting from his mouth. Afterwards there came out of his mouth golden plates about half an inch wide, and on them was written in Telugu script 'Sri Rama.' These pieces are still with us in Venkatagiri.

These fits came fairly often, but no more since 1960, when he was about 34 years old. In these trances he would remain unconscious for some minutes, but sometimes for hours. When he came to, he used to say that he had gone here or there to save some devotees. Sometimes he would give us names and places, but we never tried to verify them because we believed what he said.

We often tried to prevent him from falling, but the trance

came so suddenly that we could not do it. In these fits he would sometimes put his hair into his mouth.

On one occasion Baba had given to Gopal Krishna a sheet of stamps with a photo of his (Baba's) face printed on them.

> We were sitting in a room in Venkatagiri. I think this was in 1951 .... Baba asked me to buy a sheet of stamps as he often used to write to his close devotees. So I went and bought him one sheet of stamps. By the time I returned, bhajans were going on with my family present, and they were all singing. So I kept the sheet with me and sat down. He then asked me to show it to him, so I gave him the sheet. He took it, waved his hand over it, and lo! the whole sheet changed into stamps depicting his own head with his name and below some ornamentation in the corners of the stamps. He then gave some of the stamps to other people present but about half the sheet to me.

When Gopal Krishna described the incident to me, he still had four of these stamps in his possession (he had given the others away to friends and relatives). He gave me one as a present.

The following story reads like one of the tales of *A Thousand and One Nights*:

> On one occasion Baba opened a girls' high school in Venkatagiri. There was a large gathering of people, and it was threatening to rain. He said there would be no rain till the opening was over. It did not rain on this spot although it rained all around.
>
> Once they were preparing food for the poor people. At every *Dasara* (certain religious festival) they give food to the poor people outside on the bare ground in front of the mandir. Then we saw the rain coming, but Swami said: 'You just cook.' We started cooking, but by then it was raining all around. Only around the mandir it did not rain, not a drop of water. The water was flowing all around. It rained for nearly half an hour; it was not just a passing shower. It was raining, raining all around but not a drop here. It was as if a canvas had been placed over us. That was the greatest thing I ever saw. Baba stopped the rain from coming.

If these stories and experiences that Gopal Krishna told me were true and as he interpreted them, did he then have any clue as to why Baba possessed these seemingly remarkable powers? He responded with the explanation Baba himself had given him:

Once I was alone massaging his feet and asked him: 'What is the difference between you and other great people like Ramana Maharshi and Sri Aurobindo?' His answer was something like this: 'These people have with their penance and meditation gone from your level to the godhead, but I have come from God to redeem mankind and with all the powers so I need not do any *sadhana* or to acquire powers.'

We never saw him do any sadhana (spiritual or religious practice) or sit regularly in meditation. Still he was an endless source of miraculous powers.

In those olden days he told us what was going to happen in the future: that we would have to see him through a binocular, we would have to sit far away from him, and the whole world would come to his feet.

Finally a story that illustrates one of Baba's ways of modifying his devotees' behaviour:

One day in Venkatagiri we took Baba to the jungle. There were then many deer in our forest. About four or five deer came near to our jeep, and I said that if I had a gun I would shoot them. Swami felt so bad about this that he did not eat for two days. From that day onwards we stopped shooting deer.

The following paragraph from one of our interviews probably best sums up Gopal Krishna's attitude toward Sai Baba:

I have not studied philosophy or religion, but I have faith in Baba, nothing else. I do not go to see any saints or swamis, or visit temples. Baba is so humane, so universal, he loves everybody. That is why I revere him and worship him, not because he is a god or miracle maker. You feel some solace and comfort when you are with him. You forget everything.

9
The Raja Of Venkatagiri

The late Raja of Venkatagiri died in 1971. His eldest son and heir to his title was born in 1924 and is hence two years older than Sai Baba. I had met the present Raja a few times in Madras and Puttaparti, but it was not until September and again October 1981 that I had the opportunity to talk with him at length about his experiences concerning the swami. Dr Thalbourne was present on both occasions and participated in the interviews. In December of the same year we met again, and he showed me his personal puja room at his residence in Madras where he kept a collection of items that Baba had presented to him or his family on various occasions.

> We first met Baba in July 1949 in Bangalore where we used to go for the summer with the family. There is a famous race course in Bangalore, and my father used to take a polo team there.

> He was 22 years old, although he looked much younger. He was very frail. All the members of our family went to have his darshan at bhajan-time. Baba was staying with Sakamma, who was a big tea-estate owner. After bhajans, Baba came and called my father, and we all went with him. Since this was our first darshan, we were naturally very shy. The first time we meet any stranger, we normally feel as if we are talking with a stranger. But with him it was not so: he called us, and after our *namaskaram* (prostrating to him) he spoke to us as though we had been acquainted with him for a very, very long time. Everybody seems to have this experience with him; for him, time is no barrier. He greeted us and talked to us as if he had known us for a long time and we were old devotees.

He went to Puttaparti with his family for the first time some

weeks or months before the inauguration of Prashanti Nilayam
on 23 November 1950 and stayed there more than a month.

By then, we were quite devoted: we went, we saw, and we were
conquered. That is all. By 'conquered' I mean that we
surrendered. It is very difficult to explain what caused this:
either it was his attraction, or his personality. He attracted our
devotion, and we became his fervent devotees. When we had
first gone to see him, we did not go as devotees; we were simply
reverential, as when we go to any other saint. In Hinduism it is
said that all sages should be respected. But personal devotion is
different from honouring a sage, paying obeisance or being
respectful to a person. Here, we surrendered: it was absolute.

Was there any particular event that triggered the 'surrender'?

In the beginning, in those days, he used to give many more
presents than now from his 'Sai Stores'. He used to materialize
objects more frequently. The first thing that he materialized for
me on my first visit to Puttaparti was a photograph of himself,
which he gave to me and which I still have. I don't remember
exactly how he produced it: he just moved one hand over the
other, and he materialized it. It is the size of a playing-card, and
I keep it in my puja room .... Materializing objects is a part of
Swami's nature, quite natural to him. If he wants to, he can
produce anything.

At that time, Prashanti Nilayam was under construction.
There were no cranes then. It so happened that the iron beams
for the roof of the new mandir could not be lifted. So the
masons sent a word to Swami, who was away, I believe in
Bangalore, and asked him how they should get them up. Then
Swami said that he would come.

These iron beams were huge: they are as long as the width of
the mandir; and there was not just one, but a series of them
which were to be positioned at regular intervals. Swami told
some of the people to go and tie a rope to a beam. 'Lift it', he
said. And they went up easily, as if they were a piece of cork,
whereas before that they were struggling and couldn't do it at
all. Swami was not helping to pull the ropes, but simply
directing operations. The workers were up on the terrace,
which had not been completed at that time. They lifted the
girders and didn't feel the weight at all.

Baba and his devotees went regularly to the Chitravati River.

It was almost a daily routine in those early days ... the pattern was generally the same. First, he would talk about philosophy and narrate some story on a religious theme for some time. Then there would be some singing of bhajans. And then he would suddenly ask some person to ask questions, or something like that. Next he would place his hand into the sand, or make a small mound of sand and then put his hand into it. We would be watching, because we knew that he was going to take something out of the sand. He was playful and used to try to create suspense in us. Sometimes he would make no mound, just put his hand into the sand.

And what would he take out?

Innumerable things: so many things, so many times, all sorts of things, from sweets and other eatables, to objects of worship. It all depended on what he wanted – on sankalpa, a Sanskrit word the nearest English term for which is perhaps 'wish'. But it is more than 'wish', because kalpa means 'creation', and 'wish' doesn't denote 'create'; sankalpa means 'creation along with the wish'. As soon as the wish enters his mind, it is fulfilled, as in the materialization. He may create a material thing, anything.

Swami would produce from the sand all sorts of images, chains for the neck, jewels; he gave us a number of them. And when he took out food from the sand it would be hot, as if it had just come from the oven. And he would distribute it to everybody. Though it came from the sand, there was no trace of sand on the food. And what flavour! It makes it so unique. We had never tasted such flavour before. It was Indian food, but that quality – the taste and the aroma – was not of this world.

It was generally sweets that he made. Sometimes this would be in a liquid form we call amrith. He would just pull his hand out of the sand, and it would be full of amrith. We used to go prepared with plates as we expected some eatables.

I was once or twice with Swami when he went to the Kalpavriksha tree, which is near the top of the hill that lies close to the Chitravati River. I think the tree is still there, but it is now very much smaller. He used to ask the devotees to ask for any kind of fruit, even if out of season. I am a serious type, and so I did not ever myself ask him for fruit out of season, but I was present when other people did. Many people would ask for something, and whatever they wanted, they got it. They did not get it from Swami's hand, but from the tree itself. Swami would be sitting far away from the tree. 'What fruit do you want?' he would say. 'Then go and get it' he would tell them.

The Raja had this observation to make:

Going to the river was only a pretext to keep us devotees away from boredom and to create some enthusiasm. Also, unless he performs miracles, we will not develop faith in him; they are a necessary ingredient to inculcate or inspire the devotees to have faith in him. No amount of telling the devotees who he is and that he is 'a great one', a *Bhagavan* (godly person), will be sufficient. By observing him and coming to know him, we obtained the conviction that he is an avatar and developed faith in him as a godly person, a Bhagavan.

He gave some details of the times when Swami produced statues on his visits to Venkatagiri.

Swami has produced several small statues during his visits to Venkatagiri, and they are still kept like treasures by our family.

On 10 or 11 September 1950, we, a group of people in three or four cars, went from Venkatagiri Palace to the Pellakur Garden on the bank of the Swarnamukhi River. There Swami produced from the sand a statue of Sri Rama. First he made a drawing on the sand in front of him, and then he took with his hands the statue out of the sand. The statue was about ten inches high. On another visit a year and a half later, he produced, during bhajan singing, statues of Sita and Lakhsmana. These three statues are all exquisite pieces made of metal. These three deities form a group according to Hindu beliefs.

Baba produced other things as well:

Till 1966, every time Swami used to visit us, he would take us at least twice to the Swarnamukhi riverbed, where he would produce things from the sand. If I remember right, there was a Peace Corps mission of Americans staying with us from 1964 to 1967 – five people. Their names were Stanley Tyrrell, Wiley Craig, and Janet, Amist and Phyllis, whose family names I no longer recall. They came to the riverbed also. Swami gave one of these people a cross, and to another, a ring. Why, out of five people, he gave something to these two, I don't know. Why he gives to one particular person when there are hundreds of people there, we don't know.

The Raja recalled Baba's trances.

One day, I think in the early 1950s, we were all in the house of Hanumantham Rao in Madras. It was on Sri Krishna's birthday, which falls in either August or September. Swami went into a trance. This is another phenomenon that we don't see now. He used to leave his body, which would become stiff; this used to be very common in those days. Sometimes, by the look of his eyes, we would be able to make out that he was about to fall into trance. But not one of us ever caught him while he was falling; he would fall abruptly, and with a bang, and sometimes he would even hurt himself. Sometimes he had convulsions, in both arms and feet, and his limbs would be very rigid and not flexible at all. It is very difficult to describe this and it was also very painful to look at.

There was no particular pattern to his trances. Sometimes there would be no movements at all while he was in trance; he would just fall down and be still. But sometimes he would be very violent. Then there would be jerks in his limbs that might be very strong and violent. He would then get abnormal strength. Sometimes he might pull out his hair with his hands. He would, as far as I remember, never bite his tongue so that it would bleed.

In these trances he would sometimes take on some ailment from others and have it for some time after he returned from trance. Sometimes these ailments were serious, sometimes only light fever. The malady would pass from a devotee into his own body. Once in Delhi, for example, he had paralysis for some time after he returned from trance.

A few times in trances articles would come from his mouth. Once we saw small golden leaves shoot out from his mouth. As they came out they would scratch the edge of his lips. We also saw vibuti come from his forehead and his feet many a time. I remember particularly one incident in Hanumantham Rao's house when vibuti came from his feet.

Most of the time when Swami came back from trance, he would tell us where he had gone, but sometimes he would not.

He remembered one particular incident:

… that happened at Hanumantham Rao's house. I was present, and my brother might also have been too. Many people were there, but my cousin Madana had just left when the incident occurred, after bhajan. A basket of sweets 'came' towards Swami's hands as he was lying on a bed, in trance. We could see it coming. We did not follow the basket from where it came – it was very difficult to judge what distance it moved because it was inside the room. Our physical eyes have their own limitations. But the basket did come to his hands. After it came, Swami got up.

What the basket was made of I can't remember, but it was full of Indian sweets. Some of the sweets were given to us, and we brought them home and distributed them later to some people. I don't recall what sort of sweets they were, except that as usual they had a special taste; whatever comes from 'Sai Stores' is always special.

Had he seen him change things without touching them?

I have seen Swami change things at a distance – not stamps, but some other things, such as a ring. A normal ring would be there on a person's finger. Swami would say: 'Do you want a new one?' 'Yes, Swami.' 'OK'. And the ring would be changed, right there on the finger. I have not experienced this myself, but I have seen it. But generally, what he does is he takes the ring, holds it between his fingers, blows on it, and it becomes a different ring or changes in some way. For example, I was a cricket player at one time, and I had a ring. But there was a difficulty as to what to do with it when I was playing, since I couldn't have it on my hand then. So I asked Swami. He said 'OK. Do you want it enclosed?' 'Yes, Swami.' 'Then give it to me.' He caused it to be fitted with a little case and gave it back to me. On the ring was a photo of himself, and now it was fitted with a cap that could be closed over it. This ring is still in my possession.

The Raja himself had been witness to no unusual things with motor cars. However, he added:

Two things have happened which many reliable people have seen: one was when his car ran out of petrol, and he asked the people with him to fill it up with water, and it ran on water. The other thing is that without touching the controls, the car went by itself. Swami sat cross-legged, no feet on the clutch or on the brake, hands never touching the steering wheel. The car went; he drove the car like that! He was in a playful mood.

Swami would also produce eatables when we were in the car. Somebody might say: 'I am hungry.' 'What do you want?' Swami would ask. 'I want a cake made out of such-and-such a crop', pointing to what was growing in the fields we were passing. And Swami would create such a cake, as though he had sown the crop, harvested it, and cooked it.

The Raja did not remember who had witnessed the incidents of water running the car or of swami's driving without touching the controls. The incidents were not recorded as far as we know. At one point he said what, in some form or another, we would hear often:

> The problem is that at the time we never thought that Swami's history would be so valuable; otherwise we would have noted all these incidents down. There are innumerable items that we saw. But sometimes what remains of our memories is the remnants of remembrances. The incidents were too numerous to remember them all.

Two events occurred in Kanyakumari, the southernmost tip of India, where Baba took a group to the seaside.

> He went to the water's edge, and three or four other people also went with him in the water. I stayed up on the beach, waiting, just a few yards away. There were quite a few of us there, including B. Ramakrishna Rao, who was then governor. Swami went into the water, and when the wave receded, there was a necklace of pearls stuck around his feet. Everybody saw it, and if I remember right I think he gave it to Mrs Ramakrishna Rao.
>
> Another incident occurred at Kanyakumari. There is a temple there at Cape Comoron, where there's a beautiful statue of a deity …. Swami told us a story, that there used to be a diamond on the nose of the statue (it was a female deity), which had been stolen by the Portuguese in the 1600s, (a fact that) seems to be quite correct historically. This statue is just like any other orthodox Hindu statue, but such a beautiful piece – the life in it! But the point is, that the diamond was definitely gone, and Swami somehow materialized it. He gave the diamond to that deity.
>
> Similarly he gave a present to Shiva at Benares. It was a huge thing, a full necklace to be worn. He presented it to Lord Vishnaiva; he himself (Sai Baba) put it on the lingam for in that temple there is no statue. The necklace was made of a variety of precious stones. This was in 1960. I was there, as was Raja Reddy, the singer B. V. Raman, and several other people.

The Raja gave us his version of his father's missing passport:

> My father was always an absent-minded person. (He) lost his passport and couldn't find it for days. He eventually found it. Upon his return to India, Swami told him: 'You lost your

passport. You were always like that – forgetful. You dropped it somewhere, and it came to your room.' That means that Swami himself got it back to him.

He described a tonsillectomy.

I do not remember the name of the patient, but I think he was a young man. Two others were present, one of them being the singer B. V. Raman. He was asked to bring a basin. He held it, with some water in it. I was holding a towel. No anaesthesia was given. Baba told the patient: 'Open your mouth.' Then he produced some sort of three-pronged instrument, and also a knifelike thing. He inserted these into the mouth and made a cut. It was done all of a sudden. Blood came out. B. V. Raman is a Brahmin and not a tough man; he almost fainted. Swamiji joked and shouted at him: 'Don't be afraid.' The patient did experience some pain, but before that Swami had applied vibuti, which mitigated the pain. The pieces of tonsil were thrown out, just like after any other operation. After the operation, the patient suffered, so Swami just brought some vibuti, applied it on his throat, made him eat some, and the pain left in a very short time.

In those days, the Raja told us, Swami used to be carried in procession by the devotees, from the old mandir to the new mandir.

This would take place in the evenings. Because there was no electric light, many people used to carry gas light and Petromox lamps, as well as dried dung patties, which put out a lot of light, and a type of firework which gives a brilliant glow and which we use during festive times.

It may have been an optical illusion; we can't say. But for many people, Swami would appear in different colours, different hues. Though I myself didn't see him that way, he used also to appear as *Amba*, that is, as a Devi (Hindu goddess) sitting there, a female form. And a change that was obvious to everyone was that vibuti used to come from his forehead. And more than that there was a sort of lustre on his face – something like a shining, but not exactly. It is very difficult to describe, but the nearest Christian terminology is 'beatific vision', an aura. But I have never seen any halo or bright light around Swami.

The Raja had never observed any change of bodyweight in Swami. He had this to add:

I have experienced a peculiar sensation from touching Swami. It is a very difficult thing to describe; one has to feel it oneself. But as far as I was concerned, it was a pleasant sensation. It makes you feel elated, but in a sense it is not elation. The nearest description that I can give is that it is a feeling of general well-being; you feel very happy. It is an electrifying experience.

Baba had not visited Venkatagiri since 1970, and things in Puttaparti were very different from the early days. The Raja told me:

I used to spend a lot of time at Puttaparti in those days, especially from 1950-56. Whenever Swami used to go on tours, I would accompany him. At that time we were with Swami during the whole day – not just me alone but all the devotees; no secrecy and nothing to hide. But now it is impossible; there are too many people. Nobody is allowed to go up to him in his room now. If all were, there would be a stampede. But sometimes in the old days, just as now, we might have to wait days together; he wouldn't even look at us.

Physically, we are not as close now as we once were. But still, his grace towards us is being reflected in some form or other, and in that sense we are still very near to him. I sometimes feel his presence. In some little ways he makes his grace and presence obvious to us.

Our class has been virtually destroyed, by political, social and economic changes in this country. If our family is one of the few holding on to the older traditions, it is entirely because of Swami, because he wants these traditions to go on. He is the custodian of Dharma. He is Rama Himself.

Swami has neither birth nor death. His body is merely, for the time being, serving his purposes. Swami is not Swami's body. With our limitations, the name and form are very important for us. We haven't reached the stage where we can really know Swami. Swami is the absolute Brahman in his original form. Because of his *deva sankalpa* (that is, his divine wish), he has taken this form and this name. But actually he has neither name nor form, except for the benefit of people. This is according to the Hindu philosophy which we believe in.

There are so many pseudo-Bhagavans now. They are there against the injunctions of Scripture. Our Scriptures have described the qualities of a person who is really divine. Only if all those qualities fit the man will we orthodox people recognize him as an avatar, and Swami has all these attributes. Lord

Krishna is the clearest example of an avatar in our history.

Ordinary human beings who attain *siddhis* (psychic powers) can create things. But if they use this power that they have acquired through penance and austerity, they will exhaust it. It is not good for them. They will try to demonstrate it for those who go to see them, for their own publicity and for selfish reasons. But Swami does not do one thing for himself. That is the difference between him and others. Whatever he does is solely for the benefit of others. He does not call anyone to come to him, nor anyone to give anything to him. Only Bhagavan should produce miracles, as he is omnipotent, omniscient, omnipresent.

10
'Ask For Whatever You Want'

In the Telugu-speaking area just within the borders of the state
of Andhra Pradesh is the small town of Kuppam, some fifty
miles east of Bangalore. There lived the family of Mr
Radhakrishna Chetty. The members of this family were some
of the very early devotees of Baba, or 'Bhagavan' as many of
them prefer to call him.

Mr Radhakrishna, his wife and children visited Puttaparti
for the first time in 1946, when Sathya Sai Baba was only 19
years old. They became so attached to the young swami that for
many years they stayed with him six to nine months of each
year. Mr Radhakrishna ran a stone-cutting and granite export
business and could therefore stay for longer periods in
Puttaparti by leaving day-to-day operations to his manager.
Mr Radhakrishna had died a few years prior to the time when
Dr Osis and I first met his family in 1975. We visited Mrs V.R.
Radhakrishna in her home in Kuppam and later also in
Whitefield, where she frequently stayed with her daughter Mrs
Vijaya Hemchand.

I soon became acquainted with seven of the eight sons and
daughters of Mr Radhakrishna, who are now all married and
living with their families in localities far apart. The eldest,
Suseelamma, widow of Mr Venkatamuni, is now living in
Madras with her son Eswar and his family. She was born in
1913 as the daughter of Mr Radhakrishna's late first wife. Mr
Radhakrishna had seven children with his second wife,
including Krishna Kumar (born 1930) living in Coimbatore,
Vijaya Hemchand (born 1931) in Whitefield, and Amarendra
Kumar (born 1934), living near Kancheepuram. The youngest,
Muralidhar, born in 1945 lives in the old family home in
Kuppam, where he continues his father's business.

Because of the Kuppam family's early and long association

with Sathya Sai Baba, I have found their testimony about Sai Baba's early days to be of outstanding importance. It has made things easier that all the members of this family, except for Mrs Radhakrishna, have a good command of the English language.

When Dr Osis and I first visited Mrs Radhakrishna in Kuppam in early February 1975, her youngest son, Muralidhar, acted as our interpreter. In September 1981, after a second independent translation of the transcription of the interview, Dr Thalbourne and I went through a draft of this chapter with Mrs Radhakrishna, with the help of her daughter Vijaya.

In the first interview Mrs Radhakrishna wanted to know the purpose of our enquiries. After we had explained our intentions to her and told her about the several interviews that the swami had granted us, she spoke to us freely and obligingly. She had some extraordinary incidents to relate, the most baffling perhaps being Sai Baba's sudden disappearance from one location and reappearance at another:

> I will say as much as I remember. Almost every day all of us in the ashram used to go for a walk towards Chitravati in the late afternoon. As we were approaching the river and passing a hill on our right-hand side, he (Baba) would sometimes suddenly disappear. He would, for example, snap his fingers and ask those around him to do the same. And hardly had we snapped our fingers when he had vanished from amongst us and we could see him on the top of the hill waiting for us.

Mrs Radhakrishna stated that such disappearances and reappearances were common with Baba in the early days, namely, in the late 1940s. More rare, however, was when he showed them a dazzling light from the top of a hill:

> One day when we were walking with him towards the riverside, he told us that he would show us the 'third eye.' Lord Shiva is supposed to have the third eye. On a previous day, he had told us: 'One of these days I will show you the third eye.' So that day when he said: 'I will show you the third eye', we knew that he was going to show us something. Just as we were looking at him on the top of the hill, we could see a brilliant light resembling the rising sun, and the rays of that light were unbearable. This brilliance of light started from his head and fell all over the place. There was suddenly a lot of light behind him as if the sun had risen.

Before the light came to its full brilliance, people began to say they could not bear the light, and the women almost fainted. Because they started complaining and before they could think what might happen, he was with them again on the riverbank.

We asked Mrs Radhakrishna to describe what the light looked like, such as its form and colours. She said:

There were colours, but they could not be distinguished on account of the brilliance of that light. There was so much brilliance that we could not see properly what the colours were. The light was right behind his head; it was a sort of a rising sun behind his head. There were so many colours, the centre being very dazzling, and they could not be distinguished. It was so bright, and before anyone could think of colours, he was back again. This incident was about 6.00 in the evening. It was slightly dark that day. The radiance was more brilliant because there was some darkness in the sky behind.

We asked her for more details. Where were they? Where was the swami? How did he disappear? How quickly after his disappearance did they see him on this hill?

We were just about reaching the riverbed when he suddenly told us: 'Look, look, I will show you something', and immediately in a matter of seconds he was on the top of the hill. And the people were just standing there at the foot of the hill. As we looked towards him on the top of the hill we saw a dazzling light. It looked like a ball of bright redness and emitted colour rays which could neither be distinguished nor counted on account of its brilliance. One could not look at it. It was so red and bright, and before anyone could think of colours he was back again with us. This incident occurred at 6.00 or sometime after 5.00. It was overcast that day, and the brilliance was greater due to that slight darkness.

Later in the book we will describe how other witnesses reported this dazzling phenomenon.

Mr Radhakrishna fell sick several times when he was in Puttaparti. His widow told us of one such incident which is of particular interest as it involved and apparently led to Sai Baba's sudden disappearance from the Chitravati River and reappearance at the bedside of Mr Radhakrishna. This event occurred the day after he was allegedly healed of a serious sickness by Baba (see the chapter 'Raising the Dead?').

The very next day after this incident (of being 'raised from the dead') happened, the people asked Swamiji: 'How about going to Chitravati this evening, Swamiji?' He answered: 'Why, poor Radhakrishna is so ill, how can we leave him and go? Let him get well; we will go later and take him with us.' Then I said: 'It does not matter. I will look after him. You can all go to Chitravati.'

When Swamiji goes to Chitravati, the ashram is completely empty – everybody follows him. Everybody left, only me remaining with my husband. They reached the riverbank, and he sat amongst them on the sand, talking to them.

At that time, I was giving my husband something to drink when he fell into his chair unconscious and the drink came out of his mouth. Then I cried out: 'Swamiji, something has happened, something has happened.' Next moment, the swami was at my side and said: 'Nothing has happened, stay quiet.' He put his hand on Radhakrishna's forehead and gave him some Horlicks (a beverage widely used in India) and he recovered.

According to Mrs Radhakrishna, the swami appeared at her side immediately when she shouted out for him. She knew that he had gone to Chitravati, and she was sure that he was not in the old mandir before she shouted for him in panic. To go from Chitravati to the old mandir takes at least several minutes if one runs fast. Mr Radhakrishna and his wife were the only people in the ashram when this incident occurred; their daughter Vijaya, the only other member of the family at Puttaparti at this time, had gone to the river with Sai Baba and the group. Mrs Radhakrishna told us:

At the riverbed, Swami had suddenly vanished. They were all looking around searching for him, looking if he was on the hilltop. After searching the whole area at Chitravati, looking this side and that side, they came running towards the ashram. As they came to him and asked why he was there, he answered: 'A small thing had happened so I had to return urgently. Everything is all right.'

Did she know of any other case of this kind happening to somebody else? She replied that Baba used to do many things, but that she had never asked other people what had happened to them. She herself had not witnessed any other case like this. The swami used to say: 'I will protect till the very end anybody who believes in me.'

Near the top of the hill above Chitravati is a tamarind tree. We had heard from other devotees and had read accounts in the books written by Kasturi (1974) and Murphet (1971) that Sai Baba had many times in his early days produced things for his devotees from this tree in some remarkable way. This is how Mrs Radhakrishna remembers it:

He often used to go with us up the hill to the tamarind tree. Then he might tell us to pluck leaves from the tree and keep them in our hand and close it. Then he would say: 'Ask for whatever you want', and when we opened our hands, the thing we asked for was there. Sometimes people did not believe him. They would think of some object, but before they opened their hands, they would ask Swami what was the object they were thinking of. He would answer correctly as to what was in their hands, before they had opened the hands.

The older people would ask for an idol, *saligram* (statuette) or lingam for pujas. The young might ask for chocolate, peppermints, sweets or fruit.

We would just close our hands, think and wish; that's all. Where the things came from, we could not see. We just saw it when we opened our palms. The leaves would no longer be there; in their place would be something else.

Then Swami himself used to pluck various fruits from that tree – apples, pomegranates or mangoes. It is a most surprising thing when an apple comes from a tamarind tree. But he could pluck any fruit from that tree or from any tree. And if we asked for a particular fruit, say an apple, he might say – especially to people who would not believe in him – 'You go and pluck; you will get an apple.' And they would find an apple on the tree.

Almost daily he would show some miracles. It was a very common affair for the people with him. Sometimes he would also produce hot things from his hand. When he was walking on the Chitravati bank, he might suddenly bend down, take some water from the river in his hand, and say: 'Yes, nectar.' And so it tasted when he gave it to someone to drink.

In those early years, there were usually some 30-40 people with Swami in Puttaparti. A number of people of our family were there, including my daughter and sons. We all used to sing devotional songs, bhajans. That was the main activity. Swami would lead the singing. Once we were singing a song in which a snake was mentioned (the snake is a symbol of Shiva). Then a snake was suddenly there with his hood open. The people shouted: 'Swamiji, there is a snake there!' He said: 'Don't get agitated, simply sit down; it will not do you any harm.' The snake was there till the song was over. Then Swami told the snake: 'Go, go, go.' It just disappeared and we could not say afterwards where it went.

11
He Vanished Before
His Devotees' Very Eyes

In 1946, when the Kuppam family first went to Puttaparti, Vijaya was only about 15 years old. Now Mrs Hemchand, Vijaya currently lives in Whitefield with her husband and children, and her mother frequently stays with her when the swami is in Whitefield. Our first interview with Mrs Hemchand took place on 21 January 1975. Between that time and September 1981, we had a total of four interviews. Apart from these formal interviews, I have had informal visits to the Hemchand family during almost all of my visits to India since 1975. Hereafter I will refer to Mrs Hemchand as Vijaya, as she is called by her friends.

According to Vijaya, Sai Baba would vanish before his devotees' very eyes. These astonishing disappearances occurred many times during the period 1946-48, sometimes once or twice a week. They were allegedly observed by all the devotees present.

> We used to go with Bhagavan to Chitravati every day, usually about 4.00 in the afternoon. On the way there, he would be walking with us, ladies on one side and gents on the other. As we were passing the hill, and before we had crossed the river, he would suddenly vanish from our sight. He would then, in no time, appear on the top of the hill and call us: 'Here I am, on the top of the hill.' Sometimes he would suddenly disappear before our eyes without saying anything. We would start searching for him, look this side and that side, but then he would clap his hands from the top of the hill.

We asked how Baba came down again?

He might shout: 'I am coming down,' and by the time he had finished the last word, he would be in our own midst.

Did he then reappear at the same place where he had originally disappeared?

He would reappear in the same area, but perhaps not on exactly the same spot. For example, sometimes he might have been next to me when he disappeared, but might reappear next to another person.

Vijaya took almost daily notes when she was with Sai Baba, and every few days when she had free time she would write them up in a final form in her diary, but undated in the beginning. Unfortunately for us, the diary was written in Telugu and she used to write more about what Sai Baba said than what he apparently performed in the way of miracles. The books she has filled are now between 30 and 40 in number. She has refused several people permission to publish extracts from them and says she will continue to do so until Sai Baba asks her to act differently.

My acquaintance with several members of the Kuppam family grew into friendship, and in the end Vijaya did me the precious favor of looking up a few things in her diaries. She also allowed me to photograph a few relevant passages which I later had independently translated by two academics at the universities of Bangalore and Madras.

At my request she went through her diary up to 1950. The single record of Baba's alleged sudden disappearances concerned the incident with her father, described earlier by Mrs Radhkrishna.

According to Vijaya, the disappearances no longer occurred after 1949, with one exception in 1950, the year when the new mandir, Prashanti Nilayam, was inaugurated on the swami's birthday (November 23rd). At the time this incident occurred, Vijaya's father was sick and was being attended to by his wife. Mrs Radhakrishna was giving him a cup of Horlicks to drink when he suddenly lost consciousness and appeared to be lifeless. Mrs Radhakrishna's account of this incident was given in the last chapter. Vijaya described this incident in her diary as follows:

It was between 6.30 and 7.00 in the evening, and we had just crossed the Chitravati River on our way back to the ashram. Baba was talking to us as we were walking along. He was in the middle of the group when suddenly he disappeared and was no more there. People started searching for him but could not find him. It immediately struck me that something must be wrong with my dad, and that this must be the reason why Baba had disappeared. So I ran straight to my father's room in Prashanti Nilayam, and it took me nearly ten minutes to get there from the river. Baba was sitting there near my dad and was wiping some sweat from his face. He himself was sweating profusely. I asked him why he had disappeared and he said: 'Your mother was shouting at the top of her voice, "Sai Baba!", so I had to come and rescue your father.'

According to my mother, as soon as she had shouted this, Baba appeared at Dad's side. He just patted him on the shoulders and said: 'Come on, get up.' Then my father opened his eyes and asked: 'Baba, where am I?' He answered: 'You are with me, don't worry, nothing is wrong.'

The text cited above is the only contemporary written evidence for the sudden disappearances. Later we will learn what other people report about this claim.

When we asked Vijaya if Sai Baba might have suddenly run away rather than have physically vanished, she rejected any such interpretation. According to her, the swami vanished in a split second from the sight of those around him. He was always the centre of their attention, and so there was no question of him somehow slipping away in a normal manner. He simply vanished.

The early devotees of Baba believed that he could also suddenly appear at distant locations. The Hemchand family reported one incident which in their view showed Baba's sudden appearance in the faraway city of Madras, where they then had their home. Mr Hemchand relates:

We were living in Madras at that time when we received a telegram from Bhagavan to start immediately for Puttaparti. So we went away. Then, two days later, we received in Puttaparti a telegram from one of our neighbours: 'Your house burglarized. Come immediately.' Then Bhagavan told us: 'Don't worry, nothing has gone, but if you had been there your life would have been in danger. So I have saved you by sending you a telegram. But for your conscience, you have to go there to see for yourself that nothing has gone.'

I went back to Madras. Everything was there, but the thief

had bundled up some things but then left them behind in the back yard. The thief had put in a bundle all the things he wanted to carry away, but he had left them there. We did not understand why he had left the bundle in the yard just outside the house.

After three or four months the thief was caught, and he was brought by a policeman to show where he had robbed. He came to my house and then he said: 'Here, I took all the things and tied them up and was about to take it with me when I saw a person in a white robe with tuft hair and he shouted: "Hemchand, thief, thief", and I got frightened, threw away the things and ran away.' The thief's description of the figure fitted the appearance of Bhagavan as it was at this time, white long robe and tuft hair.

The incident occurred over 30 years ago, too far back to trace the policeman who had brought the thief to the house.

Much more rare than Baba's bodily disappearances, however, were the occasions when Baba showed what Vijaya called 'the visions' when he showed them 'the rising sun', 'the setting sun' and 'the third eye'. He would show the devotees these visions at dusk after the sun had set but while there was still daylight.

On one occasion he was on top of a hill and the devotees were below, when a dazzling light shone forth from him. The swami showed such visions on three occasions at most, but Vijaya had witnessed them only once. In one of our early interviews with Vijaya she had given an account of this phenomenon, which was much the same as that of her mother but more elaborate. In 1977 she went through her diary and found there a passage in which she gives a contemporary description of this event. She kindly allowed me to photograph it. Here is a translation of this text.

This time when we went to Parthi (Puttaparti) by train, we learned that Sri Baba had gone to the sand banks of the rivulet. Therefore we went straight there, sending our luggage to the ashram. By the time we reached there, Baba was already on the hill. All devotees had gathered at the bottom of the hill and were watching him. Already it was sunset. This is the hill on which Baba had been previously. Sri Baba could be seen by all from there. Behind his head bright red rays, which resemble the rays of sunset, were shining. After some time, they disappeared and were replaced by a bright powerful light that was emanating *crores* (tens of millions) of blinding sun rays and that was glistening like a diamond on the head of a snake. Looking at it and unable to tolerate the brightness, two people collapsed to the ground. All the people were staring with wide open eyes, overwhelmed with joy. Immediately the light disappeared and there was pitch darkness. Suddenly going from very bright light to darkness, our eyes were blinded, but we recovered our sight in a little while. Before we could open our eyes, Sri Baba stood amidst us and was laughing aloud. All our hearts were filled with joy. He went to the people who had collapsed and applied vibuti, which he had materialized in his hand, to their foreheads. They regained consciousness and offered salutations to him.

It was not until 1950 that Vijaya started to write down dates in her diary. By calculating from easily datable events in her diary (such as festivals), she believes that Baba showed the light from the hill sometime between April and June 1947. Vijaya told me that her older sister Suseelamma had also seen it once but on a different occasion, so it has happened at least twice.

Why has Baba stopped producing these two sorts of phenomena – the disappearances and the visions? Vijaya informed us that the only reason the swami would give was that the crowd around him had become too large. Also at that time – the beginning of the 1950s – he gradually stopped going to the Chitravati River with his devotees. 'At first he used to visit almost every day each of the families in their rooms in Prashanti Nilayam after we moved there from the old mandir, but as the crowds grew larger these visits gradually became fewer and eventually stopped.' In the 1940s and 1950s most of the devotees came from relatively distant places, like Bangalore, Madras, Kuppam or Venkatagiri. None, Vijaya tells us, came from the neighbouring villages or from the small towns of Anantapur or Penukonda, which are also close to Puttaparti:

> In those days, they were all 'anti-people' who did not like Baba much. People in the neighbouring villages talked so badly about him. They used to say: 'He is after all just a boy. We have seen him from his birth. We know what he is. How can he become a god?'
>
> So, whenever we went to Puttaparti, they said: 'Why are you spending so much money? Why have you come down here where there are no facilities, nothing?' So they used to grumble

He Vanished Before His Devotees' Very Eyes   107

at us. At Dasara time Bhagavan used to come out in a procession during the night. It would start at about 10.00. Again, by the time we came back to the mandir, it would be 3.00 or 3.30. When the procession came all the villagers used to close their doors. Nobody would come out.

She described some incidents from the processions.

The procession would go from the old mandir and through the two streets of Puttaparti. Every day of the ten-day festival we would make a different type of flower decoration, and he would be sitting on the top of the palanquin and the men used to carry him. So that we could see Bhagavan we would walk backwards in front of the palanquin. We would be singing bhajans. From the top of the palanquin, Bhagavan used to guide us, go left, go right, this side, that side, because we could not see the road ahead of us.

Those ten Dasara days we could often see vibuti just showering from his forehead forming the three stripes of Shiva, as if somebody is pouring the vibuti. It would be full of fragrance. It would come as if someone had put a lot of powder on the face. His face would become full of vibuti. It wouldn't be falling down, it would stay on his face quite thick, it would form on his face. We thought the particles would fall away but they did not, and the face remained full of vibuti. If something fell off it disappeared on the way down.

Then some people used to see Baba take on the form of Rama, Krishna, Shiva. Once we saw that Ardha Nareeswar, that half Shiva and half Parvati – the whole body divided in the middle. One side of him had the form of a lady (Parvati), the other that of a man (Shiva). Most of the people present saw this.

Mr Hemchand, who first came to Puttaparti in 1948 and only during festivals, added to his wife's description:

Half of his body will be Shiva, half Parvati. As he turns his head to the right, his head will be like that of Shiva with all its characteristics, and within a few minutes he will turn his face to the left and it will change into the face of Shiva's female counterpart, Parvati.

We will see appear on his forehead the three wide stripes of vibuti that are characteristic of Shiva. First, there was nothing and then suddenly, we see these three bright stripes of vibuti. And after a few minutes it will disappear and then we will see on his forehead the sandalwood paste (chandan) and a round spot of kumkum[1] that is characteristic of Parvati.

Vijaya reported one most remarkable incident that happened sometime before 1950. They used to go with Sai Baba to the Chitravati River and stay at the time of the full moon until late in the evening, talking and singing bhajans. Before they left in the afternoon, the ladies would normally have prepared food for dinner, which they brought with them in several vessels in a bullock cart. This group could number 50-60 people. This day it was different.

> Before we left, Bhagavan said: 'Today is a special day; you do not prepare anything in the house. I will prepare something.' We said to ourselves: 'How is Bhagavan going to prepare it at Chitravati?' Then he said: 'You load all the empty vessels on the bullock cart.' Then we were there till 10.00 or 10.30. We had been singing bhajans, going up the hill, coming down, running on the Chitravati banks, and we were so tired. We told Bhagavan we were really hungry. He told us to bring the empty vessels.
>
> All the vessels were placed in a line, and he asked us to put the lids on to close the vessels. Then he went to a nearby tree and took a small branch from it. He walked by the vessels, touched each with his stick, and said: 'rasam, sambar, rice, chapati' and so on (these are names of Indian dishes). As we uncovered the lids, the smell was coming beautifully out of the vessels. Even the rasam was bubbling hot. And then big lotus leaves were picked by the boys in a nearby lake and used as plates. Bhagavan made us all sit in a line, and he himself served the food for all of us.
>
> It was wonderful. We had never eaten such delicious food in our life. For two days after we did not feel like eating much. Then Bhagavan said it was just like amrith (nectar).

Vijaya was not able to substantiate this account by a passage in her diary. She told me it had not been recorded. This particular incident had earlier been independently reported to us by Mrs. Radhakrishna in her home in Kuppam.

Vijaya told us of another experience:

> My husband was not well at that time. He had had a cough for some time and so he went to our doctor, who examined him and told him that the eosinophil percentage (of cells in his blood; an indicator of conditions like asthma) was far too high and that he was having asthma and had to undergo treatment. He was very upset about this. That night, before going to bed, I prayed to Baba to bring him relief. During the night, I had a

dream. I was telling Baba about my husband's worries and told
him I did not know what to do. 'I will give you vibuti', he said,
'which you should give to him.' I held out both my hands, and
vibuti was pouring into them. Then Bhagavan told me my
husband will be all right.

That was the end of the dream, and I woke up and found that
my hands were empty. But then I looked at my husband and
was going to wake him up to tell him the dream when I saw
vibuti on his forehead. You know the way Bhagavan with his
thumb puts vibuti on people's foreheads? It was just like fresh
vibuti. I asked my husband if he had put it there. 'No, I have
been asleep.'

The very next day my husband's cough was much better. In
the evening of that day, he went to the doctor who had
examined him. He said the eosinophil percentage had gone
drastically down and was asking him what he could have done,
for it never goes so quickly. From that day onwards there was
no cough and he was hale and hearty.

Mr Hemchand remembered this incident well:

> I had a severe attack of asthma, and the doctor said it will take a
> long time (to recover). He asked me to have my blood tested. A
> high eosinophil percentage was found in the blood, which
> meant my cough was related to asthma. After that night (of my
> wife's dream) I went to the doctor. No trace of the sickness was
> then found, but it is almost impossible to cure asthma.

According to Vijaya, every day she was with the swami, he
produced a variety of things, such as vibuti, sweets, fruits,
rings, or medallions, wherever he might be. We will report just
one example:

> Sometimes when Bhagavan was sitting in a chair talking to us
> or sitting on his throne with the bhajans going on, he might
> take a leaf of jasmine in his hand, between his fingers, and it
> would become vibuti or amrith of beautiful smell, and no
> longer would there be a jasmine flower in his hand.

Vijaya usually spent nine months of the year in Puttaparti, and
there was, she told us, no time at all to read and study for
school. But Sai Baba forced her to go and attend her exams,
though she at first refused to go since she was sure she would
fail and since she did not want to feel ashamed afterwards. Sai
Baba said he would help her, and he ordered her and her
brother Krishna Kumar to go and take their examinations.

These were final high school examinations. We started to attend
school shortly before the examinations, and everybody was
laughing at us: 'Look at these people. They are coming at the
end of the year, and they want to pass the examinations.'
Everybody was teasing us. I felt so bad and cried like anything
and told my dad that I am going back to Puttaparti, I am not
going to school. But my father told me that I had to go to
school and that I had to obey Bhagavan's orders. We had these
big books, and we did not know anything that was in them, and
on top of that, they were in English.

She and her brother prepared by taking one chapter from each
book, preparing 10 questions based on its contents and
studying the answers to those. They went to take the exams.

Before we left Puttaparti, Bhagavan created two small stamplike
pictures of himself and gave one to me and one to Krishna
Kumar, and also a pen to each of us and told us to bring them
with us to the examination hall. The photos were just like
stamps.

When the examiner came and distributed the question paper,
we were so scared and sweating like anything. In the first
examination, which was English, then you won't believe me,
whatever questions we had selected and prepared, all the ten
questions were on the examination paper. We were quick to
answer them all, and we were in ecstasy. And immediately when
we came home, we wrote to Bhagavan. Like this all but the last
examination were over. There only came questions that we had
prepared, and we wrote beautiful examinations.

But things were different with the geography exam.

When we saw the examination paper in geography, nothing we
had prepared was there.

That day the examiner was a Moslem. He was going around
and came to me. He said: 'What is wrong with you?' Then I did
not say anything. Then he looked at the picture of Bhagavan
and said: 'Who is this cinema actor?' I told him: 'This is not a
cinema actor, this is Bhagavan Sri Sathya Sai Baba from
Puttaparti.' 'Then why are you not writing anything?' he said.
'Because I have not prepared properly. I do not know any
answers; I feel helpless.' Then he went off. After a few minutes
he brought a sheet of paper. On it were answers written by a
clever student. He put that paper under my paper and told me
to finish it. Then he would bring me another paper. After 10-15
minutes when I had finished that sheet, he brought another

one, and a third and a fourth till I had answered nicely all the
questions. And he also gave me help with a map. After the
examination I told Krishna Kumar and learned that the same
thing had happened to him, although he was sitting in a
separate hall.

So we passed our examinations with Bhagavan's help. I stood
first rank in the district, at the top of several hundred students
and received a shield for my examination, secondary school
learning certificate.

The same day, in Puttaparti, Bhagavan was telling Mother
about the examination and the examiner, how he helped me,
how he was asking about the picture.

Sometimes Sai Baba used to talk to his devotees about his
future. This is how Vijaya remembers it:

We were all sitting at the Chitravati River. He said: 'In the
future so many thousands of people are going to come. Even to
have one *parnamaskar* (to touch his feet) will be very difficult for
you.' He even drew a map, on the sand, of Prashanti Nilayam.
It had then not been built. He was telling us that such huge
buildings were going to come. He did not say much about this,
just that thousands and hundreds of thousands of people were
going to come to see him.

In those days we used to have parnamaskar so many times a
day. Whenever he sat down all of us would do it; when he got
up, we did it. When he came into the room, when he left the
room. Like that we touched his feet so many times a day. Then
he said: 'Just to touch my feet once will in future be very
difficult.' Like that he used to tell us but not often. Now we are
realizing how difficult it is to touch his feet. Not once in three
months we are getting it now.

Mr Hemchand was also present on these occasions, probably
sometime in 1949-1950.

'My work has not yet started' Baba used to say, 'but it will start
in due course. Then it will be very difficult for you to come near
me. There will be thousands of people. Whatever programme I
have in coming here will start in the near future.

Note
  [1] Kumkum is vermillion powder and is considered auspicious by Hindus.
The small red spot many Indian ladies have on their forehead is made with
kumkum.

12
'You Will Not Be Able
To Explain It'

Krishna Kumar was born in December 1929 as the eldest son of Radhakrishna Chetty and his wife. He visited Sai Baba with his family in 1946, when Baba was only 19 years of age. From 1946 to 1950, he spent about six months of each year with Baba. He lives now with his wife and grown children in Podanur near Coimbatore, a small city one night's train journey to the south of Bangalore. There he runs a small factory with a few employees. He has invented some machinery that he uses to produce ready-made foods and other products. I first met Krishna Kumar in his home in October 1977, and interviewed him twice thereafter, in October 1981 and July 1983.

According to Krishna Kumar, his half-sister Suseelamma had gone to Baba before the rest of the family. Their father had been suffering from an incurable stomach ailment, and they were seeking help from 'philosophical people' who might give his father some peace of mind so that he could forget his disease. Baba then asked Suseelamma to bring her father to Puttaparti. Krishna Kumar recalled:

> When we first got to know Sai Baba, he was almost childlike, a very flimsy, tall, thin, bony-like figure. Very thin. I don't think he would have weighed more than 50 to 60 kilos.
>
> He used to perform many miracles and cure incurable diseases, but he was also very fond of playing games with people. We used to have bhajans in the evenings. Baba was a very good singer, our family was also good at music, and this fact made us more attached to him than anything else.

He described a typical day:

In those days, Chitravati was a picturesque place, full of these tamarind trees and gardens, and we had beautiful shades. We would go to the riverbed after eating, at about 3.00. We used to make 'country cradles' – hang two ropes from the branches and make a kind of swing – and get Baba to sit on that.

From there he used to throw sweets; he would simply throw his hand, and everyone could pick up a sweet for himself. There would be just enough sweets for everyone to have one each – no more, no less. So in this way we used to spend our time, up to 6.30 or 8.00.

In the evening we would come back to the ashram. As soon as we arrived home, we would sing bhajans for about half an hour. He used to have a fancy that we should all prepare the dishes for the evening meal. He would ask everyone to get together and make the whole thing, and then he used to serve it himself. He took pleasure in serving us.

Then we used to make him sit in the centre, and we would form two lines – one row ladies, one row gents. He would talk about his philosophy and tell us about a number of stories from the Ramayana, Bharatam, Bhagavatam, and so forth; he used to tell beautiful small stories.

Thus did we spend our time, till 10.30 or 11.00. Then, tiredness forced everyone to go to bed. By 4.00 a.m., some people were up again. Those who liked to sing would then do so for Swami. This is what they call the 'suprabartham.' Baba didn't sleep much himself – only till 5.30. Even now, I don't think he sleeps much. Like that the days were passing on.

Things were much different in those early days in Puttaparti.

The old mandir was just a small hut-like thing when we first came to Puttaparti. It was gradually expanded, and only after these baktas and rich people came did it become a fine large building. But even then it could only accommodate about 100 people. At that time Baba would very seldom leave Puttaparti. On important occasions there would hardly be there more people than 150-200 and many of them used to stay on the outskirts. They would hire small huts in the village and use them simply to sleep in at night. Many people would stay rather closer, putting up tents or making some sort of shelter for themselves. That is how life used to be in those days. We always stayed within the ashram.

Baba would speak of his future:

> He was telling people that after some time they might not be
> able to come close to him because of crowds around him, and
> as his volume of work will be increased, and because of the
> plans which he had for the future.

> We were unable to understand (these plans). We never thought
> that he was going to construct schools, colleges – we never
> thought that it would develop into such a big affair as it has. He
> also used to tell us that he would not be seen in this country for
> a pretty long time – that he would be going abroad. I think he
> has plans to go abroad for some time, for preaching or
> propaganda or something like that.

Occasionally he would send people away.

> After some time, whenever Swami feels that it is necessary for
> people to leave because of their family responsibilities, he will
> send them away. Being sent away is not a pleasant experience.
> He will create a fight with you. He will not reveal to you that he
> is sending you away. He will throw the fault on us, saying: 'You
> have not followed my instructions', or something like that, and
> that this is the reason why he is sending you off. But the real
> reason is that he is so kind to you that you would not like
> leaving him. So he will create a small fight, calling the parents
> and saying: 'This fellow has done such-and-such a thing. I
> don't like him. Send him off.' That is how he used to clear
> people. After some time he used to make them realize why he
> has done this.

Krishna Kumar described some of what he saw in the way of
miracles.

> For example, when we were walking in the evenings at
> Chitravati, Baba would pick some wild plant, and immediately
> it would become apple, or orange, or some other fruit. We used
> to coax him. Suppose somebody says: 'Swamiji, this is not the
> season for grapes. We want grapes.' He would therefore
> immediately say: 'Pluck a leaf' and there would be a bunch of
> grapes in our hand, without him touching the hand.
>   Suppose you were a good bakta, and you wanted a ring or
> something like that, with a photograph of Swamiji embedded
> in it. You might say: 'Swamiji, I would like to have a ring.' He
> would then tease you, saying: 'Why do you want that?' But then

immediately he may say: 'Go and take that flower.' You pick the flower, and he will not touch the flower himself. As soon as you have plucked it, he will ask you to close your hand around it; and when you open your hand, you straightaway find a ring, and with the image that you wanted. He has given things in this fashion to a number of people.

There were more:

> On special occasions Baba caused the colour of his gown to change, especially when he was in the procession and on the palanquin on the last day of the Dasara. Also sometimes on the way to Puttaparti. Suppose he was wearing a green gown during the procession. It would turn into another colour, but by the time he reached home, the original colour would be back. I saw this a number of times.
>
> In those days, we used to have processions on Thursdays and also at festival times, and sometimes we might go on any day if there was a good gathering of people. The baktas would decorate a palanquin with flowers. We would place Baba on the palanquin, and baktas would carry him on their shoulders around Puttaparti for one or two hours. When we came back to the mandir, we would make him stand and sing bhajans, and he would play along with us what we wanted him to do. Then, suddenly you would find on his face vibuti, or kumkum, or sandalpaste[1]. If he wiped his sweat off with his handkerchief it would keep appearing. We saw this on a number of occasions.
>
> Baba explains the appearance of the material on his forehead by saying that some of the baktas wanted to see him in that form, and so he appeared like that for them. And especially during festivals, but not at ordinary times, we could see his face in full illumination – very bright. So if people are really lucky, they can have a darshan like that; it appears for some people, and not to others.

> Whenever we departed from Swami, he would produce vibuti, or kumkum and bless us. That is a very common thing with him.

Vibuti was sometimes produced in large quantities.

> For pujas he will just close his fist, move his hand in throwing moves, and out will come a shower or spray of vibuti. Baba calls this latter *abishekam*, which means 'giving a bath' .... In Baba's vibuti abishekam the holy ash comes out in full force. It can be any quantity; there's no limit to the amount – it depends

on the idol we are worshipping. If the idol is big, then a huge quantity of vibuti will come forth and almost cover the statue; and if the idol is small, only a small quantity will be poured over the idol. There's no limit for Swami.

He also used to perform vibuti abishekam during Sivaratri festival. There would be an empty vessel, and Swami would ask two of his attendants to hold it upside down above the idol. He would then just put his hand into the upturned vessel, move it around a little, and then hold it there. The vibuti would start pouring out, and by the end there would be, I would say, about three to four kilos of vibuti.

Did Krishna Kumar ever see Sai Baba produce something unnatural, something neither nature nor man produces?

Once a botanist came from Bangalore and was challenging Baba to produce something not normally found in nature. So Swami asked me to bring something from nearby wild cranberry-type bushes. I picked a handful of leaves and brought them to Swami, who told me to give them to the botanist. The botanist took them and started laughing, saying: 'What is this? I ask you for some unnatural thing, and that is what you give to me!' 'Have patience' Swami said, 'look inside the leaves.' He did and found inside the bunch of leaves a small apple.

'Apples are common' said the botanist. Baba then replied: 'Don't be in such a hurry, open it.' When he cut the fruit open, we did to our surprise see apple on one side and sapota on the other side, but the whole fruit was under an apple peel. Finally Baba said to the botanist: 'See, my stores produce very unnatural things.' He used to name the place where he got his objects 'Baba stores' or 'Sai stores.'

Unfortunately Krishna Kumar did not know the name of that botanist but thought that he had been a lecturer in the Indian Institute of Science in Bangalore or from some other institute in that city. This incident, like most of what he reported here, happened in the late 1940s and some in the early 1950s. Nor did he remember the names of anyone else who had been present. Most of the people around Baba at that time were older people, and over thirty years had passed.

Baba was also challenged by a *sadhu* (Hindu holy man) from northern India:

I remember when a big sadhu from Kashmir came to Puttaparti. He was a tantric – that is, he was himself able to perform miracles. As soon as he arrived at Puttaparti, he challenged Swamiji, saying: 'I can do better things than you can.' He demonstrated his abilities. For example, he used to take an empty pot, pour from it, and out would come water, and he says it is from the Ganga. And he used to open his hand and reveal kumkum. He was a well-built large man with a big beard. He was a good musician too, had a big steel rod, called gazale in Hindi, that is used as a musical instrument. He played on that gazale, attracting most of the people.

At that time there was with me in Puttaparti the old pujari Seshagiri. I did not feel bold enough to talk to the tantric by myself, but the pujari came with me and we asked the man: 'What do you mean by doing all these things?' He said: 'I am challenging Swamiji to stand before me instead of the other way around.' And he told us to tell this to Swamiji. Swamiji replied by saying: 'Wait for three days and then we will see to it.' Then, one day, when bhajan was going on, the man suddenly got up and just fell at Baba's feet. He started crying – that big tantric sadhu. Everybody had been scared that he was going to harm Swamiji or do something. We never thought that he was going to surrender himself. We expected that he might be playing some trick to harm Swami. But instead he started crying like a child. Swamiji started laughing.

The tantric said (I remember his words even now): 'I am a fool. I never realized that you were Narayana.' Narayana is the same deity as Rama. He was from Bhadrinath, where the population is predominantly Vaishnavite.

From that time onwards he became like a docile cat. He was there for more than seven days. He started preaching that Swamiji is God. He told us: 'You are all very lucky. I have been to so many hills and places of pilgrimage and done all these pujas and tapas (religious austerities), and it is only now that I am able to see the real God.' He then took his leave and departed, saying he would not come back.

Had Krishna Kumar at any time seen Baba produce large quantities of food, instead of just the usual handful?

Baba is very fond of having the poor fed. He would ask us to prepare a quantity of sweets, say ladus, for feeding of the poor. But then we would realize that we didn't know how many people to cater for. He would just ask us to bring one basket of sweets, and would keep on distributing from it. The basket might not hold more then 200 pieces, yet he would distribute a piece each to as many as 500 people. I have seen a number of instances like that.

I remember another incident. There was a festival where he was supposed to get up early and be bathed by all the baktas. The usual procedure is that everyone has to pour some water over him and get his blessings.

On festival days Swami is expected to get up by about 5.00, but on this particular day he got up very late, and he said he was not going to conduct this festival. People started complaining and said: 'It is a very auspicious day; he cannot behave like that.' So he said that he would have his bath and that nobody should prepare any food.

Then, at lunchtime – about 12.00 or 12.30 – he asked everybody to bring empty vessels. I saw this incident clearly and with my own eyes, so I can't forget it. Baba just made a movement with his hand right over the empty vessels, and I could see the food rising up from the bottom! I would say that he produced about a dozen varieties of dishes in this way, one in each vessel, and it came up in a matter of seconds .... Then Baba told us: 'This is why I told you not to prepare any food. I was intending to give you something divine, prasadam.' That was one of the incidents where you could not forget him; where you have to come to the conclusion that he is really a miracle man.

Major incidents were few. It was on only some occasions, when Baba felt like it, and when he was in the right mood, that one could see such major things as these. Krishna Kumar remembered another major incident from the time when the new mandir was under construction, apparently the same recalled by the Raja of Venkatagiri.

The large hall of the new mandir is some 40 feet across. There was a girder that weighed several tons, and to lift it by mechanical means was not possible. It went half the way, and as the men were struggling to lift it up, the heavy weight of the girder caused the sidewalks to crack ... they were not able to pull it up. Baba was away at that time in Bangalore. This beam was standing there half the way; they were unable to bring it down and unable to put it up. So they immediately sent a message to Swamiji ....

Upon his arrival back two days later he came immediately to the construction site. He just said: 'Come on. Lift it now.' And as soon as he said this, within seconds they were able to lift it and keep it in position. Perhaps he gave them some superhuman strength, or he made the beam light. After they had lifted the first girder, they changed the mode of lifting them and had no problems after that.

Construction of Prashanti Nilayam began in 1948, and it was still being built when I had to leave Puttaparti in 1949 or 1950 to take care of the family and business affairs because my parents were staying most of the time with Swamiji.

What did the people in the village think of all the stories about his miraculous feats that they must have heard?

The village people didn't have much faith in Baba in those days. They were against him, because they were under the impression that he was a miracle man who could cause them harm if they got into trouble. Now all the villagers and neighbours have great faith in him.

We asked Krishna Kumar if he had seen Baba become unconscious or fall into trances.

Swami's trances used to occur quite often, generally once a month or once a fortnight, sometimes even two or three times in a single week. It would depend upon the 'calls' that he would get. He would just say: 'I am feeling uneasy,' or, 'I am feeling unwell,' and immediately we would arrange his bed in his private room, and he would lie down to rest. As he went off into trance he would forget himself. His whole body would go cold to the touch, and there would be no proper movements of the limbs.

The first time I saw this I thought he had collapsed. I didn't understand these things in the beginning. In those days, there was an elderly man there, Mr Seshagiri Rao, and we used to call him when Swami fell into trance. Then Seshagiri Rao caught hold of my hand and said: 'Don't fear. Just be here, that is all.'

We never used to come out of that room at all while Swami was in trance, and we kept it locked from the inside. We would come out only after he had returned to consciousness and instructed us to come out. Sometimes he would come to within one or two hours; at other times it would be considerably longer. The maximum period I have ever experienced is one occasion when it lasted nearly one and a half days. During these times he would be without food and all. The amount of time he spent in trance would depend upon the nature of the trouble of the person whom he was 'visiting.'

Did Baba sometimes say what had happened to him while he was in trance?

He would not tell us much in detail of his 'rescues'. He would frequently just say that he had been to some place and helped some people and that those people would be arriving before long. But he did not give any names. And sure enough, those people would come. They would express their gratitude, receive Baba's blessings, stay there a while, tell us baktas what had happened to them, and then go home happy .... Occasionally he would say he had been to countries far away.

Sometimes Baba would appear to people in distant places in his normal form, sometimes in a disguised form. I know an example of the latter. An old man and lady were coming to Puttaparti from somewhere in Andhra. They were changing from one train to another, and since they had a big bundle of luggage, they were too lazy to cross over the bridge and were instead walking across the railway track and their son following behind them. Suddenly, there appeared a train engine. The couple later said that some 'young man' (they were unable to describe him further) pulled them off the tracks and just managed to save them. As soon as they got to Puttaparti, Swami said to them: 'What kind of fools are you, to cross the railway lines in that way?' He scolded their son. These people were very surprised that Baba knew what had happened. I was present when Swami talked to these people.

I must say I don't remember who this family were. I did not see them after that, and so many people used to come. There were a lot of cases like that one, but we used to just enjoy the story and then forget about it. Still, a lot of people used to tell how they had been saved by Baba. They came to this conclusion because as soon as they would arrive at Puttaparti, Baba would start questioning them about their incidents. The way he was questioning them naturally made people think that if he knows what happened there, then he must have been the one who was there.

People have also told us that he has appeared in full flesh in another place when he was actually in Puttaparti or in Bangalore, but I have not had any such experience myself.

Krishna Kumar's mother, his sister Vijaya, and his brother Amarendra Kumar had all told us that sometimes Baba would suddenly disappear and then reappear on a hilltop near Chitravati. Krishna Kumar told me that he had witnessed such incidents *before* I mentioned to him the experiences of his relatives.

I have seen him say that he will go up the hill, and suddenly he would be up there ....

There is a place that is called 'Kalpavriksha.' This was a tamarind tree which Baba used to call his 'Kalpavriksha' because it used to give him whatever he wanted. On the western side of the banks of the Chitravati, and close by the river, is this small hillock, further up from where the well is. It was a beautiful place, with a big flat rock near the top; it was like a beautiful garden. It was the only hillock that you could easily reach from the river. Behind the present mandir near Kothacheruvu village there is a row of hills but they are about three miles from Puttaparti.

In those days, at the time of Sivaratri, Baba used to tell us: 'I will show you the divine light.' At about 8:00 p.m. we would all walk towards that faraway hill, and we would go with Baba close to the hill. Then he would disappear – he was not to be found with us – and within seconds there would be seen a bright light shining from the top of the hill.

We did not actually see him appear on the hill, and in fact we could not see his form there at all because of the distance and the darkness. All we could see was this very powerful light. It was not lightning. Nor was it white. It was a yellow light, something like a huge candle flame. Baba would be up on the hill for two or three minutes, and then suddenly he would be with us again. He would ask people whether they had seen the light (*jyoti*), and some people, if they were not cautious enough, would say no, if they had not seen it because of some obstructions blocking the view. So Baba would say: 'Watch. I will now show you the light again,' and he would immediately disappear again.

As soon as he disappeared, we could see the light shining on the hill. This phenomenon I have seen two or three times. We have seen him make light on both hills but more on the Chitravati River hill.

When I say he 'disappeared', I do not mean that he would vanish into thin air. He would say that he would just walk ahead of us, and within seconds he would have reached the top of the hill. Whether he got there by flying or by walking, we don't know. But it must be miraculous how he gets there so quickly. He is on the top of the hill within seconds.[2]

Another time, it was going to rain heavily, although none of us actually knew that it was about to rain. We were all on that hill which is right next to the riverbed. It was early in the evening, if I remember right. It suddenly became dark. Baba then asked the people to get down from the hilltop without a moment's delay. We had about half a dozen old people with us, and it would take about half an hour to clear the hill. Ninety percent of the baktas were elderly people, and most are no more. Baba brought them all down, just by lifting them under the armpit and got them down within seconds. We don't know how he got them down so quickly. Baba helped the heavy ladies to come down, whereas I was helping some other people. Only these fat people had difficulties in coming quickly down. Anyway, having reached the base of the hill, we had not walked a furlong before we suddenly saw lightning strike one of the rocks on the hilltop, causing it to break, and one part of it rolled down the hill. Then Baba said: 'If you had been there a few minutes longer, I don't know what would have happened to you.' But of course, he knew.

Some older followers of Sai Baba told stories of how, in the early days, he dealt with what they term spirit-possessions. Krishna Kumar described one such case:

We believe that spirits of the dead can enter the body of a living person and start acting very differently from what these people normally do. Once there was a fat lady into whom some spirit had entered in this way. When she came to Puttaparti and Swamiji started the bhajan, this spirit used to take over her, and she would start singing her own tunes. Swamiji used to warn her: 'Either you keep quiet, or get out of here.' She used to argue with Swamiji, but it was not the woman arguing but rather the spirit. She would change the tone and the way of talking.

There was a small hall in the mandir, and we were just taking our food there. Then suddenly the spirit took over the woman, who said: 'I must have food with Swamiji.' Swami said: 'You are unfit to be here. Get out.' Then, to our surprise, he told all of us to clear the place, but I remained with him. He asked me to bring him some saffron rice, which is used to give blessings. I brought a small quantity from the puja room.

He sprinkled a little over the lady and then took hold of a little strand of hair in the middle of her scalp and just lifted her up, this heavy lady. I think she must have weighed about 250 pounds. He just lifted her, swung her in a circle around him, and dropped her on the floor again, pulling out this bunch of hair, whereupon the lady fainted. He knotted the hairs and said to the lady when she had regained consciousness: 'It is all over now. From now on, you will not be taken over by this spirit, because it has been caught here', by which he meant that the spirit had been caught in the knot.

This is the only case of possession that I have seen him deal

with in this particular way. In other cases, he would ask us to
get a small stick, as soon as the spirit comes, and he used to give
the person a good beating. The person being given the beating
would cry and bellow like hell. The spirit will answer Baba who
he is, where he is from, what he died of, and so on. As soon as
Baba had finished the beating, he would just break the stick,
saying: 'That is enough. The spirit will not come back again. It
has reached its salvation.' And the spirit would not affect that
person or anybody after that.

According to an Indian popular belief, spirit-possession is not
really a mental illness. What did Baba do for those mentally
ill?

Many mentally sick people came to Baba, but none of them
were healed. Baba said they would have to suffer. He would not
heal these people.

Krishna Kumar related that Sai Baba in those days never
used any perfume or powder. In spite of that he would
sometimes suddenly smell of beautiful fragrance. The smell
suddenly came, stayed for a few minutes and disappeared. It
was mostly of sandalwood and musk. It was not uncommon at
the beginning of bhajan sessions. Krishna Kumar used to help
him with his bath, and sometimes immediately after Baba's
morning bath he would also smell these beautiful perfumes for
a few minutes.

Many devotees reported that vibuti had appeared in their
homes or in puja rooms on photos of Sai Baba or other
religious figures that they have hung on the walls. Krishna
Kumar had both heard about and seen such incidents:

I first heard about vibuti appearing on photos at a distance
from Baba somewhere around 1949 or 1950. The first instance
that I heard of was in Bukkapatnam with the Yadalam family.
The people involved are no longer alive. They initially thought
that it was simply dust, which had collected as a result of
negligence. But as it continued to come, they told Swamiji
about it and he said: 'No, no. It is not dust, it is vibuti. You
may remove it and keep it, and give it to people who are sick.'
So that is how it started.

The distant vibuti seems to come to people who are, as you
would say, not particularly close to Baba. He says: 'It does not
bother me whether the person is a disciple or not. He can be

anybody. If he likes me, I like him; if he does not, I still like him.' That is what he used to say. 'Whether you pray to Christ or someone else, it does not matter to me. I have no caste, no creed, nothing like that. Whoever has a real love of God, I am always with him.'

The puzzling phenomena around Sai Baba caused many to ask him: 'How do you do it?' Krishna Kumar said he had answered:

Baba used to say: 'Are you able to see a song? You can only hear a song. How can you see a song, or hear light? You can only see light. Miracles are like that; you can only experience them.' He says that all these articles that he produces come from somewhere. They are just transmitted from another place. We cannot say how they come. They come in a fraction of a second.

Many people would say: 'Baba, you must show me some miracle.' He would say: 'I show you something, and you still do not believe in the miracle. What am I then to do? You should learn how to do this for yourself. It is possible. But even then you will not be able to explain it to others. You can only enjoy it.'

Notes

[1] Vibuti is greyish-white, kumkum is red, and sandalpaste is yellow.

[2] Dr Thalbourne, then 26 years old, tall and used to running, ran the distance as fast as he could and reached the top in one minute and thirty seconds. It may take most people 5 to 10 minutes of strenuous walking to reach the hilltop by the steep, winding footpath that now finds its way up the hill.

13
Figs From Any Tree

Amarendra Kumar is the second eldest son of Mr. and Mrs. Radhakrishna in Kuppam. He had a long and close association with the swami, staying with him, usually as a personal attendant, over long periods in the 1940s and 1950s. He lives now with his wife and children near Kancheepuram some 50 miles inland from Madras, where he runs a small stonecutting and polishing business.

The four interviews with Amarendra Kumar took place between November 1977 and July 1983, at his home and in Madras. He always received me with great hospitality and spoke freely about his association with the swami. He was particularly articulate about his experiences, and he seemed at the same time much concerned to be as accurate as possible in his statements. His fascination with Sai Baba was evident, but his independent mind could see the pro and con of any issue. His first trip to Puttaparti in 1946, when he was 12 or 13, came about because of his father's poor health.

At that time, my father was not keeping good health. He had gastritis, or something like that, but it could not be diagnosed with certainty. He was under treatment for quite some time, and then somebody casually mentioned Sathya Sai Baba to my father.

My father was engaged in quite a lot of social work but would not spend much time in prayers and suchlike. He was, though, by no means an atheist; he was a god-fearing man, but he did not like to waste his time going here and there. Instead he used to say: 'Service to humanity is service to God.' When somebody suggested to him: 'Why don't you seek help from Sai Baba?' he refused outright, saying: 'I will not fall at anybody's feet. Sai Baba is probably a great man and a mystic, but I do not believe what people say about his miracles and godliness.' But eventually he was cajoled into going and seeing Baba. Still, when we first went to see Baba, it was purely out of a sort of academic interest rather than spiritual love or the urge for spiritual healing.

He recalled the family's arrival.

In those days, getting to Puttaparti was a Herculean task. We had to take a train to Penukonda. From there we had to go by bus, and the last part of the way by bullock cart. Many times we had to walk as much as 18 miles through the forest, and finally over the Chitravati River to reach Puttaparti .... As we arrived for the first time, we were surprised to find that Baba had crossed the river to receive us. He was actually waiting for us. Baba immediately came up to my father and asked him: 'Are you not Radhakrishna from Kuppam?' My father said yes. Then Baba said: 'Come on, prostrate yourself. Touch my feet. All your problems are over.' My father answered: 'Sorry, no. If my problems should be over, simply as a result of touching your feet now, I will have to touch them later.' Baba said: 'You are certainly going to touch my feet. Forever you will remain my disciple.' This statement came true; until my father breathed his last, in spite of so many things, he remained a firm devotee. Baba went on: 'I have come all the way from the ashram to receive you, because you are all my children.' And we said: 'Good. Thank you very much for all your hospitality' and we went to the ashram.

At first Baba used to talk just with my father. Later on he asked us to sing a few songs as the whole family were good singers. We started doing bhajans, which used to last us for three or four hours a day.

Our first visit to Puttaparti lasted for nearly twenty days. In those days it was very difficult to stay there for even a day or two, with all the inconveniences. Yet despite all the inconveniences we felt really happy to stay there; we never minded them and often didn't even notice them.

Gradually my father's faith in Baba developed. On my part, I would say that from the beginning I felt a personal attachment to Baba rather than spiritual faith. But naturally, as the attachment grew and as we came to understand him better, seeing him from day to day, our faith also increased, most definitely. That is how we became devotees.

The size of the crowd around the swami had greatly changed since that time.

It was a very small circle of devotees around Baba in those days. We would remain together all the time, day in, day out, except for perhaps when he was taking his food, and even then most days he would eat in the company of the others. The group never exceeded more than a hundred in those days, which then was a huge crowd at Puttaparti. But now at festival times we number the crowds in hundreds of thousands (lakhs), and 'hundreds' have lost their significance. The minimum number of people I ever witnessed around Baba in those days was about 30 to 50 people. Then the crowds started growing and growing.

What did the inhabitants of Puttaparti think of the swami in the early days?

At that time people in Puttaparti did not like Baba. People who visited Swami had to go through lots of hardships. Not only that these people did not like him, they gave us a hell of a treatment. They would not give us water, did not want to sell us anything to eat, no transportation. Anybody who called himself a devotee was done with in Puttaparti. And they would give you trouble and harass you. Even the bus drivers in Penukonda would give us trouble, give us the worst bus, which we might have to push half the way. When we went to Puttaparti, whole families used to go together.

The village *munsif* or *kamam* (chief) was one Mr Gopalraja. He had been Baba's classmate in school if I am right. If you happen to know our scriptures, you will know that Kamsa was Krishna's main opponent. So we used to say: 'If God is here in the form of Baba, then Gopalraja is Kamsa, the demon.' Such difficulties he gave us. Now, I have been told, he has become very much devoted to Baba and comes to see him quite often.

Whenever we went with Swami in procession through the village, a number of us had to stand as guards; otherwise they would throw stones at us. And before the procession started some of us had to act as intelligence fellows and try to check up if anyone was planning to throw stones, beat us, obstruct our way or disrupt the procession in some way. They harassed us a number of times. One or two devotees were hurt on one occasion. But whenever a stone was thrown it would never hit Baba, however carefully they tried to aim. It would just stop at a distance. There used to be a lot of tensions and politics in Puttaparti in these early days. But Baba always said: 'Just don't bother. I am too great for them to touch me.'

He described Baba's behaviour as he knew it.

Baba was quite boyish in those days. He was hardly 19, if I am correct. Every evening he used to take all the devotees with him down to the river bank. There we used to sit, sing or just chat. Baba used to come out with miracles, one by one. He would produce, out of nothing, some beautiful, wonderful, delicious eatables, such as jellaby, marzipan, ladu. Such beautiful sweets, as if fresh from the oven, and sometimes so damn hot – too hot in fact, as if you had just taken them out of the frying pan. You know what Indian sweets are like: full of ghee (melted butter), full of spices – they were really delicious. Baba's sweets were as though they had just been brought from the kitchen. So nice! And all these things he would produce from the sand and the river.

He would just make a heap of sand where we had sat down, put his hand into it, asking us: 'What would you like to have?' We were several children of about 10 to 12 years old, so unmindful of his greatness. We were small, and we always used to say: 'Swami, we want this, we want that.' Just like that, and he would produce for us every damn thing, out of the sand on the river bed.

Then often he would just be walking, and pluck a leaf or something from any plant that he might come across. From it he would then create some fruit for you – wonderful fruit, sometimes apples, sometimes sapotas (yellowish-brown small fruit). And as far as he was concerned, there was no such thing as a fruit being 'out of season'. The fruit was in his hand when he opened it just after he had plucked a leaf. And the leaf had disappeared. Anytime, anywhere, he can produce anything. That is the thing. Many times he would give us figs that he plucked from some ordinary tree.

Near Puttaparti there is a hillock, on which there is a tamarind tree known to us as 'Kalpavriksha'. Even as children, Swami used to take us and we would climb up that hill. Vriksha means 'a tree', and according to our ancient Puranas, Kalpavriksha is in the heavens: whatever you want, whatever is asked for, the tree gives it. From that tree on the mountain Swamiji used to produce idols for worship. Then, suddenly, he would produce a sort of a bracelet, or even a brooch, or a pendant, a locket – so many things, according to his own whims and fancies. He would be the one to make the choice. He would give the objects to several people there, sometimes saying: 'You pray, you keep it in your puja room, you do this, you do that. All your problems will be over.' Sometimes he produced things as large as 9 to 12 inches in height: idols. And good idols. The metal was good, and the figures were extremely beautiful. Baba would make such exquisite, lovely things.

We asked about the relationship between Baba and the young people who were close to him and attending him.

In the early days Swami was amongst us right from the time (we) got up at 5.30 to 6.00 till that time he went to bed. In those days at least, we, the boys, did not bother to give that much respect to him. We were a sort of a group of friends. Nowadays the situation is very much different. Now he is quite aloof from us.

But still, with him we were always on the guard, always prepared for the next move.

People like me are rather outspoken. I believe that unless you are outspoken and frank you will in life not get the right answers for yourself.

Swami was often moody. Through one remark he might not talk to you for hours. Sometimes there were days when he would not talk to you at all. Once he is out of mood he may not even talk to anybody, or it may be only you that he does not talk to. There was always a scare in you that he might change his mood. Though we were close to him, we were always on the guard; much though he gave us liberty, we were always careful to mind our position. This fact was always there. He might ask you: 'Did you have your food?' Sometimes when in a good mood he might say: 'Why don't you come and eat?' Then he himself would come and sit with you and even serve you. Then he might say: 'Come on, have a little more.' Thus he could be extremely obliging.

When he asks you on another occasion if you have had your food and you answer yes, then he might say: 'You stupid ass, have you no other business except eating?'

And suppose somebody asks me why Swami is out of mood, the only answer I can give may be: 'Because I took my lunch.'

Why he can react to an answer to the same questions so differently, I do not know, but such is the spirit of the man. When he is out of mood and not talking to anyone, he may be sitting numb or putting up a serious face. Anybody will be scared of approaching him. He will look very serious and terribly irritable.

It never occurred to us that he was Baba the Great or Baba the avatar. Of course, my mother and father often used to scold me: 'Why are you behaving like that? He is an avatar, you should remember.'

Different people have different ideas; some things we take for granted and other things we do not agree with. I have gone so far as not to acknowledge him as an avatar or incarnation of

Shirdi Baba, though for me he is really great beyond any description.

In the course of a public speech he used to quote from the Bhagavad Gita. Then during his speech, he (would) start to talk as if he were Lord Krishna at that time: 'I was telling Arjuna ....'[1] Then after the speech I would get up and tell him: 'Look, I am sorry. What Krishna has said we can accept, though we do not really know after thousand of years; but our scriptures are there, so we take it for granted. But how dare you say that you are Lord Krishna?'

Swami would then answer: 'You shut up, you are only a schoolboy, a kid, only a child still in the kindergarten. Suppose I try to tell you what Krishna was, who he was and who I am. Surely you are not going to understand me; you have not risen to that level.' And somewhere in our arguments he would say: 'I am great, I am God incarnate' and I might answer that just because he is great, he cannot ask me to digest anything he may tell me. On some issues we did not agree. I always called him a mystic and still maintain he is a mystic. Whether he is God incarnate, can we really say yes or no? I feel that we are not competent to discuss that issue. How many of us have contacted God or seen God, so how are we to judge? The question of him being an avatar is also beyond our jurisdiction even to discuss. Let us admit our ignorance. As far as I am concerned, the important question is not whether he is God incarnate or an avatar or an ordinary human being. For me he is Baba, which means love and affection, a unique personality.

The young people lived closely with Baba.

In my opinion, we were rather too close to Baba. We used to sleep in the same room with him, eat with him, play with him, stay with him utterly and completely. There was hardly a single minute when we were apart, day and night. We stayed with him like that for months on end. It was probably because of this intimacy, or something like that, that sometimes when we asked him for anything specific he would say: 'I need you. Why do you bother to have any this or that?' Even so, he has given me a raksha, which is a sort of a talisman. I still have the raksha in my possession. That is the only thing he actually gave me on his own initiative, apart from the usual food and so on. The sight of these miracles was very common for us, and later on we did not even ask of him to produce things, because a number of times every day we were seeing all these sorts of things.

We were overjoyed whenever he gave us something. We, who were around Baba in those early days, were simple folks from small towns. For us Baba was always great, and the idea of research, the idea of finding something out about these phenomena, or recording them, never entered our minds.

When I was a boy, my job used to be to act as a sort of attendant to Baba, carrying things for him, especially to the river, such as his *chappals* (sandals), towel and the napkin that he used to have. In those days he used to eat or chew a lot of betel leaves - just hundreds and hundreds of betel leaves. All the time he would be munching, munching, munching. These leaves were kept in a box, and this box was my main charge. Thus, almost all of the time, I would naturally be by his side.

He then mentioned the disappearances.

On many occasions, especially when we were walking by the river, he would suddenly vanish from sight. As he vanished, he would be walking with us in a group and talking to us. We would not see him or find him. But then he would be calling me or someone by name, and when you looked for him you would find that he would be on the top of the mountain. All this would happen within seconds.

We asked Amarendra for more details.

We would all be walking together, Swamiji leading us with the band of devotees closely behind him or at his side. And suddenly we would not see him but would only hear his voice calling some of us by name. Yet we had seen him just a second before. We had just been walking with him, and suddenly he would not be there. Then we would hear his voice calling us, we'd look this way and that, and then we would see him sitting on the top of a tree or on the top of that hill by Kalpavriksha, for example. He would just be clapping his hands, saying: 'Come on. All of you. Come on.' He could be anywhere.

Just like that, he would be sitting at the top of a tree, calling us, saying: 'Come on up, come and join us, anyone who can climb this tree.' And in a flicker of a second, you would see him elsewhere.

Did Baba disappear often in this fashion?

I have observed this phenomenon many times. In the span of my association with Baba I must have observed this hundreds of times. The first time I ever saw it was in my first visit to Puttaparti.

Could Baba have diverted his attention and been quick to slip away?

I did not have the impression that he was simply very fast in moving. No, that was just not possible. For example, we would be at the foot of the hill, perhaps even 100 yards away from the foot of the hill. Baba would be with us talking. We would be speaking to him, and even before you finished your sentence you realized that he was not with you. All this would happen in a flicker of a second. We would not actually see him disappear, but neither would we see him running away from us, yet he would be calling us from the top of the hill. Had he just been running away from us, we the boys were naturally going to follow him and try to catch him. He would never run away from us. We simply would not see him anymore, but (we would) then hear him calling us from the hilltop or some other place.

It would have taken me a minimum of a few minutes to reach him at the point where he was on the hill: first you would have to run to the hill, then climb the steep hill, which was covered with a lot of boulders, around which you would have to negotiate your way. (Most of these boulders have now been taken away and used as building material). It would be simply impossible even for a superman to go up the mountain within seconds. Sometimes it would take as much as an hour for all the people to get up to the top of the hill. (Every afternoon it was a regular routine for us to go to the river and then go up the hill). If some of the people were elderly, he would come down from the top and help them in their climb. But when he came down to help, he would do this normally, which is to say, walk like us.

Sometimes, however, he would disappear from the hill and then suddenly appear on another. You see, we would see him on the top of the hill, and he would tell us to come on up. He would wait for us. Sometimes he would come down halfway and help the ladies and the children and old people to climb up the hill, and he would rejoin us at the top. Then sometimes he would say: 'Come to the other hill' pointing another place out to us. 'Come and join me there' he would say. But before we could start going in that direction, we would see him already standing there and calling us.

Such incidents happened at a particular time of day.

These things would occur in what we Indians call the evenings, by which you mean late afternoon – about 4.00 to 5.00 p.m., a little before sunset.

How were the lighting conditions at that hour?

Baba's 'disappearing' would not normally happen when it was dark, but rather before that, when there was still at least an hour to go before sunset. As a number of people were going up the hill, it was imperative that we all find our way back before it became dark. We would arrive back at the ashram by dusk, and immediately afterwards would conduct bhajans.

Over how long a period did Amarendra observe these disappearances?

We experienced these disappearances definitely up to the time when I went to college in Madras in 1949. After that I did not stay as long with him every year as before.

Earlier, Amerandra's mother and sister had described Baba's creating a great light around himself. Had he seen such an incident?

There were some instances, when Baba was on the top of the hill near Chitravati, that he would create or produce light. I have seen this on two occasions. As we have been discussing earlier, Swami would sometimes disappear from us. We used to go to the riverside about 4.00 or 4.30 and return about the time of sunset, when it had not become quite dark. Then he would sometimes disappear from the crowd and suddenly call from somewhere, clap his hands, and shout like: 'Look, I am here.' On two occasions when I was there, something extraordinary happened. We looked into the direction where his call came from. We may not have been able to see Baba or see him in full. But you could see someone standing on the top of the hill, and from that figure would emanate a bright light, a halo we might perhaps call it. On one of the occasions it was a beam of light, just flashing like from a lighthouse.

This did not occur on any special day. These events, like most of what I have been telling you, happened in 1946-50, that is before the new mandir was built. I was then 12 to 16 years old.

You tell me that my sister Vijaya described these incidents when Baba produced the light in a more dramatic way than I do. I am three years younger than Vijaya. For some reason it probably did not have the same impact on me and does not come to my mind as flashy as it does to some other people. It was extraordinary all right, but the significance of it probably did not occur to me as it should. I had become too used to extraordinary things.

I have heard some people describe this as Baba having shown to them the third eye, the rising sun, the moon and so on. As we (Amarendra Kumar, Michael Thalbourne and Erlendur Haraldsson) are discussing these events, we are only three of us talking together. But imagine we were 30 in a group and were seeing this light phenomenon. Suppose I say: 'Look at the halo of light.' Then someone else in the crowd may say: 'No, no, you see, it is the rising sun.' So somebody might have seen it as the third eye, another like the rising sun, and so on.

As others did, he had observed changes in Baba's personality.

There was a gradual change in Baba. In those early days he was just a sort of a boy. He was really boyish – sometimes naughty, mischievous, most uncontrollable and very jolly-going. It was in the early 1950s that I had my college education, and by that time he was changing fast. We had observed by about, say 1952 or 1953, that there was taking place in him a gradual change. He was becoming more sober-minded, more reserved, rather more philosophical than he had previously been. I would put this change somewhere in the mid-1950s.

Had he ever witnessed changes in Baba's appearance?

I have witnessed Baba change in appearance quite a number of times. That would normally take place whenever he was taken in procession. You see, in those days, normal person though he was, we used to take him in a sort of procession, especially during the Dasara – on each of the ten days of that festival. Every evening then, we used to dress him in finery. He would not normally have gotten dressed up that easily, but we would bring all our pressure to bear on him – enjoin him, make him dress up. Then we used to have a large beautiful palanquin built. We used to make him sit on the palanquin, and we would take it round the village on our shoulders. Puttaparti was a small village in those days, containing scarcely 60 houses if memory serves me correctly.

While the procession was in progress, we used suddenly to see him change, or rather perhaps I should say, we could see a change in his appearance. A few people would say that Baba assumed the form of Lord Shiva; others would say: 'No, no. He looked like Lord Krishna.' I for my part have not seen the many appearances that people used to talk about, but even so, I have definitely seen some things. I was able to see a lot of vibuti falling from Baba's forehead; this I have observed many times, and also many times seen sandalwood paste appear on his face. Sometimes I have observed stripes of sandalwood paste forming an *ardha chandra* (crescent moon, symbol of Shiva) on Baba's forehead. And many times kumkum started falling from his forehead. I have seen it on many occasions. This sort of thing went on for quite a number of years, up until the 1950s.

All these phenomena were occurring during these Dasara functions. But gradually he started giving up these processions; he became very sober. Yet I would say that in his heart he really liked these processions and that he was probably just making a big show of it that he was not interested. But he would ultimately consent to take part in them. Some people used to say that they would – during these Dasara processions – see Baba's face or body change into another form, like that of Lord Shiva or Krishna. That I have not seen, only the formation of vibuti, kumkum and sandalwood on his forehead.

There was in Amarendra Kumar's opinion, an explanation of why different people saw different things.

In India we have Shivaites and Vaishnavites (who pray to Krishna) and so forth. And those who believe in Krishna may be darned allergic to Shiva; they will not recognize Shiva as god at all. Seeing Baba appearing in a different form depended, I think, on your psychology. A staunch Shivaite might have seen Shiva in him; a strong Vishnavite might have seen Krishna. But since I was neither Shivaite nor Vishnavite I would only see him as Sai Baba. Also only some people claimed to see these changes in his form. When they were describing them, others were complaining that they had not seen anything of the kind.

He had seen the swami's robe change colour.

Yes, one of the very odd things we observed about Baba was that sometimes the colour of his robe would suddenly change. Nowadays he wears gowns of very few colours, mostly saffron and sometimes red, and white sometimes on festival days, but in his early days he would wear any colour. Sometimes baktas would come and beg him to put on a gown they had brought, and to please them he would wear it.

We who attended him at that time were so close to him that without our knowledge nothing would happen to him. We boys were there for everything. We would help him change and constantly be close to him, carrying his betel leaves and handkerchief, and help him with everything. But sometimes, suppose I have dressed him in a blue gown, then in about an hour or so, I suddenly notice that he has a red gown on.

I would for example say to him: 'Swamiji, this morning I put on you a blue gown, didn't I?' 'Yes' he would answer. 'Then what happened? Now you are in a red gown' Of course, sometimes he would give a reasonable answer, but more often the answers would not be convincing though we tried to digest them. He might say: 'I went to such and such a place to meet so and so, and there he gave me a new gown.' But the place he mentioned might be hundreds of miles away, such as Madras or Bangalore, and we knew well enough that he could not possibly have travelled to that place on that day.

Sometimes he used to fall into trances. As he woke up, he might tell us that he had been to a far-off place. Sometimes he might connect the change of colour of his robe with a journey while in trance.

Was it possible that Baba might simply have changed clothes?

Impossible. It would have been impossible for him to change clothes without us noticing it. Most of the time we even used to keep with us the key to his room. As soon as he went out, we used to lock it. In the old mandir he lived in a small cabin-like room with a simple cot. The place was such that when it rained, myself or my brother Krishna Kumar had to place a bucket to catch raindrops from the leaking roof so that the water would not disturb him. He used this room to take a siesta, and there we kept his garments. At night he used to sleep with the devotees in the hall or upon the roof.

In those days we were attending to Sai Baba so much that he would not do anything for himself. He used to chew betel leaves a lot so that he would be red around his mouth. I carried them for him. He did not even carry his own handkerchief. One of us always had it hanging on the arm ready for him to use. And when he had used it, he would hand it back. Like that we always used to move around close to him. For anything and everything we were there. He was being attended to all the time. Even for the smallest thing, we boys were there. He would not even know where his gowns were kept or his purse or anything, so we were with him all the time.

He had also seen the swami produce food on a large scale.

It was at Dasara or some such day that Baba once said to us: 'You do not have to prepare anything for lunch. We are going to the tulassi garden. But before we go, you wash the vessels. We will cook when we come back.' So the ladies cleaned the vessels and kept them ready, thinking that they would have to cook when they came back.

We went to a huge garden of tulassi plants that was in Puttaparti and plucked baskets full of tulsa leaves. In the story of Lord Krishna we read that Brindavan, where he lived, was full of the tulassi plant. This plant is used for religious purposes, and we make garlands from it. Baba would himself make such beautiful garlands that no lady could compete with him.

When we came back that day to the old mandir, Baba said: 'The food is ready, let us have lunch!' We replied that the ladies had not prepared anything, so how could we eat? 'Why don't you look into the vessels?' he answered. As we did, we found them full of food. It was smelling so nicely, such beautiful food had been made. He had produced all the various dishes, rice, sambar and all that. It was to our utter surprise that this food was there ready for us, for only one or two old people who could not walk were left in the ashram while we went to the tulassi gardens.

Everyone who was not sick used to follow Swami whenever he went out of the ashram. These one or two sick people had not noticed anyone cooking, and cooking for 50-60 people is no small job. Things like that could happen with Swami.

Once, on a car trip to Kuppam, Baba apparently changed the contents of a sealed water container.

At my sister Vijaya's marriage Swami agreed to come to Kuppam. At that time he was generally not attending any marriages. When he went to somebody's place outside, he used to act very moody and funny and very reserved. My brother Krishna Kumar and myself brought Swami by car to Kuppam. Once on the way we saw some rabbits in the forest, and Swami said: 'Come on and let us have some fun.' So we started chasing the rabbits and went quite far from the car. There we sat down and Baba said we should have a meal there. My brother or the driver went and brought a carrier in which we kept our meal. Then I happened to take too much chilli into my mouth, and it felt burning hot. I complained to Baba.

We carried with us a mug full of water, and he told me to drink from it. I said there was only water in it. 'Does not matter,' he replied, 'open the mug, drink the water, and all the chilli will not harm you.' I did, but then the water tasted so sweet, so extraordinarily good, similar to coconut water. He did not touch the mug that had a screw top. Before we left on this trip, we had definitely filled it with ordinary water. And when I had drunk from the mug, he again filled it up with water, though there was no water at hand.

Water was also changed into petrol.

I have also seen Baba pour water into a car's petrol tank. Or rather I poured the water into the tank myself. We were short of petrol so he told us to take the car to Chitravati. We poured buckets of water into the tank till it was full. 'Fill it up' Baba said, 'fill it up.'

First we said: 'Not only is he mad, he is making us mad; what is all the nonsense?' Since I was only a boy, the driver or Baba would call me to pour the water, and I thought this was a lot of fun, and was always laughing while we were pouring the water. I think my brother Krishna Kumar must also have seen this.

Whose car was this?

As far as I remember this was Akkamma's car. She was a lady who used to come to Puttaparti in a car along with Sakamma, who was a well-to-do lady in Bangalore and a great devotee of Baba. Both of them are no more. I also remember Akkamma's son Srinivasan Reddy, but I have long since lost touch with him. I think it was into their car that we poured water.

This happened in the 1940s, before the construction of the new mandir. We have travelled long distances on Chitravati water. Later on Baba became more sober, that playful childishness was no more to be seen, and he did not engage in such acts. After he got his own car, he always used to tell us: 'Go to the petrol bank and fill up.'

I poured the water on only one occasion, but I have heard about this happening at least two or three times. It was not an ordinary experience, but once in a while it happened. We often had lots of fun with Swami, just like schoolboys.

More about Baba's personality in his youth.

Baba could be really boyish, naughty and mischievous in those days. For example, we believe in the evil eye – what we call *dhristi*. In order to avert these evil powers, it is a custom that when you are coming in from outside and cross the threshold that we take camphor and perform *arati*, a light ceremony. Because of the light, because of the camphor, because of several holy things used in the ceremony, it is believed that the evil spirits will not touch you.

In the evenings when we came back from Chitravati, there was always a rush, especially with the ladies, because each would vie with the other to do this rite of arati as Swami entered the main door. In this rush he would be amidst us and so many people would be surrounding him. Then suddenly we would not find him. And as we went inside the front gate or door, we would find him coming walking from the back of the ashram, as if he were jumping from the backside wall. Or he would just be sitting in the prayer hall even before people started entering from the outside. But everybody would be looking for him. Thus in a mischievous way he would slip by the ladies who wanted to perform arati as he entered.

Many times too he would tease us, especially the boys, and make fun of us. For instance, he still calls me Nalladora, the black lord. I am the only one in the family who is rather dark-skinned. Nalla means dark, dora means lord or someone high up. We came to use the word telladora, light lord, (tella means light), for the British when they ruled over us. Thus he would always tease me by calling me Nalladora: 'Nalladora, come here.' I would naturally feel offended if someone else called me by that name, but some way or another we were happy just for getting his attention. He could make terrible fun of people. Of course we were boys only and used to take it lightly and jovially.

In those days Baba very seldom used to take a bath. In one of our songs we have mentioned how it is not necessary that one should always take one's bath, always sit for prayers, and so on and so forth, because, as we have seen, Baba doesn't take a bath every day, yet still he is clean, still he is sacred, still he is holy, still he is great, despite being in this state. Bath, prayers, sitting in meditation – all those things are only 'enactment,' as we would call it, because Baba didn't find them essential, and still he is great. Even so, at least half a dozen of us used to hold him by his arms and legs and virtually throw him, physically, into the bathroom, bolt the doors, and pour oil or water over his head. He would eventually submit. But at first he would try to give you the slip. He was just like a child, as when a mother takes her child into the bathroom by force, bolts the door, and gives it a bath. So in that way he was mischievous.

He used to sleep all night, but I would say that he would not fall into a deep slumber as we do; all the time he was alert, even in his sleep. I know this because we used to sleep by his side, all the time, and if ever we used to get up during the night he would open his eyes and ask: 'What is it?' You see, we used to sleep on the top floor, on the open roof, and we used to have quite a number of dogs in those days, and whenever these dogs started barking we used to get up. By 'we' I mean the three or four people who were very closely associated with Baba; we used to sleep alongside him. There was my brother Krishna Kumar, another Mr M. Krishna now living in Hyderabad, one Mr Ramu, and a boy by the name of Natraj, who was from Bangalore and is now professor of electronics or something like that. Except for my brother and Krishna, I have lost touch with these people.

Did he ever see the swami produce any rare objects?

Most of the things that Baba produced were natural things, for as long as I can remember. To be frank, we were all like children in those days, and it was only after we had grown up that we started questioning whether this object is something from nature or that object is something unnatural. So I do not recall Baba producing things that we do not find in nature.

As for the fruits that Baba produced, there was nothing especially unusual about them, except that some of them were unseasonal; he would produce a mango, or a sapota, or an apple when you would not find such fruit anywhere during that particular season. Also, I found that almost all of the edibles he produced – fruit or whatever – were extremely delicious.

Had he ever seen Baba produce an animal?

I have not seen Baba produce any living creatures. But it may be of interest to mention that we have seen a whole family of scorpions living within that bush of hair on his head. You see, he not only seldom used to take a bath; he seldom used to brush his hair. So it was rather difficult for us to know what was in that big bush there. Once, when we started brushing his hair, we found a family of scorpions living there quite happily, crawling around and playing. We were actually rather awed and wondered whether they would sting us. All of us saw this: the group of boys who used to stay with Baba. And we asked Baba: 'What's all this? Have they not done you any harm?' 'Oh, what can they do to me?' he replied.

We were rather scared to try to remove them, but we did it very carefully without them stinging us. I think Baba was happy to have them. He said: 'What can these things do to me? Nothing. Forget about them.' Then we said: 'If we have to comb your hair, we have to make sure to take precautions lest they sting us'.

Baba's response to being photographed was described.

Baba was very averse to photography in those days. He would
not normally allow anybody to take photographs of him; it was
only later on that he permitted this. In our experience, he
would not pose for the camera unless you obtained his
permission well in advance. Many times, when people tried to
take his photo without him noticing, they would have a very
strange experience: either they would not find the roll of film in
the camera – that is to say, the film would be missing – or they
would end up getting a blank, and nothing else. We have seen
this happen even to expert photographers; if they had not
obtained Baba's approval, then they just would not have any
success in their attempts to film him. I have seen this many
times. Even very experienced, professional photographers from
Madras or Bangalore were there. It even happened among our
group of boys, all of whom were from college, like Varadu.

People used to ask him for his permission, saying: 'Baba, you
must allow me to take a photo of you.' He would say no. Then,
very surreptitiously, these people would take a photograph,
and he would immediately say: 'All right. You can take as many
photographs as you want. Show me the results tomorrow.' The
photographer would immediately complain that he couldn't
find the film roll that had been in the camera. And on many
occasions Baba would produce that film roll from his hands,
saying: 'See, here is that roll of film' and he would give it back
to them.

As far as my own experience goes, whatever I have
photographed has come out. But finding these blanks was quite
a common thing. Rather uncommon was the claim that some
extra thing which wasn't present at the time the photo was
taken had appeared in the picture. I have not had any personal
contact with such incidents.

Had he observed any striking case of healing?

As regards disease and physical disabilities, he used to cure so
many things. He conducted operations. He once operated on a
case of appendicitis. The beauty of it was that he didn't do any
such thing as open the abdomen. What actually happened is
this: Baba told me to go out and fetch some water, some Dettol,
a towel, some cotton wool, and all that. So I ran out of the
room and brought back everything that he had asked for. I
don't remember the name of the patient – only that he was a
middle-aged man from the village (that is, Puttaparti). Baba

just pulled up the man's shirt so that he could see his stomach. Then he suddenly put his hand like so, moved it this way and that, and then took a lump 'out of' the man's stomach; but the stomach was not open. I saw a lump of flesh coming out, and there was blood on it. Baba's hands were all smeared with blood. He put everything into the basin, washed, and said to the man: 'Come on. Get up and walk.' The man was quite happy; he was immediately able to get up and move around, and after that never complained about abdominal pain. Baba used no knife – nothing at all for this purpose. In some of our songs you will find that we have sung in praise of his feats in this area: 'You see, without a knife, without forceps, without anything, he is great enough to conduct an operation.'

As to the question of other miracles, it is very difficult to say anything in particular, because the whole damn thing was a miracle. I do not know how to expand it or add any more to it. Everything he did was really miraculous; there is no plausible explanation for it. He was performing these miracles several times a day; it was a very common thing in the 1940s and 1950s. He would be producing something throughout the day, as many as 20 to 30 times a day. They just happened according to his whims and fancies, not at any particular hour or at any particular occasion.

Did the swami sometimes read or study?

He never had a book in his room. I have never seen him going through a book, nor did he read the newspapers. But he would receive quite a bit of mail, and usually he would not even read his letters. Suppose he would receive a bunch of letters and we would say: 'Swamiji, you have letters.' Many times he would not open any of them. He would just scan through the front of them unopened and leave them there. But if you ask him what has happened to so and so, he may give the entire message in the letter. We tried that out, because we used to read most of the letters. For example, someone was sick or something happened in his house. His wife writes to Swami about the problem in the family and asks for his blessings. He would then, after scanning the mail and without opening the envelope, simply tell us Mr A is sick and so on. Then we open the envelope and read the letter to him and find that what he had said was correct.

To the suggestion that Baba could have known the contents, more or less, simply by recognizing the handwriting, Amarendra said:

I can answer that the same person could write for a variety of reasons. Suppose I would write him a letter. I would not only do so when someone is sick; it might be about a marriage in the family, about someone being promoted in his job, how someone is doing in college, that I plan to visit Puttaparti, and so on. There may be many different reasons. Then he would receive letters from total strangers who have heard about him and never written before, and he will also say what they have written.

My mother keeps hundreds of letters from Swami to my family, most of them addressed to my father or me. She keeps all the treasures and does not want to part with even my own letters.

In those days Swami used to spend an hour or two every day writing to his devotees. He would tell us about developments in Puttaparti, what has happened, sometimes ask us to come; he would write about so many things.

He thought he knew when Baba started performing miracles.

The miraculous side of Baba started I believe in 1943. Till then he was an ordinary boy. We have authenticated information from his mother, father and brothers, for that family used to be close to us, just as if we were one family. So naturally we exchanged our views, and we were able to have first hand information about when that great change took place in his life. They always said that he was a very normal boy except that sometimes he used to talk to himself, or sit alone in thought, do praying and bhajans, more than children generally do. Apart from that he was a very, very normal boy.

The change came all of a sudden. You must have heard that he was bitten by a scorpion. The transformation in him took place after the bite. Only after that did he start performing miracles. If I remember correctly nothing unusual took place before 1942. It probably started only in 1943. Then he was around 15 or 16 years old.

Did he remember some devotees who were with Baba before his family met him?

My family was one of the first batch of devotees to come to him. When we came, Sakamma, a well-to-do lady from Bangalore, was the first and most important devotee. She was just like a mother to Swamiji. Shortly after came the Raja of Mysore and his group. They have since all died. Sakamma passed away

sometime in the 1950s. In her later days she was not as much
attached to Baba as earlier.

**Did Baba in the old days ever describe any episodes in the
life he claimed to have lived as Shirdi Baba?**

To that question the answer is yes, many times. I have been told
the following story by some people concerned. You may have
heard the story of the Rani (queen) of Chinjoli when she came
to Swami for the first time.

The Raja of Chinjoli had been a great devotee of Sai Baba
from Shirdi, who used to go and stay with him. After the
demise of the Raja and when Shirdi Baba was also no more, the
Rani learned from two of her sisters living in Bangalore that
there was in Puttaparti a young Baba who called himself an
incarnation of Sai Baba of Shirdi. These sisters, Rajamma and
Sitamma, visited Puttaparti quite frequently.

The Rani told her sisters that she did not believe the young
swami could be Shirdi Baba reborn, and they left the topic.
Then Puttaparti Baba came to her in one of her dreams and
said: 'Why don't you come and visit me? I am Shirdi Baba born
again and living in Puttaparti.'

According to what these people told, the Rani shortly
afterwards contacted one of her sisters in Bangalore and asked
her what that Puttaparti Baba looked like. And as her sister was
describing him, she exclaimed: 'Yes, that is the very same man
that was in my dream.' Till then she had not met Puttaparti
Baba and she did not have much knowledge of him.

The three sisters went to Puttaparti together. As soon as the
old Rani appeared, Baba said: 'You have come at last. But what
has happened to that mug I was carrying all the time? What
about my kamandala?[2] Have you brought it with you?' The
Rani asked him: 'What kamandala? Tell me.' Swami replied:
'Have you not kept it at such and such a place in the palace? I
used it so often. Every time I sat for a meal, water was only kept
in that kamandala. Don't you remember?'

The Rani was taken aback for a minute for she remembered
this, but she was not fully convinced. She probably thought that
her sisters might have told him something.

Next Baba asked her: 'What are you doing with my tonga (a
small horse-driven cart)?' Only Shirdi Baba used to ride in a
certain tonga that was kept at the palace for his disposal when
he visited Chinjoli. The Rani said that after Shirdi Baba's death
they were not using the tonga. 'Instead of keeping it idle in
Chinjoli, why don't you bring it to Puttaparti?' Swami
suggested to her, and she had the cart brought to Puttaparti.

(The tonga is a beautiful piece of work and was still in Puttaparti in 1981).

Like this Baba was giving her incidents from the personal life of her family and Shirdi Baba: 'Do you remember this and that situation? Was I not there to tell you what to do?' The Rani went flat on the ground and prostrated to him.

The Rani has died, but one of her sisters may still be alive.

This incident leads one to assume that Sai Baba may be an incarnation of Shirdi Baba. Otherwise, where did he come to know all this? But how can you or me or anyone else claim with certainty he is Shirdi Baba reborn?

Amarendra said more of Baba's effect and personality, adding some personal details.

Baba is a very magnetic personality, to put it in a nutshell. Very magnetic. Whatever assumptions or presumptions or convictions you have for yourself, the minute you see him, something overpowers you. This was so very much in the early days. But for us, no doubt we were overpowered by his personal affection; we became more attached to him on a personal level. Our contact with Baba consists basically of a sort of attachment. You felt that you were missing something when you were not with him.

And when he would not eat, we virtually used to weep, for no good reason. Whenever he said: 'I am not feeling hungry. I am not going to eat anything,' we used practically to cry and beg him to eat. So it is this sort of attachment that I would emphasize in our case, rather than that he is a great man or a mystic or an avatar.

Of course, we have the greatest regard and respect and even fear for him. In a sense, he is too great to be hurt, he is too great to be offended; so we all have respect for him as a very great man. Sometimes we were also a bit casual, maybe because of our close association with him. People used to wait for him for hours and hours – for days even – just to get a glimpse of him. But we had all the privileges. Suppose you were a newcomer to Puttaparti, and a very moody, temperamental type. Baba might not even say hello to you for days on end; he will just not bother about you. People feel slurred because of this; before long, they start feeling that they have done something wrong or made some mistake. Later on, Baba may decide to talk to them, or he may not even talk to anyone. For days people might stay before having to leave. Again they might visit, and sometimes he will choose to talk to them. He is like that.

But we rather felt: 'Well, that's our Baba after all.' We took things easy, probably because of our close association with him. Sometimes he would be talking to you so nicely and all that, and on the next occasion when you go to Puttaparti he will just not bother about you: he will not call you, he will not talk to you. And, well, I will not keep it a secret: in my case he used to call me names. All that we had to bear with. But still there was that attachment; it's this love for the man, this affection we have for one another, all these things bound us together, as they still do today, even though we are a long way from each other. And even when he was calling me names, true, sometimes, in fact many times, it seemed unreasonable on his part. I have many times quarrelled with him and argued with him; we more or less used to fight with each other. That is probably one reason why I started keeping myself a bit aloof from him.

There is never any reason to his actions, never. Thinking back on it all, we were probably rather too silly or narrow-minded. We were just human, we had our human failings. Baba is too great to be questioned; that is what he always said to me. People frequently do not believe him. And they are too inquisitive, and they come with a preconceived notion. They think that he is really not great, that he is bogus, that he is a fraud, that he is only an impersonator, that he is a cheat. People who come to him with such misconceptions will really find it difficult to get along with him, isn't that so? Baba will then give them a harrowing experience. He is not an easy man. My, he can be a terrible man.

An example of how he could be a difficult man would be if suppose you tried to outwit him. Before you manage to plan it out, he will just draw a blanket over your vision; he will just make you go all topsy-turvy.

We all have our own weak points, of course, and he will put you in some sort of situation where you will have to go and see him and say: 'Baba, I'm really sorry. I never wanted to do this, and please don't do this to me.' You see, he would expose you in front of a crowd of people – sometimes your weaknesses, sometimes your purposes. So in this way you are put in a tight corner and feel embarrassed. And then, naturally, you will go and say to him: 'Enough, enough.'

But he is not blackmailing you; he says it is to make you understand what you are and what he is, and that sometimes he has to follow certain tactics. Probably this was one of his tactics.

This was all a long time ago. Personally, I have seen such a great change in him; he has become so sober-minded.

Among those who have been close to the swami over a long period, were there, we asked, some who have lost faith in him or question him in one way or another?

Of course, Baba has now an enormous number of devotees and admirers, but there are also many people who very much disagree with him. Even I, to a certain extent, started questioning him. As I told you, he may or may not be an avatar. The fact is also this: if they have got something against him, they will prefer not to talk about it for the love of the man. That is my impression.

But I am sure Mr Krishna in Hyderabad, who was very close to Baba at one time and left him, would speak freely about his experiences. He is also such an honest fellow and would never say a word outside the truth.

Do then some of these former devotees question the genuineness of the miracles?

As far as the physical miracles, the materializations, are concerned, the group of people that I was with share almost the same view. As far as I have seen, the materializations are a hundred percent genuine. I believe this also to be Krishna's opinion. He, myself, my brother Krishna Kumar, and several of our friends know every inch of Baba. None of us would dare to say that the physical phenomena are not genuine because that is not the truth. I do not know of anybody who may be able to substantiate any claims that the phenomena are fraudulent. If someone says they are, he must be able to substantiate his remark.

Recently I met accidentally Mr Varadu and Mr Krishna at the railway station in Madras. We are old friends through our common association with Swami but had not met for a number of years. Both of them left Swami after being very close to him for some years. We had a lot to talk about. None of us found a reason to question the genuineness of the materializations. In that way he is powerful beyond question. What we talked about were his actions, his words, his claims. That is where people disagree. All of us three were such that if we do not agree we say no, if we agree we say yes. That is one reason why I am also keeping aloof (from Baba). After a certain stage, we the old devotees have seen a different kind of group gather around Swami, yes-men. We always called them the fifth columnist. You cannot say yes to something you do not agree with, be it Baba or someone else who says it.

Swami can be an endless subject for discussion. There are

plus points, there are minus points, yes and no, this and that. So many aspects of his life and personality.

Of himself he said:

I am not as close to Baba as I used to be, and for very good reasons. One reason was my education. Another is that lives change and we have our business; and nowadays I live too far away, so I don't find the time to go out there and see him. Whenever he wanted me in later years to stay for some time, I was simply not able to do so. It is like that.

An excerpt from an earlier interview forms a fitting conclusion to this chapter devoted to Amarendra Kumar.

You must notice that I am keeping aloof, not meeting him as often physically as I used to. Still, there is not a single night when he does not come into my dreams, not a single night. (In my dreams) we talk to each other (and many times we still quarrel with each other), we go for a picnic, and so on.

My wife used to say to me: 'You dream of him because you recall those days with him just before you go to sleep.' But to be honest, most of the time I do not think of him at all, (I do) not recall those older days, unless there is an occasion like now to meet people to talk about him, and that is rather seldom.

This I tell my wife, and often go to bed with a thousand and one worries and no thought of Baba, nor do I ask for him to come into my dreams, but still, he comes.

Notes

[1] Arjuna was Krishna's chief disciple and brother-in-law. The Bhagavad Gita, the most popular scripture of Hinduism, contains Krishna's exhortations to Arjuna on the battlefield at Kurukshetra as the latter suddenly became despondent and refused to fight.

[2] This is an object that is used to keep water. It looks like an ordinary water mug but it has a long spout, just like there is on a coffeepot.

14
'Enjoy These Days Now'

Mrs Kamala Sarathy is a tall, slim, graceful lady who speaks excellent English and lives with her family, including two college-age grandsons, in one of the suburbs of Madras. Kamala Sarathy is one of those people on whom a lifelong interest in religion (and in her case also in classical music) seems to have had a marked and very positive effect. I think it is fair to say that I met several such people among the Sai devotees.

I also learned, probably from her brother Dr C.T.K. Chari (retired professor of philosophy at Christian College of Madras University), that throughout most of her life she has been an active member in the Ramakrishna Mission, an organization that was founded by the disciples of Ramakrishna Paramhamsa (1836-86), who is considered by many to be the greatest of all Indian saints and mystics of modern times and who caused in India a revival of interest in the ancient Vedanta philosophy. It was his disciple Vivekananda (1863-1902) who made the first major effort to make that Hindu philosophy known to the public in the West.

Several of Sai Baba's more prominent devotees have been followers of other religious leaders and philosophers. Many of them have, after joining Baba's fold, continued their former associations. Prof Kasturi, for example, held for 17 years a leading post in the Ramakrishna Mission in Mysore, and Dr Gokak was an ardent follower of the movement of Sri Aurobindo (1872-1950).

I interviewed Kamala Sarathy in Madras in November 1977 and again in September 1981 with Dr Thalbourne. She first met swami in 1949 on a 'lightning trip' to Puttaparti, based largely on curiosity created by the comments and conversations of two musicians – B. V. Lakshmanan and B. V. Raman (they describe their experiences in the next chapter). She stayed a month.

> I can't say that I went out of faith or anything. I really don't know what it was that took me there. I cannot say that I was very interested for the first two or three days because I had not had much contact with great people of this type. In those days, when Baba was very young, he used to spend all his time with us. The first two or three days he spent talking to us in a very nice way. He would take us to the river and do some miracles there. For example, he would take out of the sand a statue of Krishna, or sometimes some sugar candy, or amrith – anything, all kinds of things.

Her knowledge of music gave her a somewhat special view of Sai Baba.

> The first time I went – in fact for the first three or four days – I was rather upset, because all the songs of Thyagaraja (the greatest of all South Indian composers of classical music and songs) used to be altered, so that the name 'Rama' would be changed to 'Baba'. Being a student of classical music, I did not very much like that. It created rather a conflict in me. But that time my violin master was with us, and he, who was a classical musician, became impressed with Baba's music so I decided to let it be, thinking that perhaps Baba was as great as Rama (God) and that therefore it was all right to change the names. Later I became convinced that he was as great as Rama.
>
> When I first came to Puttaparti, Swami used to sing many songs of classical Indian music as an experienced, trained singer. Our family and the Kuppam family were both trained in music, but still Swami would sometimes correct us, also on the text of the songs and the timing of the music. He was a very good singer. My late music teacher, Mr Chidambara Iyer, who was a violinist with All India Radio in Delhi and once went with me to Swami, was much impressed with his outstanding knowledge of music, although he had never had a music teacher. Sometimes he would sing some rare compositions of Thyagaraja that only learned musicians would know.
>
> Now they no longer sing classical songs at bhajans, only popular bhajan songs. In the evenings when my music teacher used to massage Swamiji's legs, Baba would often sing some rare compositions of Thyagaraja. So my music teacher asked him: 'Where did you learn these songs?' Baba then answered: 'Thyagaraja had these songs from me, Thyagaraja was inspired

by Rama', meaning that Swami was the origin of Thyagaraja's music.

Thyagaraja composed a great number of pieces. Many are commonly known and sung by all, but some compositions are rarely played and only known by learned musicians. That Baba knew these rare pieces so well much impressed my music master.

My music master, who died a few years ago, became very attached to Swami through music. He was very psychic himself. Around Swami new bhajan songs were constantly being made at that time. My music master, who was with me in Delhi, used to have dreams about this music, and he would put down the notations for these songs in the mornings and then teach all of us. When we next came to Puttaparti, we could already play and sing the new songs. In that way Swami taught my music master in his dreams.

Now nobody sings these old songs. Raja Reddy used to sing them, but now they sing simpler songs. In the old days we all used to sing classical songs, and I used to play my violin, but now Swami says we shall only sing the name of God. Recently the singers Raman and Lakshmanan were in Puttaparti, and they started singing a long classical song, but Swami stopped them and told them only to sing songs with verses that only contain the various names of God, namely musically simpler songs.

Kamala Sarathy explained her fundamental reason for becoming a constant member of Baba's group.

For the first few days I did not think much of Baba. What really impressed me was the following. I was thinking: 'There is one thing very spectacular about this ashram.' In those days, only about 25 or 30 people would be there. They experienced great difficulties in getting there, having to use bullock carts for example. Yet when they left, they would have tears in their eyes. Baba used to see them off in the olden days and lift the children into the bullock carts, help them to get into the carts, and all that. Everybody would be in tears. And Baba too. He was quite visibly moved.

Then I was sitting on the veranda in Puttaparti one day and thinking to myself: 'Many people come to my house as guests, but when they leave I don't think they are so sorrowful or that I am so sorrowful. What is it that makes people sad to leave Baba? What is it that they get?' Pondering along these lines I just thought: 'It is the love which he gives, probably, that is the great thing about Baba.' While I was thinking this, Baba came

from behind and told me: 'You are thinking along the correct
lines, Kamala.'

It was not easy to bring Kamala Sarathy to talk about the
miracles she had observed. That question had to be repeated.
She was an admirer of Ramakrishna, and his group always
belittled the importance of miracles; in fact Ramakrishna
'strongly discouraged the use of occult powers' (Swami
Akhilananda 1948/1965, p. 149). Apparently he shared the
approach of Patanjali (the author of the most famous of
ancient texts on yoga), 'who states definitely that they (miracles)
are great obstacles to higher spiritual experiences and mystic
realizations' (ibid. pp. 148-149).

I was not a great one for miracles. But gradually I knew that he
could do anything. My one-month stay convinced me of that.
But even so, the funniest thing happened. Prema, my younger
daughter, who now lives in Boston, was a very tiny girl, still at
school. For a long time she had been troubled with stomach
gripes. As we started for Puttaparti, she had an attack and was
not well at all, but we went nevertheless. I had wanted to ask
Baba before leaving Puttaparti whether there was anything
seriously wrong with the girl. But I quite forgot. Yet later he
told me: 'You know, you remember you wanted to ask about
your daughter, but you have forgotten? I have not forgotten.'
He gave her a *tayithi* (something blessed), a talisman, and he
enclosed the talisman in gold and gave it to her. Surprisingly
enough, she got over her trouble.

As for other miracles, he used to take things out of the air – I
mean, anything from statues of Krishna to amrith nectar, and
various kinds of things. But I think that the most miraculous
thing is his ability to make his presence known in faraway
places – not that I have experienced this, I must hasten to add.
We have all had guidance from him in dreams, and this is very
accurate.

My elder brother was for the last two years of his life
paralyzed in the arms and legs. I don't know the exact cause of
the condition; it was progressive and had something to do with
his muscles. He had undergone some sort of spinal operation
at Christian Medical College Hospital in Vellore, after which he
regained the use of his hands, but slowly his legs started fading.
He wanted to go and see Baba, but Baba said: 'No, he can't
come; he's in a wheelchair. I'll come to see him.' Because he
was ill he was staying with me, and so Baba came to my home to
see him. Then Baba did something strange for him. My brother

had a severe pain in his knee; Baba went across to him, and before we all realized what had happened, he had produced some vibuti and rubbed it onto my brother's knee. And you know, that pain completely disappeared. Until the time he died, the knee was free from pain.

Had Kamala Sarathy ever seen any of the extraordinary phenomena that some of the older disciples report, such as seeing his face change form or seeing him vanish and then appear at a different place?

As for other miracles, I have never seen Swami's face change or anything of that sort; nor have I seen him disappear suddenly in one place and reappear in another. But there are other things that I have seen. One time he took a statue of Vishnu out of the air after we had visited, with him, the temple of Badrinath. He then said that we should sing bhajans and that we were going to do a puja. Next he just waved his hand while we were singing the bhajans, and he materialized from the air 108 golden tulsi leaves, all at the same time (Hindus consider 108 to be an auspicious number). Worship followed with Swami performing the rites. He gave a gold tulsi leaf to all of us to keep, but unfortunately, through my own carelessness, I have lost the one he gave to me. All of us who were present received a leaf. Then he also produced 108 bilva leaves made of gold and gave one each to various people. This is one way in which Baba brought life back into the temples.

I remember too that when we went to Benares with him he took a necklace out of the air. I was there. I saw it. We have also seen Swami stop rain from coming. It was in Puttaparti. We were feeding the poor in the open, for then we had no place inside for this. It was cloudy and started drizzling. We became so worried. Then Baba came, extended his hands like so, and then, you know, the drizzling stopped.

Kamala Sarathy did not, however, remember any case of Baba stopping the rain in a limited area when it was still raining all around.

Another incident occurred when we were returning from a trip to Badrinath. Swami was saying to us: 'You must all hurry, hurry, hurry! We must go! All the cars must go! You must go, go!' We didn't know why Swami was hurrying us up like that. He was very angry: 'Come on! Come on! Quick, quick, quick!' he was saying. All the cars drove further, and then we stopped and were asked (by swami) to get out and walk. I was very tired, but Swami said to me: 'What is this? You are walking so slowly?' So we all had to rush, rush, rush. Swami was the last to leave; the whole group of 120 of us crossed over a bridge, and only then did Swami leave. Then a boulder came down; the whole thing dropped, and the entire road was blocked. Had we left five minutes later, we would not have been able to cross the road. These things I have seen.

I have now to rely on my memory of these events. As my brother C.T.K. Chari says, I don't note things down, and he is always angry at me. He scolds me because I don't write down the dates and time of all these incidents. He says: 'You are most unscientific.' But I am very bad at figures, and I say to him: 'Yes, we are not temperamentally alike. I am not a scientist, just an ordinary person. Why don't you go and stay in Puttaparti and do it yourself?' 'Oh, I don't like to experiment with Swami' he says. He does not like to go as an investigator, because he is one of those Indians who have regard and love for Baba.

I was also present in Puttaparti when Swami turned a sheet of stamps into a picture of himself. I think my brother (C.T.K. Chari) has got a copy of one. I am afraid that I have lost the copy that I had; I am very bad at keeping things. I don't rightly remember who it was who brought the stamps to Baba. I think it might have been my nephew Varadu – one of my cousin's sons – he came with me on the first trip to Puttaparti. But maybe he only procured one of the changed stamps for my brother C.T.K. Chari. I am really not sure.

Baba also cured this same nephew of mine of TB – he had tuberculosis. Baba performed a miracle and cured him, and to this day he is well.

Baba once gave me a ring which I subsequently lost, but there is one thing he took out of the air which I have retained, because he said: 'Keep it in your shrine' so I have still got it. It is a picture of Baba in the mantra 'OM'. He gave it to me in the first interview I had, when I went to Puttaparti the first time. So that I still have. As for the tulsi leaf, my brother is very angry: 'How can you go and lose it?'

I have seen Baba taking out of the air for Indira Devi (an American devotee of Russian origin now living in India) an atchaypatram, which is a special kind of vessel, or casket, in which we keep vibuti. It was quite big and full of vibuti. I was with her when Baba produced it with a wave of his hand. We thought that at any second it would turn the other way and vibuti would drop out of it, but no, Baba deftly caught it. He just moved his hand in a circle and caught it. I saw it with my own eyes. It was remarkable; it was such a big thing.

One item worth mentioning came up in our conversations about Kamala Sarathy's first visit to Puttaparti, something several people had told me earlier:

> We were perhaps 25 people with him, and he was telling us that lakhs (one lakh is 100,000) of people would be coming to see him and that I would live long enough see him in all his glory. I did not believe this at that time. Then I did not have so much faith in Swami. 'You will then only be able to see me from a distance,' he said. 'Enjoy these days now for they will never come again.'

15
The Singers

The twin brothers Mr B. V. Lakshmanan and Mr B. V. Raman are by profession singers of classical Indian music. They came to know Sai Baba in February 1948 when they were asked to sing at the inauguration of a temple by Sai Baba in Guindy, Madras. After the inauguration Baba came to them and asked if they would come to Puttaparti for the Sivaratri festival.

What follows are excerpts from interviews taken in their home in Madras in January 1976 and November 1977 and at the home of Mr Gopal Krishna Yachendra in November 1980. Mr Lakshmanan:

> We went there, both of us. We stayed for a while around Sivaratri and were frequently in Puttaparti after that. Then Baba did not talk much – he was a little shy – but he used to sing much, sing bhajans. He looked somewhat timid in those days and did not reveal himself much.
>
> Subsequently we became quite close to Swami. My brother stayed more with him at that time because I was for some time with the family of Kamala Sarathy, who was then living in Delhi. But for all big occasions, festivals and his birthday, I used to come from Delhi to Puttaparti.
>
> What impressed us right from the beginning was his very presence. Whenever he came, the whole atmosphere would change as soon as he appeared. We had resonance with him and were impressed by his universal love for all of us.

The singers became very close to Baba and served as personal attendants of a kind. From 1949 to 1963, they stayed with him several months a year and led the singing of the bhajans. When Baba went on visits, for example, to Madras or Venkatagiri, then they, especially Raman, would accompany him. 'In those days we saw so many miracles' they stated, 'that it is hard to remember what we saw first.'

Frequently he will produce eatables and give rings and lockets. Then he may produce idols of different sizes, small but also large sizes, for pujas and temples. One big idol from him is in Venkatagiri. We saw him produce some large idols at some big festivals like Sivaratri. But we often did not know to whom he gave them. We may all see when he produces a large idol, but then he may give it to some devotee during a private interview.

He used to do a lot of miraculous things just for fun. Now he has no time for that. For example, he might create something, show it, take it in his hand, close it. And when he opened his hand, there is nothing there. He was very joyful and playful.

Then he has also taken a great number of things out of sand, like a hot cake to give to others to eat, and it would be clean and fresh.

He produced so many things, hundreds of them, so many that it is hard to remember individual cases. Once when we were with Baba in Venkatagiri, we all of us went to some riverbed where we spent quite some time. He talked to us and chatted about many things. There were lots of people, perhaps a hundred of them. Then he made a heap of sand with his hand and took out of it a beautiful large statue of Sri Rama Lakshmanan.

The memory of one incident was particularly vivid.

Once we were having a meal with him in Madras. Then he took up a piece of rice from his plate, held it in his hand, and said: 'Bring me a magnifying glass.' It was brought, and he invited us to look at the small grain of rice. As we looked through the glass, we saw that on that grain of rice was engraved a carved picture of a girl with Lord Krishna.

This happened in the house of Mr Hanumantha Rao in Madras. He and his wife were there. He was a great devotee but has since died. Many of these old people have left (died). This was a carving into a soft small piece of rice. We needed a magnifying glass to see it.

The singers said they had seen Baba remove a man's tonsils. Lakshmanan also related a personal experience of apparent healing:

Once we were on a tour with Swamiji somewhere in Nellur District. All of a sudden I had a pain in my stomach. I was walking a bit behind because of the pain so he asked me: 'What is the matter?' I said pain. Then he produced a ladu-like sweet and asked me to take it. It was quite hot, as if it had just been

prepared at the oven, quite sweet also. The pain then
disappeared.

All people who were with Sai Baba in his early days report
having observed him fall into trances fairly frequently. The
singers stated that they were told that he had been going into
trances since the age of 14 or 15. He was leaving his body, it
was said, and going somewhere.

In the 1950s, when we were there for longer periods, he
frequently fell into trances. In a day he might go twice, but then
he might not go into trance for a week. You could not tell when
he might fall into trance. The trances might be short or long.
He might stay in trance for hours. Once in Puttaparti in the
early 1950s he was in trance for two days. His trances came
suddenly. Once we were in a village in Velur, on a veranda on
the second floor, when he suddenly fell 15 feet down. But he
was never hurt from falling. As he went into trance, he fell
down suddenly. There were no convulsions, no movements at
all till he would come to himself. As he suddenly came back,
there would be a little tremor in his body, a slight shiver, and
he would get up.

When he woke up from trance, he did not say anything about
it. Sometimes he might later give some casual remark such as:
'I have been to this or that place, somebody is having
difficulties, and I have helped them.' These were private things
that were occurring to people, and only seldom did he talk
about them. But sometimes after two or three days a letter
might come from someone who was ill. 'I have seen your
presence. I am now much better.' There were many incidents of
this kind, but we did not care to memorize them and did not
prepare for being questioned about them. To some people he
might say where he had been if they pestered him, but we never
did. No one kept any record of these events.

Around his 32nd year these trances stopped. It was about the
time he started giving public lectures.

The singers observed vibuti phenomena, as did so many
others:

Previously during festivals like Dasara and his birthday, we
used to carry him in processions through the village during the
night. Sometimes during the procession, we would see vibuti
appearing on his forehead. This we have seen many times. We
have also seen kumkum appearing on his forehead.

According to the singers, the maximum number of people attending festivals in the 1950s would be 100 to 200, and between festivals there were much fewer. Then there were no public meetings or addresses, no preaching. Baba would be quite informal, spending almost all the time with his devotees, taking his food with them, and so on. From the singers we heard again:

> We did not realize in the early days that the crowd around him would grow to such a magnitude. But he told us then that there would in the future come a huge crowd, that we would only be able to see him from a distance, and even that would be difficult in due time.

16
An Ex-Devotee

So far we have presented accounts only from Sai Baba's followers and admirers, who probably give a rather one-sided view of the enigmatic personality that is Sathya Sai Baba. In my discussions with the devotees I gradually came to know about a few people who had been close to Baba at one time but then left him for various reasons. It was not easy to find these people. Either the devotees were reluctant to help me find these ex-devotees or, more commonly, they had lost contact with them many years ago and no longer knew where they lived. Two names of ex-devotees came up more often than any others: those of Mr Varadu and Mr Krishna. For quite some time I could find no one who knew their whereabouts. Finally Gopal Krishna Yachendra made some calls for me and found Varadu's address in Madras. He even accompanied me there in November 1977 and introduced me to Varadu. Gopal Krishna had not met him for twenty years or more. At this meeting I learned that Varadu was related to Dr C. T. K. Chari and Mrs Kamala Sarathy.

Varadu, a bachelor, lives with his sister's family. He looked rather thin and not in the best of health. He received us warmly, and quickly we were in an animated discussion about his days with the swami. Varadu is a lively person and spoke so fast that I sometimes had difficulty understanding him. One soon had the impression that he was a man of many interests who enjoyed discussions and was active, outspoken and independent.

Varadu presently holds a senior post with a manufacturing firm in Madras. His relative, Dr Chari, told me later that Varadu had very much wanted to join the Indian army but that he was not accepted because of his health. That, Dr Chari told me, would probably have been the kind of life Varadu would have most enjoyed.

During the course of this and two other long interviews over a four year period, I had the impression he enjoyed recalling his time with Sai Baba, but he also expressed concern that everything he said, down to the minutest detail, be correctly presented in our manuscript. Two times we went carefully, word for word, through the text that follows. I obtained most of the information in my first interview with Varadu, but as we went through a write-up of that interview, he added further details that I have also included. All the questions have been dropped from this text.

It was quite a long time ago that I was with Baba – from May 1949 to 1953. I stayed with him for quite some time. I would stay for a month at a time and then go away for a while. It was quite an interesting experience, but then I was not fortunate enough to continue being with him. I still pray to him, but as far as personal contact is concerned, we stopped all that in 1953. He had told me that when the time comes, I would have to go away from him, but his grace would always be with me – I do believe that. Sometimes when I feel bad and depressed, I just think of him, and I get some sort of relief.

How I came to know him in the beginning was just out of sheer curiosity. My aunt, Kamala Sarathy, had come from Delhi, saying that she was going to see the Swamiji. She asked me: 'Why don't you come over and see?' But I had never believed in such people, so I said I wasn't interested. Then my cousin said to me: 'Why don't you come? It's a picnic' and at that I said okay.

So we went. Quite a few things happened – I mean, things which you cannot explain normally: miracles, mind-reading and all that. Nobody can read your mind, surely? For example, a few trivial incidents occurred on our way to Puttaparti. Our bus broke down. It was quite late in the evening – about 9.30 or 10.30. I got out, tried to fix the bus, and before long the bus started again. We reached Bukkapatnam, and there got hold of a bullock-cart. We crossed the river and were walking across the sand, and I was carrying my cousin's violin in my hand. (My cousin, Kamala Sarathy's daughter, Prema Bose, was a violinist.) We reached Puttaparti at 3.30 in the morning, so it was too late at night to see Swami. We went to bed, and got up about 6.00 to have darshan.

When we met Baba, he just looked at me and laughed, saying: 'You have come to me not out of faith in me but to test me.' And he told me how we had come and how the bus had broken down at Bukkapatnam and that I had been carrying my cousin's violin. 'And you're now thinking that I am reading your mind, aren't you?' he said. And that's exactly what I was thinking! I said: 'It is obvious you are reading my mind.' Then he laughed, and said: 'As far as that is concerned, you have made your own test.'

We stayed there for some time. Next morning I took some photographs of him. You see, ever since my childhood I have been a photographer. Now there is a story that if you take a picture of Sai Baba without telling him, it will not come out. So I took five pictures of him when he was doing puja. Then he said, smiling: 'You have taken five pictures, but they won't come out. If you want to take pictures, I will come and sit for them. Now you can take pictures.' I took three photographs and made a note as to which they were on the roll. I developed the film myself. In the first five pictures there was nothing, but the later three came out. One is with Kamala Sarathy. I gave all the negatives to Kamala Sarathy.

Swami used to produce things from the air. He would ask: 'What do you want?' He used to produce sweets for me; the sort of sweets we make here in India, such as jellaby, ladu, gullabjamun. If he gives these sweets to you, you have to eat it yourself; you are not supposed to share it with anybody. My mother sat next to me, but I would still eat it all myself.

Once we all went with Baba to the river Chitravati, and there we were sitting. I was not very well. At that time I had tuberculosis, and I was undergoing treatment which was called 'pneumothorax'; they pump air into the pleural layers and keep the lung collapsed. It had to be done to me every thirty days. On this occasion it had been twenty days overdue for treatment, and I was worried that I had not gone back for the rest of the treatment. I was scared of cold and rain in those days, because of my TB. We were sitting around Baba in a circle about 20 feet in diameter. Baba knew I was scared of rain and cold. Rain clouds were gathering, and it started to drizzle all around us. And believe it or not (I am telling you what happened, not hearsay) we saw the wetness all around us, but not a drop fell on us! We were all dry!

Baba then laughed and said: 'Go and fetch some water from the river.' So I went down to the Chitravati and collected some water in a bottle. When I brought it back, he said: 'Pour whatever you want.' I was staring at him. 'You still have no faith in me' he said. He asked me to give some of the water to each of the baktas (20 to 25 were there), and yet even after doing so there was still some water left in the bottle. Furthermore, the water tasted sweet – it was not pure water. That bottle I later took back with me to Madras and gave it to Dr C.T.K. Chari. I told him that it was water from the river yet it tasted sweet, like sherbet, though it looked just like clear water.[1]

After we had been to the river, we went back to the mandir, and Baba asked me whether I was worried. 'Yes, Swamiji.' 'Your lungs?' 'Yes' I said. 'Well, go back to your doctor and if he gives you an injection, take it. I am always there with you.'

So next day I went to Madras and from there to Tambaram. That night I had a dream: I go to my doctor, and he says to me: 'You have come too late for the injection.' My doctor, Dr Das, had been giving me this injection for the last three years, so he was quite expert at administering it to me. But in this dream he goes through the pleural layers and pierces my lung, which, naturally, made me spit out some blood. In the dream I feel that Baba comes to take care of me. My doctor is scared, but I laugh, saying: 'Relax, I am OK.' That was the dream I had.

I thus did not want to go to Dr Das by myself. I called my friends and persuaded five to come with me. One of them subsequently became a bakta of Swamiji's; he was much bigger in Swamiji's eyes than I ever was. That was Krishna, who was one of my classmates in Madras Loyola College before he became a Sai Baba bakta. Later he left Baba and is now a Christian and living in Hyderabad. Then there was Venkatesh and his brother Balu. They all picked me up in Tambaram and brought me by car to the doctor's.

The doctor said: 'Why have you all come?' I didn't tell him anything about the dream. When he gave me the injection, he did indeed pierce my lung, and I spat out blood. The doctor was worried, and I told him to relax. Swami had produced some vibuti from the air when I had been in Puttaparti. I swallowed it and the bleeding stopped.

When I got home to Tambaram, I found two people waiting for me in the house, saying that Swami had already arrived in Madras and wanted to see me immediately. I went to see Baba. He asked me if the doctor had given me the injection, and I told him that the doctor had not been able to do so because he pierced my lung and became scared, whereupon I had taken the vibuti. Swami then told me: 'You don't need any more injections; you are cured.' After that I remained free of TB until 1953.

Once in 1949 I happened to be in Madras going to the station in a bus to go by train to Christian College in Tambaram. I coughed and brought up some blood. At once I prayed to Sai Baba and took some of the vibuti he had produced out of the air, and the bleeding stopped. At that precise moment, Baba was sitting in Bangalore with my mother, her cousin, and Kamala Sarathy and her daughters, and a few friends of mine. He told them that at that moment I was in a prostitute's house and had started bleeding and that I had prayed for his help and that he came to my rescue. The only explanation that I can give you is that one factor common to both a prostitute and a bus is that they are paid conveniences.

Another such instance was at Puttaparti. I used to smoke a lot; I don't smoke much now, but in those days I smoked nonstop. Baba said that I should stop smoking, but I didn't. He also said that I should not swim, and I took this advice. I used to go swimming in wells. Anyway, on this occasion in Puttaparti three of my friends and I went to a well; they were swimming, and I was just sitting there, smoking. At the same time, my auntie, my mother and all the others were sitting around Baba (at the ashram). When we returned to the mandir, everyone was silent, and my mother was looking sad.

I said: 'What the hell have I done now?' She said: 'Where did you go and swim?' I said: 'I never went in the water.' 'Well, that is what Swamiji says.' So I went and asked Swamiji: 'When did I enter the water? When did you see us?' Swami said: 'I didn't say anything like that.' I went back and asked my auntie, and what she now said was: 'You should see a deeper meaning in what Swamiji says.' I said: 'My brain is too small for conducting examinations into the esoteric meaning of Swamiji's words. I am just an ordinary man. That is beyond me.' Weird things like that were going on.

Then I went to my friend Krishna to discuss this. Swamiji was always insisting that I give up my friendship with Krishna, Venkatesh and Balu. This was a bone of contention between Baba and myself, and we used to have a lot of arguments over it. He gave no reason for wanting me to do this. All he would say is: 'They are not good for you. Cut off the friendship.'

You see, Baba's idea is that there must be absolute surrender. Unfortunately, having been trained entirely differently, I must have a reason. Even God cannot make me do things like this; it is impossible. That is when the whole fight started between Swami and me. And it went on like that, and soon other small incidents took place. He and I would be sitting, talking, and we would be playing cards. And then some bakta would come who was seriously ill, wanting to see Baba. I would say to Swami: 'Swami, somebody has come to see you. Do you want to see him?' And he would say: 'No, I won't see him.' And I used to feel upset. Here we were, playing cards, and somebody who is half dying would come to see Swamiji, and yet Swami would refuse to see him. We used to have a fight, and he would say: 'Am I Swamiji, or are you Swamiji?' Then I used to say:

'Unfortunately, you are the Swamiji.'

These sorts of arguments used to go on. And finally the break came, in Mr Hanumantha Rao's house, in Madras. There was a bakta who had a daughter who was a cripple and who died suddenly. That man had come there and Swamiji didn't even see him. My mother brought the man back to his house. The same day, another boy, from Kancheepuram, was brought here, dying. Swami wouldn't see him either. Then that night when I said something, he said: 'Get out of my room' because I had insisted he see that boy. And after that, which was about January 1952, I didn't see him again for quite some time.

Then, some years later, Krishna fell into disgrace. And when Baba sent him out, the reason was that Swami accused him of misbehaving with an old woman of 60, a servant in the temple, in the mandir. And do you believe this story? I certainly don't.

That upset Krishna very badly. He came here and wouldn't even talk to me. There used to be some open ground here in Madras known as Loglands. (Buildings are now standing there.) I used to take Krishna there and make him sit down and smoke. I used to make him drink also, to make him forget. But he never did forget. Finally he met a pastor on Mount Road in Madras who apparently took him under his wing and gave him some solace.

Krishna is one of the very few people Baba has been very close to. At one time he was even carried with Baba in the palanquin during processions. 'What Arjuna was to Krishna, Krishna is to me,' Baba used to say[2]. I do not think anyone has been so close to Swami after him. Perhaps Raja Reddy later on, but Krishna was the last person with whom that close youth friendship was there.

Well, Krishna ended up becoming a Christian. But before that, we went to Puttaparti, at the end of 1953. Krishna said he wanted to see Swami for the last time. By then I'd stopped going to Puttaparti, but for Krishna's sake I went. And Baba never talked to me, though he was talking to Krishna. I gave him three days; if he didn't talk to me by then, on the third day I would leave. Came the third day, and I took my bedding on my shoulders and started to leave, when Baba saw me from his room in the mandir. He shouted to me and called me. I went over to him and said: 'I have come to your house. You have not invited me. I have no business here. I am going home.' He produced some vibuti, put it in my mouth, and said: 'Go back. You will have TB again. You will suffer a lot this time. But you will get rid of it after four or five months, and after that you will never get it back.'

I was acting as if nothing was wrong with me. I went for a

picnic to Pondicherry, came back, and then went to my doctor for my regular checkup. There was no cough, no temperature; I was perfectly all right. But I went for my checkup nevertheless.

The doctor did a fluoroscopy and said: 'You are all right.' I said: 'No, doctor. I want an X-ray taken.' He took an X-ray and found three cavities on one side of my lungs and one cavity on the other. He said: 'Look, you have got three cavities,' and I said: 'I know. That is why I asked you to take an X-ray.' 'But you are all right.' 'I know I am' I said, for I was not feeling ill. But a little later I really fell ill, and I suffered hell for six months. I was having haemorrhages, I was coughing up blood.

Half a year after my break with Swami, he had come to Mrs Chandran's house, and my mother said: 'Swami has come. Let's go and see him.' At that time, my mother's and elder uncle's (both of them have since died) relationship with Swamiji was a cordial one. But I did not go to Swami and was sleeping that evening in our house. My mother went to see Swamiji, and he had produced two or three small ayurvedic pills which we call jintan and had given them to my mother, saying: 'Give these to your son.'

That same evening the doctor had come to examine me. He had said that a lobectomy had to be done, that is, a portion of the lungs had to be removed. I said: 'No, doc. I will die with my lungs intact. Whatever happens, let it happen.' I have always believed in fate.

Then mother came and gave me these three pills saying: 'Swamiji asked that you take these.' I took them, and after a few minutes the cough stopped. And then I felt relieved and wanted to sleep, and it was the first time for a long time that I had been able to sleep peacefully. When I woke up in the morning, I was perfectly all right. My doctor came in the evening, examined me, and was surprised to find that my lungs were clear. He asked me to come with him to the X-ray clinic. Everything checked out normal: there was no lesion. He said: 'What have you done?' I said jokingly: 'Well, something science knows nothing about – I had some spiritual pills.' This was sometime in 1953. It was my last attack of TB except for a short minor attack in 1979. I somehow feel Baba did help me out. In 1958 I applied for an army commission, and the medical examiner said I was perfect. I was laughing, and I said: 'Sure, doc?' He said: 'Perfectly sure.' I just laughed and told him the story of my healing.

I must say that I never observed Swami change a sheet of stamps into stamps bearing his own picture. But I've seen him produce quite a few other things such as idols, sweets and medicines.

Varadu recalled a tonsillectomy performed on his friend Krishna (which is also described by Krishna in the chapter 'The Abandoned Brother').

For instance, I was present at an operation Swami performed in Hanumantha Rao's house in Madras on my friend Krishna, who had septic tonsils. Swami produced the knife from the air. I was shocked. (I am a doctor's son; my father was a surgeon.) Swamiji just looked at me and smiled. I understood perfectly what he meant: 'You still don't believe in me.' Then he put the knife into Krishna's throat. There was also with me another doctor friend of mine, Dr Dakshina Murthy, who was shocked. But none of us could say anything. Swami just kept going.

Krishna suffered for one day. Next day we took him to my doctor – Dr Das, the same doctor who was treating me. 'Who are the fools meddling with your throat!' he said. 'He is a great fool. What is wrong with him? This chap is going to get into a soup' he said. We were all a bit worried and kept going to the doctor for the next two days. Then on the second day the doctor asked: 'What has happened?' for the pain had stopped, the septic tonsils had disappeared; everything had gone. That is what Swami did. He didn't actually surgically remove the tonsils; all he did was make some scratches with the knife. But after two days the tonsils disappeared. To my knowledge he (Krishna) did not have any problem with it afterwards.

When I asked him why he had performed this 'operation' when he could just have willed his tonsils to disappear, he answered that Krishna wanted it this way and (that) it was his duty to yield to his wish. I think it was the next day that I told this to my uncle, Dr C.T.K. Chari, and he said something about split personalities and started talking about psychosomatic medicine in one of the wonderful digressions of his.

Swami used to go into trance, but when I was with him he never did any 'disappearing act'. People used to tell me that he would just disappear and go and help somebody somewhere. I won't and can't believe any such claims for that because I have never seen him do such a thing.

But I have seen him go into a trance and while in the trance utter certain words. For instance, the night when Ramana Maharshi passed away in Tiruwannamalai, I was in Puttaparti with Swamiji. Krishna and myself were both there. That evening, around 9.00, we continued whatever it was that we were doing (I think we were doing a puja) when suddenly Swamiji looked up at us. There is a peculiar way of looking he has which means that he wants to go to his room. The moment Krishna and I went through the door into the room and closed

it, Swami fell down. I was ready for it. Krishna and I both held
hands, and Swami was lying across them. Then he rose up into
the air, from our arms. He was as stiff as a board. He started
murmuring – something about 'Maharshi has reached my lotus
feet.' And then the sole of his right foot like split open, and
nearly two kilograms of beautiful, well-scented vibuti poured
out from the sole of his foot. I collected the vibuti while he was
still levitating in the air.

Then he came down and returned to his senses and asked
what he had said. I said: 'Swamiji, this is what you said:
Ramana Maharshi has passed away. And this is what came out
of your feet.' He said: 'Put it into packets and give it as
prasadam.'

A day or two after this incident, we learned from the
newspapers that Maharshi had died. It had been at the time
that Swami said that Maharshi had reached his feet.

Swami told a similar thing about the wife of a bakta of his,
Neeladri Rao from Madras, who was one of the early baktas
from 1949 or 1950. He died only recently. His first wife was ill
when Swami said one day: 'She has reached my feet.' The next
day Swami received a telegram saying she had died. I was in
Puttaparti at this time and heard Swami say this.

How do you explain this? All these things that I have told
you are true. They are things nobody can explain. Even today
Swamiji might not talk to me, might not speak to me, but still I
know that he has powers no science can explain. You see, if
anybody else wants to be a divinity, he can talk a lot of
nonsense about it, but I don't believe it, because truth is truth
and you can't change it. You can't change it one bit. I have told
you about his failing, of telling lies which I cannot to this day
understand.

My uncle, Professor C.T.K. Chari, thought he might be a
split personality. One moment he is the crude villager, another
moment he is that great soul that no one can fathom. It is a very
tough proposition to analyze him.

I observed him fall into trance two or three times only.
Krishna had more experiences; he was with Swami day and
night for months at a time, whereas I used to go once a year for
a month and twice a year for a week or so.

I don't know whether they still do it now, but in those days,
on Swamiji's birthday, we used to have these palanquin
processions in the night. One particular day a group of Muslim
boys – rowdies – had come from the neighbouring village of
Bukkapatnam. They wanted to create some trouble. I heard
about their plans, and I called my friends and told them to be
ready for it, so I had my own group of friends all around. I was

supposed to be the watch and ward – the security guard and what not. The baktas had lined up for the procession, which was about to begin. When the palanquin was to be lifted, I was standing next to Swamiji, who asked whether I was scared. I said: 'Why should I be scared, Swamiji? I'm making all sorts of arrangements.' 'You still don't believe in me?' 'That I wouldn't know, Swamiji, but isn't it better to be prepared?' 'All right,' he said.

These boys – some five or six fellows – were all standing at a corner of the open space at the mandir where we were starting the procession and seemed ready to cause some trouble. Swamiji then just turned around and looked at them. That precise second, not only I but also quite a few of the others saw in Swami a fearsome face, and one or two of the female devotees fainted. I tell you, the moment he turned, I thought I imagined I saw Swami's face become jet-black – become the face of the monkey god Hanuman. A fierce-looking face. Next minute, after seeing the fierce-looking face, these six boys just turned around and walked away. That's all they did. I then asked my friends what had happened. 'Well,' they said, 'we saw Swamiji turn into a horrible form.' I never told them what I had seen; I just said: 'Well, is that so?' These rowdies had just walked out. And Swamiji said to me: 'You were so worried. Now see what happened.' I said: 'Swamiji, I still don't know the full extent of your powers.'

One year I was a hotelier – I was running a hotel for Swamiji around the time of Dasara. So I had collected some money which I was to give to Swamiji. I left it on his table and went out to start the motor that was used for generating electricity in the ashram. By the time I had come back, that money was missing. I said: 'Swamiji, where has the money gone?' I became worried. He said: 'Don't worry.' I said: 'I have to worry. You invested your money, and I have got to give it to you. I left it on the table.' 'Don't worry', he said again. I asked him what had happened to the money. He said: 'An old bakta, an old man about 56 or 60, he has put all the stuff in his box; he has stolen that money and kept it in his box.' I was shocked. I would not leave. Instead I went and opened the box, and there was the money. But what could I do? For all I knew, Swamiji could have asked this fellow to keep it; I didn't know. Swamiji said not to bother about it, so I left it at that.

Two days after that, the weather was rainy. Another interesting experience happened to me. I should explain first of all that Swamiji had given me a gold locket, a talisman made of gold, and it was always hanging around my neck. Now on this particular day I went down to start the generator, and it would not start. I was trying to start it, but the damn thing would not start. Suddenly I heard a noise, but I was concentrating so hard that I didn't take any notice of it. Then Swamiji came rushing out into the rain. 'You go in, Swami, I have to get this started – it is my work.' He said: 'For heaven's sake, keep quiet and come with me.' And when I again objected, the other baktas said: 'What is this? When Swamiji tells you to go with him, why do you not do so?' And I said: 'OK.' I left the engine and went upstairs with Swami. My mother and some other people were sitting there glum-faced, and I asked: 'What is the matter? Why are you like this?' My mother didn't answer. Then the swami said: 'Give me your locket.' I put my hand up to my neck, but the locket was missing. I was taken aback. 'Swamiji, it must have fallen off as I was walking around.' He said: 'Stop again; don't run off, sit here.' Then the other people there said: 'When Swamiji was sitting here, your locket appeared and fell onto his head.' Swamiji explained: 'You were having a very bad crisis; you might have died at that moment as a result of some accident.' He had said: 'I must go down and save him now.' So he had come down to where I was, pulled me away, and later gave the locket back to me. Whether an accident would really have happened, I don't know. The generator was downstairs, and he was upstairs in his mandir room. I was rather surprised when he told me all this. He gave the locket back to me and said: 'Here it is. Now wear it.'

Another incident occurred in Bangalore. I lost a wristwatch of mine and also my purse, in which there was a photograph of Swamiji belonging to someone else. Somebody stole my purse – it was pickpocketed. I didn't know what to do. I told Swamiji what had happened, and he gave me rupees to enable me to get back to Madras, saying: 'There are 50 rupees for you. The purse is gone, so forget about it.'

Nine or ten months later Swami came to Madras, and he went to the Poondi reservoir with me. Poondi is a place not far from Madras, about 32 miles away, and near the railway. There is a dam there. In the evening we went outside to the top of the dam. Swamiji was sitting there, and we were all laughing. He started producing things, and straightaway he produced a small locket with his own picture in the centre, surrounded by lots of diamonds and other precious stones. He said: 'Whoever can hold it can keep it.' But nobody could hold it; it would slip out of your hand. Whether it was just imagination or hypnotism, we don't know. So Swami said to the locket: 'Go back to wherever you came from.' And it disappeared.

Then Swamiji looked at me, laughing. As usual, I was chewing some sweets. He produced a sweet and I ate it. I continued looking at him, and he knew that I wanted my watch and the photograph. He said: 'All right. Here is the watch and the photograph', and he materialized them for me. The watch he produced on the ground, but the photo he took from the air if I remember it correctly. (It was almost) one year later, (and) the watch was still working perfectly. And the photograph which he produced was the one which I had lost.

The locket had been around my neck, and the photograph had been here in Madras. But when I woke up one morning in my room in Madras, both were missing. I also lost my talisman. They mysteriously disappeared a week after the day I finally left Swami and fell out of grace with him.

The watch, however, was stolen by a friend of mine three years later. One afternoon this friend went into my room. I had gone to fetch something, and the watch was on the table. He pocketed it. I was very sentimental about that watch. So I went and told another friend of mine who is a very high police official, saying that this was the only chap who could have done it. So my police friend told the chap who had taken it: 'Please return the watch and we will close the case. If you don't, we know how to get it back.' The next day the watch was dropped into a flower-pot, and a letter sent to me about it (anonymous, of course). So I got my watch back. The interesting thing is that when Swami had 'produced' it for me (along with that photograph I mentioned before), he had said that it would be stolen but that I would get it back again.

I somehow feel Swami did help me out with my TB in spite of the fact that I fell out with him. According to his explanation, there are some baktas who come and go, and to some people he has got to give, due to connections in previous incarnations. But I would not accept such explanations. I used to tell Swami: 'I know nothing about previous lives. What I am interested in is the rationale for what you do to a person in this life.' And there he used to fight with me: 'What do you know about past lives? You know nothing about past and future, I only know.'

Then one day in 1953, after I had stopped seeing him, I heard that Swamiji had come to Madras, that he was at some house – so I went there. That was some eight or nine months after the break. Yes, I wanted to see him; I felt good at the thought of seeing him, so one fine day I went to the Osborne House, the Madras residence of the Venkatagiri family, when Baba was giving darshan. I waited till the last person had done his namaskaram, and then I went and touched his feet. He did not even look at me but turned to someone next to him and said: 'How is Varadu? Tell him I enquired about him.' This hurt me, and I stopped going to see him. I have not seen him since. I will not see him, but I still pray to him. I know that he can never deny me grace. There is no reason why I should lie about it. I cannot deny that I get relief. Later on, something may happen, but for the moment, I get the relief I want. And if he still gives me that peace, that is all I want.

After 1953 I had absolutely no contact with him. Once or twice Gopal Krishna or Madana of Venkatagiri rang up and told me that Baba was in Madras. I did not go because I felt he might not receive me. I am very sensitive about that because I am one of the oldest baktas. But as I said in the beginning, even today I may pray to him, but I am not bothered whether he gives me grace or not.

Notes

[1] When asked about this incident Dr Chari told me that he did not recall Varadu ever bringing him sweet water in a bottle from Baba. What he did receive from Varadu and was still in his possession (he showed it to me) was a stamp-like photo of Sai Baba which Varadu had reported as being produced by Baba. Of this incident Varadu disclaims any recall, as can be read later in this chapter.

Dr Chari is a relative of Varadu and has known him all his life. In the early 1950s Varadu assisted him in conducting some parapsychological experiments at the University of Madras. Dr Chari had contemporary notes of these experiments. From events connected with these experiments and from other events that occurred during the same time period (some of them related to Varadu's association with Baba), Dr Chari constructed 14 questions to assess the accuracy of Varadu's memories from the time of his association with Baba. The questions differed in difficulty and relevance for Varadu, such as asking him in which year these experiments were conducted (Varadu's answer was correct), the names of the investigators who assisted Dr Chari (Varadu recalled the names of half of them), and the name of a distinguished artist alleged to have belonged to the circle which had grown up around the subject of the experiments (Varadu did not remember). Varadu gave correct answers to about half of these questions; we considered this rather good considering that thirty years had passed since these events occurred.

[2] Krishna is one of the leading religious figures of Hinduism and known for his superhuman powers. He preached the Bhagavad Gita, the most popular scripture of Hinduism, to his chief disciple Arjuna.

17
The Abandoned Brother

Mr M. Krishna was first introduced to Sathya Sai Baba around 1950, through the family of his classmate in college, Varadu. He quickly became exceptionally close to Sai Baba. At processions when Baba was carried by his devotees on a palanquin, Krishna was the only person he ever asked to sit at his side. According to Dr C.T.K. Chari, Sai Baba accepted Krishna as having been his brother in a previous incarnation.

In 1957 Krishna left the swami, converted to Christianity, and became an active member of the Indian Methodist Church. I had heard about Krishna a number of times when I finally, with Varadu's help, was able to trace him and meet him in October 1981 in Hyderabad, where he lives with his wife and three children. I had two interviews with him on consecutive days, and we met again in July of 1983.

Even today I would respect Sai Baba, not for all these so-called miracles, but for the fact that he is using all the funds he is getting to construct educational institutions and hospitals, and trying to revive what you call Indian culture. This is what I understand he is doing; of course it is a long time since I have met him. Though I have become a Christian and accepted Christ as my personal Lord and Saviour, I still have respect for Indian culture. I went to Sai Baba to have peace of mind and did not find it. I found it only after I came to know Christ. Actually it was Mr Varadu's mother who introduced my family to Swamiji. My mother went earlier than we to Puttaparti with Hanumantha Rao. We were family friends of the Raos' since we came from the same area. I first met Swami in 1951 in Neeladri Rao's house in Madras, but Varadu had come to know him through Mrs Revatamma, who was a sister of the singers Raman and Lakshmanan.

He had this to say of Baba's materializations:

When I first came to know Sai Baba, he was producing things in the same way I am told he is doing now. He frequently produced vibuti by a wave of his hand, also talismans and sweets. For example, once when we were travelling, I asked Baba for an apple. He walked up to a nearby tamarind tree and picked from it an apple. He also took things out of the sand at the Chitravati River. But should these materializations be a criterion to call him a god-man or anything superior to us? Does any knowledge or ability to do something make anyone a god?

As far as the bringing forth of vibuti and various objects is concerned, somehow he is able to produce them out of nothing, and I cannot explain that phenomenon. He did that very frequently all those years that I spent with him.

I was fond of kova, a certain kind of sweet. Sometimes – particularly in Puttaparti, which is a village and where it would not be available – I would tell him that I would like to eat this sweet. He would then often say: 'What, are you a glutton?' But somehow he would always produce for me that sweet. This sweet is oily, white and sticky, and made of milk. I don't believe he could have hidden it in his clothes and always had it ready for me on these particular days when I would ask for it. Somehow he can produce these things. How he does it I do not know. But if somebody says that he is a god or a superhuman being just because he produces these things, then I do not agree.

Two frequently given explanations of the materializations he did not accept.

To the question if I have ever seen anything hidden in his clothes I can only answer no. How could he hide them? If he were hiding these things, then some time or another they would fall out. No, he does not do that. In those days when I stayed with him, he would never wear any underwear, only his long silk robe, which had no hiding places. We who attended on him kept his clothes ready for him when he had his bath in the morning – such people as Amarendra Kumar, Varadu and myself. We got him dressed, and there was nothing in the robe. None of us ever found anything suspicious as far as I know. Of course, what he may have done after I left him, I do not know.

One of the explanations someone has put forward to explain these phenomena is that people like him have the power to hypnotize you for some time not to see while they take the objects from somewhere in a natural way. But so many photographs have been taken when he is producing things, and they reveal only what people have seen as the incident occurred.

He went on to say:

Then there is an Indian religious explanation. Some people say that some people who have had great faith in Swami hover around him after they die. Somehow or other they stuck on to him, maybe he has tested their faith in him till they fully believed in him. These spirits will then give the things to him that he wants and as he brings them forth.

When I was with him, his devotees used to exaggerate. Even in front of us who were there, he himself will also sometimes say something exaggerated and will ask you: 'Is it not true?' and we all used to nod our heads whether it is true or not. In this sense none of us had the guts to tell him: 'Why are you telling lies?' I might have asked him once or twice when everybody else had left: 'Why did you say this thing?' I did not have the courage to tell him this squarely because somehow we did not want to put him in an awkward position.

Krishna's view of Baba's healing powers:

Swami has frequently promised cures and people did not get cured. For example, he told Mr and Mrs Hanumantha Rao that he would cure their son, who suffered from infantile paralysis. He never did. They left him after some years.[1] If asked, Swami would say that he would have cured the boy, but these people had left him. Finally Mr Hanumantha Rao's mother wrote Sai Baba and asked him not to come any more. After that Swami stayed with the Raja of Venkatagiri when he visited Madras.

When I was with him, there were claims that he performed real operations. I do not believe he is capable of any such operations. Of course, through faith some diseases may be cured. That happens, but it comes through our psychological capacity.

He also used to cast out evil spirits. People who are possessed with an evil spirit will start to swing or faint when they see him. That is a sign that the evil spirit is coming into them. Swami will then pull out some hair from their heads, put them (the hairs) into a talisman and give the talisman to them when they are back in their normal state. But some of the people will be possessed again and will not be healed. Then he will say that they have lost faith in him, have lost their talisman, or he will bring forth some other excuse.

He recalled Baba's surgery on him, presumably the same operation described by his friend Varadu in an earlier chapter.

Once I had myself tonsillitis and a very sore throat. Then Swami said he would operate upon my tonsils. This happened in Hanumantha Rao's home in Madras. He waved his hand, and a knife came seemingly out of nowhere. He put his hand into my throat. I said that I could not see him cutting my tonsils, that I would get frightened, so I blindfolded myself with a handkerchief. If someone puts something into your mouth, you will naturally cough. He was saying that I was not allowing him to make the operation, but after I was blindfolded I was quieter, and he did something with my throat. When he said he had finished the operation and I opened my eyes, there was some blood on a tray that someone held.

That evening I went to a doctor friend of mine and said: 'Look, Swamiji has removed my tonsils.' He remarked something like this: 'What do you say? You are a fool and he is a liar.' The tonsils were still in my throat. A few years later, about 1959 or 1960, just before I moved to Hyderabad, the tonsils were removed by a medical doctor at Stanley Hospital in Madras. The medical record must still be there.

Another incident comes to mind, though in that case Baba made no promise of healing. The husband of Swami's sister Venkamma was bitten by a dog, but nobody knew it was rabies-infected. When this news came to Madras, some of the doctors, like Dr Dakshina Murthy, said it was always safer to take injections against rabies. But in the villages they do not follow such rules, and some of the baktas said: 'Why do you talk like that? Swamiji is there.'

If the dog has rabies, the effect will not be there till after some weeks, but once the disease is manifested there is no cure for it. Then suddenly this man became sick, and I was asked to take him to Penukonda, to the nearest hospital in these days. So I and some relative, Krishnappa, took him there. When the doctors found out that this gentleman was suffering from rabies, they told us we had brought him too late and nothing could be done to save his life. Then we took Venkamma's husband back and to a hospital in Anantapur, where he passed away.

Had he seen Baba fall into trance?

In those years that I spent with him he often fell into trance. As he fell into trance, he might have tremendous strength so that several men could barely hold him. Sometimes he might start running away. For example, when the mandir in Prashanti Nilayam was still under construction, he was one day talking to all of those close to him, the inner circle, so to say. As we were sitting on the roof, he fell into trance and suddenly got up and rushed towards the edge of the roof. If he ran over the edge, he would fall to the ground. So we had to catch him and hold him back, but he would try to shake us off. Things like that he would do. Or he would fall down and kick with his hands. He would do as if he was pushing something away from him.

When he had recovered from the trance, he might say that someone was in great danger, for example in a car accident, and (that) he was trying to ward him off. That is the explanation he gave and in those days, since we believed him so much, whatever he said was gospel truth for us. Whenever he goes into trance, he is supposed to save someone who is in trouble in a far-off place. That is what he says, that he has gone to such and such a place. Afterwards some people might say: 'Yes. I was in such a trouble, I was saved' and so on. I did not have any such experience myself.

In trance he would sometimes utter some words that we could not understand, like speaking in tongues. None of us could make out any meaning for these words.

Swami often fell into trances, but he never shared the symptom of being possessed, such as speaking as if he were some personality different from his normal self. He was the same person all the time. Nor did his trances appear epileptic.

We asked if he recalled some specific comments of Baba's after his trances. He replied:

No, I don't. I have forgotten much of my life with Sai Baba, voluntarily and willingly. When I say this, I do not mean anything against Swamiji. I thank him and I thank God because I went through such an experience. Had it not been for my stay with Swamiji, I do not think I would ever have accepted Christ. God was preparing me for something better. In that way I have respect for Swami.

Varadu had described an incident when Sai Baba claimed that 'Ramana Maharshi has come to my feet' at the time of Ramana Maharshi's death. Sai Baba had fallen into trance, and then vibuti fell from his feet. Asked if he remembered any such incident, Krishna said:

I do not remember this particular incident, but there was a time when I and Varadu held him between us. Maybe it was around Maharshi's death. It might have happened. If Swami claims that Ramana Maharshi has come to him at his death, he is indicating that he is greater than Ramana Maharshi. I do not understand such talk from Swamiji or anybody else. Humility is something lacking in so-called god-men, most of those who are in India now. Take for instance that Maharshi Rajneesh, Swami Chimnayananda, even Sathya Sai Baba. Touch their ego, say that something they do is wrong. I wonder if they can take it more easily than any of us human beings do ....

In response to a later question he added this:

Actually, to tell you the truth, my experience with Swamiji, after I came to know Christ, was something like a nightmare which I always wanted to forget. I suffered a lot under him. Of course every discipleship brings suffering – yielding the self is not easy. I think in one way I was wasting my time when I stayed with him. If I were given a chance again, I wouldn't stay with Swamiji, no.

Baba was believed by many to know an individual's intimate past and be able to predict the future.

His devotees firmly believed that he could know their past and what was occurring at distant places. In private interviews he might tell people of their past, talk about very intimate incidents in their lives. Usually when he tells these things, people get interested and think, how can he know about my past, unless he has some spiritual knowledge or powers?

On the basis of this he might predict something about their future, but these predictions are only fifty-fifty correct. Many of them are utter failures. In my case, in the case of my family, of friends and relatives, many of his predictions have proved utterly false. It is possible that he might speak more correctly about people's past than future. And one thing we should remember. Mostly people who go to him are in a distressed state of mind, facing a particular difficulty, disease or poverty. If he can say something correct about them to begin, then they themselves may voluntarily tell him more about their situation.

If Swami says something wrong to a person, he may later justify his words by saying that he has had to assure the person so that he may regain confidence in life. Suppose some fellow comes who has lost his job and Swami says: 'Don't worry, you will find another job soon.' Now the man does not find any job, but then Swami may tell you that if he had told him the truth, the man might have committed suicide, so he must give him assurance. To me Sai Baba's predictions are no better than yours or mine.

Around Swami one will find a lot of exaggerations. For example, the baktas will only talk about predictions that Swami made and that came true, or of promises of healing when the patient recovered. They will not mention those instances when Swami made promises and nothing happened.

When asked if Sai Baba sometimes made things disappear. Krishna responded:

We are trying to get educated to the higher values of life, but you are always binding us to the miracles of Sai Baba.

We commented that it was what we were investigating. Then he said:

Disappearances could happen with him. The first time when I went to see him he said he would give me a ring with his photograph, an enamel thing. 'No, no' I said, 'opal is my birthstone; you give me such a ring.' He then took his hand, with the ring in it, stroked with something like two fingers up my nose, from its tip towards the eyebrows. Through this the enamel ring with his picture that he had produced somehow disappeared on my nose. Such things he does. He sometimes lets things he produces disappear. On this occasion he gave me another thing but not with an opal. I gave it away to my mother when I became a Christian.

Had Krishna ever seen a bowl full of sweets fall into Baba's hands in the house of Hanumantha Rao? This has been reported to us by others that were present.

I don't remember this incident. It might have happened, because in those days he used to produce many things.

Had he seen Baba change water into petrol?

No, that I have never experienced. I also don't believe he can do such things, only produce vibuti, talismans and things of that kind.

What about vibuti appearing on Baba's forehead during Dasara festivals?

Yes, some vibuti used to appear on his forehead on such occasions.

Did he ever observe that Baba's face would change form?

> No, I have not seen that. Of course, again the baktas will
> interpret that only those who are in a higher state can see these
> things. Maybe I was in a lower state for I did not see this.

We had been told that the swami would always have some
attendant around to do everything for him, even to carry his
handkerchief, that someone would bring him his clothes and
that he did not even dress himself. Was that true in Krishna's
experience?

> That was so all the time I was with him. Yes, we would keep his
> clothes and other personal belongings. Someone would take
> care that he had clean clothes. It is like with a raja. If you go to
> the Raja of Venkatagiri, I expect you will see his servants
> standing there ready with his clothes when he comes out of the
> bathroom in the morning. In the case of Swami, he will say that
> serving him in this manner is a great honour, a privilege.
>   I don't know if he still has that habit or not, but when I was
> with him, someone must go on massaging him when he is
> sleeping, press his legs. Poor Ramalingam, a young man
> staying with Swami at that time, used sometimes to sit
> throughout the night and do that.

Did Baba have any unusual eating habits?

> He used to eat normal vegetarian food, but he was more fond
> of some dishes than others, like any one of us.

We asked if Baba would know the contents of letters he
received before he opened them.

> I never noticed that he had knowledge of their contents without
> reading them. At that time the mail was not very large, and it
> used to be a sort of relief receiving letters. Puttaparti was an
> isolated place, an out and out village, Baba was not so
> well-known, and he had time to write to a lot of people.

Did Sai Baba ever make statements about previous lives of
himself or other people?

> According to Hindu religion and philosophy, there is a
> transmigration of souls. He always says he is Shirdi Baba
> reborn. You may have heard from his brother or someone else

how he was bitten by a scorpion. He was then with his elder brother, Mr Sesham Raju. They say that the real Sathyanaray-ana Raju died of the scorpion bite and the soul of Shirdi Sai Baba entered his body.

Did Sai Baba ever give any details about his life as Sai Baba of Shirdi?

There was one Rani of Chinjoli. I think she is no more. Her husband, the Raja of Chinjoli, knew Shirdi Baba as an elderly man. This lady came to Sai Baba. She told me that he correctly described incidents about her husband's meetings with Shirdi Baba. Swamiji told her what her husband had done and said when they met him as Shirdi Baba. She was convinced that Sai Baba had been Sai Baba of Shirdi. The baktas will believe this since they believe in the transmigration of souls.

Swami did not only claim that he was a reincarnation of Shirdi Baba. Once before we came to know Swami, my elder brother was sick. Then my mother gave a vow that we should all go to Tirupati (a famous temple city) and we should shave off our hair, as is not uncommon in India on such occasions, symbolizing that we are humbling ourselves before God. I also went but did not agree to shave off my hair. My brother recovered, but we lost our property soon afterwards. Then occasionally my mother would say that the reason for all our difficulties was that we did not keep our vow. After I came to know Sathya Sai Baba, I told him how it had happened that we lost our property when my brother who was a film producer lost heavily on a film and that my mother wanted us to go to Tirupati again. Then he said: 'Why do you want to go there? I am Venkateswara' (the god of the Tirupati temple, one of the incarnations of Shiva or Krishna).

Swami also used to tell us that he was Rama, especially to the Raja of Venkatagiri, who was a worshiper of Rama.

Did he ever give any details of your previous life as his brother?

He never brought up this topic when we were alone. He sometimes mentioned this when in the company of other people but never gave any details.

After the Rao family told Baba not to come, he would stay at the Raja of Venkatagiri's mansion in Madras.

This was also the only devotee's house that could accommodate all the baktas coming to see him, waiting for bhajan and other things. The question of maintaining Swamiji is also there. You have to take care of the bhajans, prepare the prasadam (sacramental fruits or sweets or vibuti given to devotees at the end of a religious service or meeting with a holy man), arrange for lights and so on. Not all could afford this expenditure.

Krishna had this comment to make:

Generally speaking there will be very few people who will continuously be with Swami after eight or ten years. Somehow or other they will fall off, but whatever their disappointment they will not want to talk about it out of respect for others. They will keep quiet. When we differ with someone, we often need courage to tell him. I mean healthy criticism, not backbiting. If we differ with Swami we must have courage to tell him, and he, as well as the rest of us, should accept healthy criticism. In those days, as far as I knew, he never accepted any criticism. As far as I know him, he will all the more resent criticism now when he has become an international figure.

Baba seemed to be a very strong personality, like someone possessing a genuine talent as a director or ruler. Was that true of him in the early days?

Even in those days some of us who were very close used to, without his knowledge, discuss him and say that he was more of a politician than a guru that can lead us to God, because of the terrific mind he has got. He is a great politician. He knows how to get things done when he wants something from you, how to talk to you nicely, and once his need for you is over, how to keep you at arm's length. Even in those days he was an expert at that art. He knew all the tactics of 'divide and rule'. He is also quite intelligent.

Every human being has his drawbacks; no one is perfect. So there are good points about him and others not so good. There are times when he reaches spiritual heights, but there are also times when he comes down even to a lower level than an educated human being. During my stay with him I found that the quality of compassion was not with him, but I may be wrong now. I have also learned much in life and changed, and so might he also have grown up and changed, also in spiritual ways.

What did he mean by Sai Baba reaching spiritual heights?

In the sense of producing these miracles. Also when he gives lectures, but these were mostly thoughts borrowed from Mr Kasturi, who was a very learned man and formerly a professor of a college in the city of Mysore. He had a good influence on Swami. In a way Kasturi was educating him.

He spoke of his friend, Varadu, and Baba.

He treated Varadu badly, used to attribute acts to him that he did not do. He would tell Varadu's mother to send Varadu to him as he wanted to talk to him. The poor fellow would come in the morning and wait till the evening when everybody had gone away.

I really do not understand why he does things like that. He will say: 'I am testing his faith', something I could never understand, even when I was a devotee of Swamiji. Now I will never understand it, because I have no faith in Swamiji any more.

Why did Krishna leave Sai Baba?

The moment Hanumantha Rao asked Swamiji not to come again to his house in Madras I expected that my relationship with Swamiji would become strained. It was mostly for Rao's sake that I was staying with Swamiji, as I was sticking with the faith that he would cure Hanumantha Rao's son. Sai Baba had told Mr and Mrs Hanumantha Rao that he would cure their son. But he never did. Every time Swamiji was coming to stay with them in Madras it was costing them a lot. They were also coming to Puttaparti and taking care of most of the expenses there. Mrs Rao's mother was asking them how long they were going to continue spending like that, and their boy was not getting any better.

Hanumantha Rao was then joint secretary of the Home Department of the government of the state of Madras (now Tamil Nadu). The American Consulate was opposite the house of the Raos, and whenever Swamiji came to Madras there used to be a sort of blockage of the road because of the number of the people coming to see him, and people were also there late at night. So the consul wrote a letter to Hanumantha Rao that he was causing a lot of disturbance to all the neighbours. I know this for I read the letter. Being a highly placed government servant, Mr Rao did not want to clash with the American Consulate, so they wrote to Swami that he could no longer live in their house when he was visiting Madras. In my view that was a time when he should have been all the more compassionate with them. Then there were times when I felt I should come away and accept a job, but because he was always promising to cure that boy and the Raos treated me like their own son, I felt I should stay on.

Another reason for my staying with Swamiji was the hope that some sort of blessing would come on my family, that we would somehow come out of our financial difficulties. I am not blaming Sai Baba for anything; I now think it was foolish to expect so much from him. I should have known his human limitations.

During the almost seven years I stayed with him, I often wanted to leave. If I was in Madras and did not want to go back to Puttaparti, Swamiji would request that I come; I always felt that many people were receiving happiness out of Swamiji and if he needed my presence, all right, I would go.

He explained why, from his point of view, Baba had such power over people around him.

You lose your individuality. He will only like people who do. Again, according to Indian religious tradition you have to surrender yourself totally to the guru.

Personally I feel that Swami will only like to have around him 'yes-men'. It is the same in religion and politics. We have had a Prime Minister who will only prefer yes-men.

What I found in my experience with Christ – of course I have never had physical contact – was that he gave me back my self. He does not take away my self as these gurus do. He transforms it.

In an attempt to be fair to all it seems appropriate to emphasize that the criticism directed towards Sai Baba in this interview concerns him as a young man in his twenties. Also we might keep in mind that unfortunately we are not able to obtain Sai Baba's view of Krishna's story.

Of particular interest to our central theme is the fact that Krishna's critical view of Sai Baba concerns his personality and not the paranormal phenomena. After several years as a personal attendant and his closest associate, Krishna had no normal explanation for the frequent production of objects.

Note

[1] The author has met Mrs Hanumantha Rao, who is now a widow, and learnt from her and Kamala Sarathy that Mrs Rao is still (or again?) much devoted to Sai Baba. Every time he comes to Madras, I was told, he pays that old lady a visit and sees to it that she receives proper medical treatment.

18
Baba's Spiritual Disciple

Probably no person has stayed longer with Baba as a close personal attendant and associate than Mr B. V. Raja Reddy. Raja Reddy is now a building entrepreneur in Bombay, where he lives with a beautiful wife and one child. He lived in Puttaparti from 1956 to 1973 and is still a frequent visitor there and much devoted to Baba. He is a handsome man and a fine singer, who often leads in the singing of bhajans. He is evidently deeply devoted to the life of the spirit, so much so that it was always rather difficult to bring him down to the earthly level of miraculous phenomena that I wanted to discuss with him. It was not that he was reluctant to talk about them. Rather, Raja Reddy's thinking was simply located in more elevated spheres.

His mother knew Sai Baba and had been a frequent visitor to Puttaparti.

She directed me to go and see him in Madras in 1952 or 1953 when I was a student. Later I had the opportunity to go to Puttaparti myself when I had wound up my studies of economics and was no more a student. I was in that philosophical mood of wondering about the truth, wanting to know something more constant about this world. That sort of inquiry was going on in me. I wanted solace and a realized man to guide me. I was very much off to that. So I went to Baba in 1956.

At that time there was much more time for him to devote his attention to people individually. There were very few devotees and such a small, meagre, simple mandir. In fact you can't even bring back to mind what Puttaparti was then, when you see it now. Then there were just the headquarters, just a simple block as you might have seen in old photos, and just a few plain little houses and few devotees, and Swami used to come to almost every devotee's block. So individual attention and guidance was there.

Had he observed what Baba sometimes refers to as 'small items', namely the materializations, when he first went to Puttaparti?

Yes, the miracles were there. But then I had been a sort of a devotee of Sri Ramakrishna Paramhansa since my early student days, and I was a staunch admirer of Vivekananda. I had been a frequent visitor to the Ramakrishna Mission in Mylapore in Madras. I was much impressed by their whole literature and practiced sadhana (meditation, etc.) to some extent even while in college. In the literature of the Ramakrishna movement I had read that miracles are not of great value in the spiritual field. So I approached Baba with that sort of background and would not give much importance to the miracles. Knowing that full well Baba accepted that fact.

Was Baba then producing and giving talismans?

Right from then on he was producing ashes, talismans, eatables and what not – that has not decreased. That is absolutely the same. But the magnitude and dimension in which he has been manifesting himself has increased enormously. His presence has become felt in so many places in the world. His activity is going around, his educational, hospital and other social activities is something immense. We never thought in the old days that this would happen. But Baba had been saying all along that this would happen.

What about physical miracles, producing vibuti, talismans and so on?

That has been just the same, all the time. The only difference is that he has deliberately stopped some functions, like Sivaratri, when he used to produce much more vibuti during *abisheikam* (a religious ceremony), when Baba would pour down vibuti on to the statue of Shirdi Baba, so as to cover it up in a heap of vibuti. During Shivaratri Baba used to take out Shiva lingams from his own divine person.

Did he also produce fruits?

Yes, fruits, eatables, jewels, rings, talismans, necklaces – it is too big to enlist them – too huge .... Also fruits out of season and out of place. I will tell you. For instance he will take up a slab of a stone, a small stone and in a moment it will be a sugar candy. I remember having seen him pluck a small custard apple and just with a blow of air from his mouth, he transformed it into an ordinary apple. These cases were innumerable.

For instance about four of us were near Baba's feet, and Baba, in that rare mood of his, was giving the holy name to us (mantra). So he rolled the paper he had in his hand up into a pin or needle sort of shape and then he just blew on it and it was transformed into a beautiful ivory needle, one end being pointed, and at the other end there was a Lord Krishna playing the flute, standing of course. And with that he wrote on our tongues whatever names he gave to us four different people. Then he also whispered it into our ears because that is a custom in India. A spiritual name or mantra should not be uttered loud, specially when a guru is passing it on to a disciple. There a simple paper was transformed into an ivory needle. He gave it to me later.

Mr Reddy described Baba's trances.

That used to be the way with Baba, not now though. Whenever there was any devotee in distress or any accident happening to devotees, and things like that, he would leave his mortal body. It started with a sort of sound from him like 'ah'. He would become absolutely indifferent to his surroundings as if staring into emptiness. Then we would know that he was about to fall into trance, and we would be ready to hold him because as soon as he left the body, the body would drop down, and our duty was to protect it – from falling and being hurt. And it would become very stiff and stern, almost like a rigor mortis. And sometimes even breathing might almost stop. This would last, say for instance one minute, two minutes, five minutes, or even ten minutes, depending on the work that he has; rarely longer, mostly just a few minutes. Then he would come back and his body would relax and become normal. We would ask him what had happened to him. He would narrate to us what exactly had happened, why he had to go and things like that. There were instances when he used to have blood marks on his hands.

He had seen some scars on Baba's hand after his return.

Yes, blood marks, red stains, which were never there before he went into trance. Then he would explain: So-and-so was under a blow of an axe, or something like that, and I had to save him.

He had a habit of plucking his hair during the trance, and he would take it into his mouth. On one occasion he plucked quite a lot of hair from his head and swallowed it. While in the trance he asked for drinking water, which I brought, and so the whole hair went down like a tablet. These hand movements were just reflexes, he later said, if you asked him. To start with I was not aware of all this. So I allowed him to pluck the hair and swallow. Then he came back to consciousness, so to speak, and enquired whether anything had happened. I said: 'Baba you have done things like .... You wanted water on the top of it. I gave you that to swallow the hair.' He said I should not have allowed him to do that. I should have taken his hand off the hair. Then he paused for a while and removed the top button on his robe and slowly pulled that hair straight out through his breast. It was all wet; a bundle of long hair which he pulled out through the skin on his breast.

Had there been attempts to verify any of the cases in which he said that he had been out of the body at distant places?

The verifications used to be there in certain cases, yes. We used to get letters by the victims or devotees ....

He remembered a particular instance concerning his mother.

She was travelling by train going on a pilgrimage from down south heading for Kashi Benares along with a small party. We were at that time in Kodaikanal in Tamil Nadu. Baba was in a camp there. On the way somewhere up in the north, my mother had fever, was a little sick, and she entered into the toilet of the moving train. In that feverishness and that movement of the train, she was about to have a fall. Baba said at that time to me in Kodaikanal: 'Your mother is going in a train to such and such a place. She is feeling feverish and was about to fall into the toilet. I helped her out and she is better, having no problem now.' After my mother came back, I verified the incident from her. She said that this thing had happened. With Baba's grace she could avert the fall.

How did she know that it was through Baba's grace that she did not fall?

She was about to fall and, what otherwise might have been a certain fall, was averted through a miraculous intervention, and therefore she did not fall. She felt that because of Baba's presence she avoided that fall. Something similar has happened to many.

Since he no longer falls into trances, how can he help his
devotees as he is reported to have done earlier?

> The answer is that it is no longer necessary for him to leave the
> body. Even while in the body and engaging in his various
> activities he can at the same time function away from his body.
> Also many foreigners and people in the North have
> experienced his help at a distance. If he would now have to fall
> into trance for each and every incident, then we would not have
> Baba attending to his normal functions.

Many claim what might be called distant experiences of Baba:
visions of him, vibuti appearing at a distance in their houses,
and so on. Mr Reddy commented:

> Yes, that is also there, but personally I don't give much
> importance to visions. I consider that from the Vedantic point
> of view. I am struggling to get out of the ordinary sphere of the
> mind. I know that these visions are within the orbit of the
> mind, so why should I give importance to visions? In fact I give
> more importance to peace, internal peace, internal bliss. I have
> been attached to my meditation very much. I have had very
> many blissful experiences while with Baba. I even had them
> before I met him. These spiritual experiences are what matters
> to me. The memory of them also gives me a bliss. You see, we
> are struggling all the while to go beyond our mind to what is
> REAL. It is beyond our thoughts. We think of so many things,
> so many thoughts come and disturb us. In meditation, what do
> you do? You keep away from thoughts, that is the principle of
> meditation. Just a simple calm pool of water where there is no
> ripple from the stone of thoughts, so that a clear reflection of
> the Supreme can come in the water. That is the purpose of
> meditation.

Did Swami give you any instructions about meditation?

> He does instruct people on meditation, but his way of
> moulding people is something different. A lot of people may be
> good at meditation, but fundamentally their character itself is a
> blockade. They are not able to control their minds. So Baba's
> way of moulding them is, accordingly, by guiding them along
> the right path of good character. He tackles you to get rid of
> your unwanted and impure thoughts. Once that is done,
> meditation is very easy.

I asked about swami's sudden disappearance from sight.

That was earlier to my going over to Puttaparti.

Raja Reddy believed, with others, that Baba is a difficult taskmaster.

He is a very difficult taskmaster. He is a perfectionist. You have to be very alert, do things to the point of perfection with him. And even if you do perfectly almost, there will be flaws in his eyes and he will just go straight on to that flaw and point it out to you though it will be missed not only by you but by many others. Of course what he wants is more the attitude behind, more your sort of mental make-up than what you actually do outside. He is very particular about that.

He would notice what went on within.

Absolutely, your mind is like an open book for him. If you think it is not, then your book is closed to you, not to him. Something magnificent, but then there is one thing, as he himself has been saying: 'I am just a reflection, reaction and resound.' That is what he says. As you think, so he is. You think he is big – he is very big. If you think he is a child – he is a child. You think he is a naughty fellow – he is a naughty fellow.

Raja Reddy had said during an earlier interview that when people are very close to the swami they notice not only the light but also the heat. What did he mean?

You might know, at the best, one side of Baba, the more pleasant side or the human side. And you remember his speeches. So that is the light you feel, but when you are actually with him, and day and night move with him, then you really face the task. He is a perfectionist, and every movement of your mind is open to him. Naturally, we are human. So many thoughts cross our minds, and accordingly he reacts. He does not welcome unwelcome thoughts, which you are clinging onto. So there you feel a distance. That is what I meant by heat. Just by being with him you feel he is reading your thoughts, and so much so that you are on the alert always, to keep yourself pure mentally. This is a highest form of 'sadhana'. If that is not meditation, what else is it? And not many can stick on to this for long, at least in my experience, and in the experience of others also. This is quite a task. Without his grace it is very difficult to be with him for long. At the same time he is very compassionate; he gives you a long, long, long rope while you commit mistakes. He corrects; there are various ways of mending. This is a very big 'sadhana'.

What did he think about the claim of miraculous cures?

I believe it is very correct.

Did he personally know any instances that would not be easy to explain away?

Yes, my wife's aunt was cured of cancer. Yet another very recent case, in the month of May 1981. A brilliant young man, hardly thirty years, with a very promising career. He developed a cancer, there was a lump near his groin. And doctors diagnosed it – I have forgotten the exact name of the type of cancer, but it is said to be an incurable malignant cancer. Doctors, expert specialists, had given him only nine months. He has a family and two small kids, and they were all depressed. A biopsy was taken, and he was given chemotherapy treatment. Mind you, chemotherapy has very bad side effects, like the fall of hair and severe diarrhoea and so on. This chap was a non-believer in Sri Sathya Sai Baba, but when this particular disease struck him, he went to Baba here in Dharmakshetra in Bombay. Baba out of his infinite mercy materialized holy ash: 'Nothing will touch you, you will be all right, don't worry,' he said. He underwent the treatment, had absolutely no hairfall, not a pinch of reaction, no diarrhoea, nothing. He looks much better .... And once the tests were conducted after biopsy the result was absolutely negative – repeatedly negative. The doctors say that this is something miraculous, it can never come like that. Once that disease attacks it can never turn out to be negative. That is the verdict of the medical profession. Now he is a very staunch devotee of Baba, and his whole family sings bhajans. Such a wonderful transformation there. That is one of the many, many cases

What about those cases when swami said to someone they will be all right and they do not get cured?

There are also cases like that. That is why Baba is sort of a contradictory character from our point of view. There we must sift, there are factors which we should analyze in every way. For instance, Baba would be the last man to say to anyone that he will not live, will not be cured. No one should leave him in an unhappy state of mind, having come all the way with all that anxiety, keenness and unhappiness. To leave him in an unhappy state of mind is something not divine at all. Baba would view it from that point of view, it does not matter even if the man misunderstands him, calls him something, does not believe in him and so on.

Once I brought my son with me to India; he was then twenty years old. He had many pimples on his face. We did not ask Baba for any help but one day he came up to me and said: 'The pimples on your son's face will disappear in three days.' But they did not.

A very simple thing Baba said, in three days it will go and it has not gone. It is clear-cut, there is nothing in Baba. Any old blind lady can come to that conclusion, it does not require any intelligent brain to do that. But then, there is something more – let us enquire patiently. Could it not be a test of how your faith stands, whether it is safely and firmly rooted or whether it is a shaken faith? There may be so many reasons. There is no particular code of conduct for Baba.

Finally Raja Reddy's response, when asked why he was so sure Baba does not produce his objects by sleight of hand.

It is to be presumed that producing an object by sleight of hand implies that the object should be small and compact enough to be hidden in the sleeve or between the fingers before actually juggling it out.

Any such sly act is completely irrelevant in the case of Bhagavan Baba. It was during our trip to Dwaraka, way back in the early 1970's, if I remember right. Baba and all of us got out of the cars and set out for the beach sands, several metres away, and climbed up a hillock to get there. As is His wont, Baba Himself (capitalization requested by Raja Reddy) asked us to locate a place for us all to sit. There, when all the eyes of the observers were intent on Him, He deliberately took up His sleeves right up to the elbows, and straight from the sands He brought out a beautiful, glittering Lord Krishna playing on the flute – magnificent – a statue of solid gold of about a foot high!! May I ask the doubting Thomas what sleight of hand could explain this phenomenon!

During the Sivaratri festivals, until a few years back, Bhagavan used to take out Shiva lingams, sometimes as big as a duck's egg, through his mouth, right in front of tens of thousands of poeple. I have also seen – nay, collected – along with many others, actual pearls rolling out from His Lotus feet while (he was) walking along the sandy dunes in Kanyakumari. These are sheer manifestations of His will and have no bearing whatsoever on any sleight of hand. For years on end, day in and day out, we have been witnesses to such and such other acts; and we are as a lot no less sceptical than most others. The Reality unfolds Itself, but we do not see and feel It (Baba) until we have the right perspective, the right intelligence, and the right experience.

19
A Westerner In India:
Dr Roerich

Dr Svetoslav Roerich was born in Czarist Russia in 1904. He later studied in the United States at Columbia University and at the Graduate School of Architecture at Harvard University. After that he settled along with his parents in the beautiful Indian Himalayas. Like his father Nicholas Roerich, he became internationally renowned as a landscape and portrait artist. He is the recipient of many awards and honours from several countries; for example, he has been given India's highest award for art by the President of India, and he has been elected Honorary Fellow of the Academy of Fine Arts of the USSR. In my youth I had read some interesting books written by his father and mother, some of them about travels in Central Asia. Meeting Dr Roerich was like meeting an old acquaintance, and we soon discovered some common interests, such as psychical research.

I first met Dr Roerich and his wife, Madame Devika Rani, in 1977 and again several times in 1981. His wife is a relative of the great Bengali poet, Rabindranath Tagore, and was a famous film actress in India. They invited Dr Thalbourne and me to their estate near Bangalore. What follows is Dr Roerich's description of his first encounter with Sai Baba.

My wife went to visit Baba in Puttaparti in 1968 and mentioned to him that either she would bring me there or I would come myself. But Baba said: 'No, I will visit him. I want to pay my respects to him.' He then fixed a date and time.

When he came to visit us, he brought with him several people, among them Dr Gokak, who was at that time vice-chancellor of Bangalore University, and also Mrs Indira Devi. Visiting us at that time also were Major Talwar, his wife and two daughters, Renu and her sister Premilla, neither of whom were married at that time. And, too, it so happened that the villagers here in the neighbourhood had somehow learned that Sai Baba was coming, so they all gathered here outside to have darshan. There were a lot of people there, exactly how many I couldn't tell you now, but certainly a few hundred.

We were all in my studio, and Baba expressed a desire to see some of my paintings. So I had some paintings to show him; he talked about the pictures at length, trying to explain their meaning, and I must say that his reading of the ideas behind the paintings was very accurate. This took some time. Then tea was served in the studio. My wife asked Baba what he would like to have, tea or coffee? But he said; 'I don't take coffee, and I really don't take tea.' Nevertheless, my wife said: 'In my house you must have something, so what will you have?' So he said: 'All right, I will have some milk, and you can give it to me in your silver cup – which you kept ready for me.'

Ever since her childhood Dr Roerich's wife had owned a silver cup; she took special care that it would always be perfectly clean, and only she would drink from it. Two days before Baba's visit, she had told one of her servants to boil and clean this silver cup because she had decided that in the event Baba wanted milk she would give it to him in that cup. But the cup had never been mentioned to the swami before he himself brought it up. Dr Roerich continues:

While my wife was out of the studio seeing to the servants, Baba waved his hand (I was sitting next to him) and produced a handful of a sweet named 'halwa'. It was quite hot and fresh, so much so that when I placed some of it on a piece of paper, ghee immediately spread out over the paper. Baba put all the sweet into my hand, and I distributed it amongst the other people present, who must have numbered some 15 to 20 people. There was quite enough for everyone, but nothing was left over.

When my wife came back, I told her that while she had been out, Baba had given us halwa. So she chided Baba: 'Why did you not give me any? You give it to others and you did not give me any!' he said: 'Yes, here', and good-naturedly he produced again the same sweet, and the same amount as the first time, so that she was able to have some, and others had second helpings.

When the group went out of the house, they found a large number of villagers had gathered in the garden and under the enormous banyan tree there. Madame Devika Rani told us that she had then said to Baba: 'Sai, you must do something for these people; they are expecting something from you.' Baba then extended his hand, and vibuti came forth. A number of people came up to him and held out their hands in cup-like fashion to receive the vibuti, and they then distributed it to the other members of the crowd. Baba kept producing a stream of vibuti for quite some time, and everyone in the entire crowd received some, despite the fact that there were hundreds of people there. Dr Roerich:

Under our banyan tree is a small Munishwara temple (or rather, shrine), which is looked after by a *pujari* (brahmin priest). Since it was getting dark, Baba asked Madame Devika Rani to get him a bright lamp. Baba went under the tree to where the pujari was standing, who greeted him. Then my wife went up to the swami and said: 'Please give him something so that he will remember you.' Baba agreed and asked the pujari: 'Whom do you worship the most?' 'I am a Sivaite priest' he answered, 'but I myself worship Ganesh.' So Baba made his usual hand movements and produced a very lovely silver ring on which was chiselled a very big Ganesh. He gave it to the man, and it fitted his finger perfectly. Then the pujari prostrated before him.

Baba then sang many beautiful bhajans. As he left he said: 'I will come again, and next time I will go to that other hill which is on the other side of the lake.' This hill is indeed on our estate, yet it is not visible from either our house or the garden. He stayed the entire afternoon with us, and these were the phenomena which he produced.

Dr Roerich had a second encounter with the swami some ten years later. An important minister from an Eastern European country who had a keen interest in Dr Roerich's work visited him in November 1978. For political reasons we have deemed it wise not to reveal the identity of the minister. Dr Roerich related the following incident:

I thought it would be interesting for her (the minister) to meet Sai Baba, so we all went together to Puttaparti, I with my wife and she with some four or five members of her staff. Of course we had to let them know in Puttaparti that we were coming, so everything was ready when we arrived.

Sai Baba then invited us into his interview room, which is rather small. All of us sat on the floor – the minister and the members of her staff, my wife and myself and two friends of ours. Baba was talking in a very friendly and informal way, as he often speaks. He then put his hand on the carpet, with the palm flat, and started moving his hand in a circular motion on the carpet. As his hand was moving, I could see that the centre of his hand – the palm – was rising, as if something was forming below it. he closed his hand and turned it over, opening his palm towards us, and in it was a large golden ring which he presented to the minister. The ring fitted her finger quite perfectly and had on it a large cut topaz of at least 40 to 60 carats.

After that, Sai Baba told Madame (the minister) that he wanted to tell her something, and took her to the inner room where he spoke to her at quite some length. When they came back to the interview room, Baba gave to each of the members of her staff (except one person) a silver medallion about one inch in diameter, which he produced in his hand, one at a time. These medallions depicted his face on one side, but what was on the other side I don't remember now. Then my wife said to Baba: 'How is it that you gave a medallion to all these people but not to him?' (meaning the staff member who was missed out by Swami). So Baba said: 'To him I give vibuti.' And he produced some accordingly.

Then Baba said to the minister; 'If you want to contact me, concentrate on the stone in that ring. I will then know that you are thinking of me, and I will in some way manifest myself.'

Dr Roerich observed:

If we take India as it stands today, the most popular phenomenon is Sai Baba. There is no doubt about this; he has millions of followers. From every point of view, it is a positive movement, because he has given happiness and faith to hundreds and thousands of people. Other people should try to ensure that this faith is sustained because this world certainly needs it in one form or another.

Whether you agree that the phenomena Baba produces are necessary or not does not make much difference. I accept the necessity of the phenomena because from his point of view that is the quickest way to attract people. If a teacher did not display these phenomena, he would not make sufficient impact. There can be no doubt about it for the time being that Baba is a great phenomenon.

This visit to Puttaparti was nice because everybody was happy; everybody received something from Baba in one way or another, and the visitors returned to their country with fine mementos of the occasion.

Part Two

20
The Critics

As Sai Baba's fame for performing miracles spread in India, it did not remain unchallenged. In 1976 an interesting episode took place that developed into a major Indian controversy of that year and was a matter of hot debate among the general public.

It started at Bangalore University. Dr H. Narasimhaiah, then vice-chancellor of that university, constituted a 12-member committee 'to investigate rationally and scientifically miracles and other verifiable superstitions' (Narasimhaiah, 1976). One or two members of the committee were, I was told, followers of Baba. The committee was constituted on 27 April 1976, and the minutes of its first meeting read in part: 'It would therefore be necessary to take all steps to eradicate superstitions among our population. The following two actually promote superstitions on a large scale: 1. Super-natural phenomena, for example 'neam', tree giving milk, 2. Miracles, for example, people creating materials.'

The committee decided to investigate some claims of miracles and to promote a more scientific attitude among the general population (the latter part of this statement being taken almost literally from the constitution of the Republic of India). On behalf of the committee, Dr Narasimhaiah wrote a polite letter to Sai Baba in which he said that he would 'be very thankful if you can kindly give me and the other members of the committee an opportunity to meet you and discuss with you all these issues (miracles and superstitions) and also to conduct the investigation of these phenomena according to well established methods of science under controlled conditions' (ibid. p. 2). Sai Baba did not reply to this letter, nor did he respond to two further letters from the committee, which were widely publicized.

In the meantime the committee members investigated a young boy, Sai Krishna, who was reported to materialize vibuti, and they found him blatantly engaged in fraud. It had previously been claimed that Sai Baba had stated that this boy's 'powers' were genuine, but whether he actually did so was never fully clarified. Anyway, the case received a lot of publicity and reflected negatively on Sai Baba, though he then denied having made any statements about the boy.

In May of 1977 the committee let it be known that it would be going to Brindavan at a certain time in the hope that Baba would receive them. Off they went, in two busloads that included the committee members, journalists, photographers, and some other interested people, their expedition first being widely publicized. The guards at the gate in Brindavan did not let the group enter the premises, with the exception of the only two women on the committee, Dr Vinoda Murthy (now chairman of the Department of Psychology at Bangalore University) and Dr Anupama Niranjana. But they would not go in unless all the committee were admitted. Dr Sundar Rao, an old devotee of Sai Baba, told the committee that Baba had instructed the guards not to let them and their entourage in and that he would not come out of his building until the committee had left.

There was never any investigation. The only formal challenge from the scientific community in India came to a dead end. Perhaps all the fanfare had not been the wisest way to ensure Baba's cooperation. The negative attitude of the committee had been obvious, but Baba might not have participated in any investigation, regardless of how he had been approached. This episode started off a widely publicized controversy that raged in the newspapers for several months. Even the respected daily *Times of India* printed an editorial on the controversy on 25 July 1976, entitled 'No Miracles'. If Baba had not been known nationally before, he was now, and so was Dr Narasimhaiah.

Baba is said to have responded curtly, when someone mentioned this affair to him, by reciting an old Kannada proverb: 'Nothing happens to the sky if a dog barks.'

Of particular interest to us is what followed. The committee received an enormous amount of mail. Mr Shivapur, who was assistant registrar of the University at that time and filed the letters received by the committee, estimated that about 1,000 letters were received. During my several journeys to India, I met a few members of the committee, including Dr Narasimhaiah and Dr Murthy, both of whom I met on more than one occasion and with whom I discussed at length the work of the committee.

I had two interviews with Dr Narasimhaiah, the first in November 1980 and the second (with Dr Thalbourne also present) in October 1981 and met him briefly in 1983. Dr Narasimhaiah said that he had read all these letters and had found nothing valuable in them. One man wrote that Sai Baba had cheated him with respect to the sale of some land near Whitefield; that matter had been settled out of court. Some people accused Baba of being a hoax, undependable and not genuine; others claimed that he is really God and accused and blamed the committee, saying that what it was doing was not correct. There had also been a few letters accusing Baba of promising healing that never occurred. There were a number of letters in which people claimed that their lives had been saved by Baba, or asserted that he is God and has divine powers, or made other such amazing claims. 'The usual stuff', Dr Narasimhaiah added. 'I don't think we can find anything substantial there, otherwise I would certainly have used that material (against Sai Baba).' According to Dr Narasimhaiah, there was nothing in the letters indicating fraud by Baba.

In 1960 Dr Narasimhaiah received his doctorate in nuclear physics from Ohio State University. Since then he has devoted his time primarily to teaching. He is something of a Gandhian figure, at least for foreigners, since he lives a very simple life in a small room in one of the student hostels in Bangalore and wears only simple traditional Indian clothes. When he became vice-chancellor of Bangalore University, he did not want the salary due to him and gave it back to the university. He used the car allotted to him only for strictly official purposes; at first he did not want to use it at all. Only at the insistence of the university officials did he move to the official residence of the vice-chancellor. He left the post of vice-chancellor in 1977.

Dr Narasimhaiah is well known in India for his promotion of science and education. He is the president of the National Education Society, which runs several educational institutions that include all levels from nursery school up to college. He has organized and promoted many activities for students and the educated public, including refresher courses for teachers on recent advances in science, laboratory programmes and lecture series on the sciences, intercollegiate competitions and debates for students, and talks by leading experts in various fields. He is a man highly devoted to education in science and a great speaker who is known to be particularly outspoken. The Central Government of India has nominated him as a (non-elected) member of the Lower House of the Karnataka Parliament, though he is not known to be affiliated with any political party.

When we questioned him about his reason for establishing the Miracle Committee, he replied:

> It was largely undertaken by one man, myself. Nobody was interested. I strongly feel that we must not accept anything without questioning, without investigation. That has been my stance whatever the field, social, economic, religious. At that time Indira Gandhi had declared emergency in our country. There was no senate, no academic council; the university bodies were all abolished for some time. As vice-chancellor I therefore had full powers over university affairs, so I started the committee. Otherwise I don't think it would have been possible for me to constitute that committee because most university people would have opposed such a cause and investigation.

Had Dr Narasimhaiah ever met Sai Baba?

> I met him once in 1973. His disciple Dr Gokak wrote me a letter asking me to inaugurate an All-India Spiritual Conference. I had nothing against it being spiritual or otherwise, and so I accepted and inaugurated it. Of course I did not criticize Sai Baba directly, but I said it was unfortunate that in this age of science and technology many educated people – scientists – would follow meekly, sheepishly some person supposed to have miraculous powers. Bhagavantam was there, Gokak was there, and Sai Baba was sitting on the big dais by my side. I made the statement that we must have scientific temper, and, of course, in passing I said that I thought Sai Baba was doing good work by running educational institutions.
>
> Not one person clapped his hands at the end of my speech. There was the silence of the grave. Probably no one liked it of the nearly one thousand devotees that sat there in front of me. At the end of my speech, Baba and I exchanged a few words about the fact that I speak Telugu, and then he said I should come again to Whitefield. Later, I have been told, he reprimanded Gokak for inviting me, but if he is God (as his

devotees claim) he should have known that I had been invited, even before my coming.

There never was any investigation of Baba, and Dr Narasimhaiah never observed him produce any object or exercise any of his alleged miraculous powers. But Dr Narasimhaiah's attitude was clear-cut: 'I am convinced he is a hoax. I don't have an iota of doubt, absolutely.' And why did he come to the conclusion that Sai Baba is a fraud?

Firstly, he did not reply to my letters. Secondly, he did not give me an interview. If he is so confident of his powers, this was an opportunity for him to exhibit them publicly to the satisfaction of all the sceptics. Then I have my doubts because whatever objects he 'creates', they are always smaller than the size of his fist. And all the articles have existed on the surface of the earth; there is nothing new about them.

I told Dr Narasimhaiah that I had been unsuccessful in my attempts to examine the mail received by the committee. He told me that I would never see it, since the present vice-chancellor was a staunch devotee of Sai Baba and would never do anything that he thought might hurt his master. The committee ceased to exist when Dr Narasimhaiah left the vice-chancellorship in August 1977.

I made several attempts to get access to the letters to the committee. I approached some high officials of the university, but without success. When every other avenue seemed closed, I obtained in November 1981 an appointment with the present vice-chancellor, Dr M. N. Viswanathaiah, and I asked for permission to read the letters received by the committee. He was very friendly and immediately phoned someone and asked that they be brought over.

A little while later, at the end of a lecture I had been invited to give at the department of psychology, I was brought a thick stack of files and told that I could return them to Professor Murthy after my perusal of them. I went through this material in my hotel room and discovered that these files contained only official letters, minutes of the committee, and other documents, but not one letter from the general public. I was about to leave Bangalore, and so I had to give up further efforts to get access to this mail, which I had expected would reveal something of interest about Sai Baba.

Earlier I had met another high official of the university, whose name I probably should not mention and whose attitude seemed similar to that of Dr Narasimhaiah. He had read most of the letters as they came in and had not found anything in them that gave a clue as to how Sai Baba performs his materializations. Most of the letters criticizing Baba accused him either of unfulfilled promises of healing, or of advising no medical help, which in some cases, it was claimed, had led to the death of a patient. There had been a letter describing a dispute with Baba over money (from the sale of some land) which was later settled out of court. One letter accused him of homosexuality. Then there were numerous letters praising him, even saying: 'He is God', but my informant said that these favorable letters were not filed.

The controversy was not only about whether Baba can really perform miracles. For many people the more appropriate question was, is he God? Even the Calcutta-based popular weekly *Sunday* published a long article on the controversy (Thakur 1976) called 'Challenge to Sai Baba, Is he God?' Indians often speak of their alleged saints and miracle-makers as God-men. This thinking has its origins in popular Hinduism, especially Vedanta philosophy. (Widely different and varying approaches to the nature of reality are expressed by other classical systems of Indian philosophy). According to the Vedanta philosophy, all that really exists is God or Brahman. That reality is the essence of all things and the root of our existence, but we are not aware of it since we are emerged in Maya, the great illusion. A true saint is one who, to a greater or lesser extent, has risen above this illusion and has become aware of the true nature of things, of Brahman; at least to some extent, he has merged into the Divine and has come to know his true godly nature and the unity of all things and minds. Sai Baba will, for example, frequently say when he is asked if he is God: 'You are, too, but you are not aware of it.' This thinking was allegorically illustrated when, according to Thakur (1976), Baba said: 'Take a cup of water with sugar at its bottom. You sip the water and it is tasteless. But you stir it with a spoon and it is syrup. Likewise, the heart is like a cup and divinity lies at the bottom.' How to stir the sugar and make the syrup, that is what saints and religious leaders are supposed to know; and if they have managed to do it successfully for themselves, they are, according to popular Hinduism,

God-men. The great Ramakrishna and Ramana Maharshi, both of whom lived in the modern era, are considered by many Hindus to be genuine God-men.

Such concepts are also found in the West. In Graeco-Roman times Plato and Plotinus, the NeoPlatonist, expressed similar ideas. Appolonius of Tyana, living about the time of Christ, was celebrated as a saint and miracle-man and was considered to be a God-man, comparable to Christ (Philostratus 1970). The Christian idea that Jesus Christ is the son of God or is one with the Father is similar to the Hindu concept of a God-man. According to a Harvard University theologian, H. Cox, the word Christ, which Jesus allowed himself to be called, 'meant one who is anointed by God, a special representative of God among others – an idea not unlike that of avatar' (Cox 1977, pp. 123-24).

During the Sai Baba controversy, some newspapers in India switched sides, over to Baba. One such was the influential leftist tabloid *Blitz*, published in Bombay by Mr R.K. Karanjia. It had always been highly critical of Baba. Then Karanjia himself went to Puttaparti. Baba took him in for an interview, which Karanjia later published in a series of five articles in his widely read weekly (*Blitz*, 31 July to 2 October 1976). After that this pro-Russian, leftist and highly critical newspaper magnate became one of the admirers, if not a follower, of the prophet from Puttaparti. In an interview with Mr Karanjia I became convinced that this was actually the case.

One man, however, showed no signs of relaxing his stance against the seemingly supernatural, though he could no longer officially challenge Sai Baba. Dr Narasimhaiah, now in the Legislative Council of Karnataka, founded in 1980 a new committee under his chairmanship, to investigate the practice of witchcraft in some rural areas, especially by those who deliberately induce fear of witchcraft and then use it for their own personal profit. Dr Narasimhaiah's committee urged the government to enact a law to punish such people. That plea was rejected, since it was claimed that 'existing provisions of the law are adequate to deal with such persons' (*Deccan Herald*, 23 August 1981).

21
How Real? A Second Look

The reader has now read through a number of chapters describing impressions and experiences of Sai Baba by scientists and laymen, devotees and ex-devotees, sympathizers and critics. Needless to say, the volume of testimony could be multiplied several times. What has been presented, however, can be considered a representative sample.

What conclusions can be drawn from all of this testimony? What evidence do we have for and against the genuineness or paranormality of the extraordinary phenomena widely reported about Sai Baba? Since these phenomena are of various kinds, it seems appropriate to consider each of the major types separately.

The alleged appearance of objects (or 'materializations') is the most prominent and perplexing aspect of Sai Baba's repertoire, though he frequently refers to these productions as small items or 'mere trivialities' (Thakur 1976, p.9). Let us begin our assessment by weighing the evidence for the various alternative hypotheses that might explain this phenomenon.

First, a little can be added to our earlier discussion of hypnosis as an explanation, namely that Baba hypnotizes people not to see from where he actually takes the objects that he produces. This explanation assumes that all people are readily hypnotizable and can easily produce visual hallucinations. Hypnosis research does not support such an assumption. Sheehan and Perry, well-known authorities on hypnosis, state: 'People vary in the extent to which they respond to hypnotic suggestions, and individual differences in hypnotic susceptibility are one of the most firmly established facts of hypnosis' (1976, p. 50). Hilgard, another leading figure in this field, has found that 'probably under 5% and perhaps as low as 1% of an unselected population of college students' are exceptionally hypnotizable (1977, p. 158). Only the exceptionally hypnotizable are likely to produce vivid hypnotic hallucinations. The majority of people are only mildly responsive to hypnosis, and a sizable minority appears entirely unaffected by hypnosis. Besides, some form of induction is generally needed to produce hypnotic effects, something Sai Baba does not seem to use. Extensive filming of Sai Baba has given no evidence supporting hypnosis as an explanation of the apparent materialization phenomena. The hypnosis hypothesis can therefore safely be rejected.

Next is the question of whether Sai Baba has accomplices. During the forty years of Sai Baba's active life as a religious leader and performer of apparent miracles, he has had many close attendants and associates. Over the years their turnover has been considerable, for various reasons. At the present time, Baba has no attendant who was with him in the 1940s or 1950s. Prof Kasturi is still around, but he meets Sai Baba only occasionally, not on a day-to-day basis. If Sai Baba has accomplices to help him in a sleight of hand production of objects, he must have had a considerable number of them over these forty years. Besides, he usually has no close associate or attendant with him when he gives audiences or interviews to individuals or groups, the occasions during which he produces most of the objects. If Sai Baba was using sleight of hand, he would need not only accomplices to bring the objects to him and perhaps help him prepare his performances, but also jewellers and goldsmiths to supply the objects, as well as people to transport them to him. Baba's production of these objects is on such a large scale that a few jewellers would probably be needed to fulfill his requirements for jewellery supplies alone.

If accomplices are involved, be they devotees or jewellers, they would be in a position to exert tremendous pressure on Sai Baba, since his movement, at least a million members strong in India and abroad, might suffer a severe blow if one of these accomplices revealed his secret. Some of those who were once very close to Baba later left him and turned their backs on him; it seems unlikely that they would not reveal their involvement in a fraud of such proportions if there were one. Krishna, for example, was disillusioned with Baba and is severely critical of him; yet he freely admits that he was never aware of anything to arouse his suspicion about the physical phenomena and that he has no normal explanation for them.

There are rumours in India that jewellers supply Sai Baba with the jewellery. Three men, all sympathizers or devotees of Baba, but none of them close to him, have expressed the view to me that jewellers in Bangalore, perhaps also in Anantapur and Mangalore, may supply him with his gifts. If this were true, they pointed out, the jewellers would for financial reasons be unwilling to reveal their involvement. According to their theory, the pieces would be stored in a safe place, and Baba would then apport them from that place to wherever he is at the moment when he needs a particular piece. None of these men adhered to the sleight of hand hypothesis. They were unable to give or point to any evidence to support their view; their views seem therefore to be founded on hearsay that I have been unable to confirm.

An acquaintance of mine in Bangalore, Mr Bharat Reddy (a former devotee who left Baba mainly because he could not accept Baba's claim to be an avatar), introduced me to his close friend and former classmate Mr Narayan Chetty, who heads Krishnaja Chetty and Sons Ltd., the largest jewellery firm in that city. Mr Narayan Chetty told me that he had seen some of the items produced by Baba and that they definitely did not come from his firm, nor were there any rumours in the jewellery community that a particular firm was supplying them.

Another owner of a well-known jewellery firm (Narayan Chetty) in Bangalore, also told me that he had had no business-dealings with Sai Baba. He said that one of Baba's devotees, a lady, had once bought silverware, apparently for Sai Baba's household in Whitefield; another time she had bought a few pieces of jewellry, but none of them had borne Sai Baba or Shirdi Baba photos or engravings. Whether these items were for her personal use or for someone else the jeweller did not know. Anyway, these few pieces would have fallen far short of the great supply needed by Sai Baba.[1] Neither of the two jewellers I met in Bangalore were in any way devoted to Sai Baba. Of course, if they were really in business with Baba, they would not have told me anything.

When most people first see Baba produce an object, they believe that he does it by sleight of hand; they think he must take the object out of his sleeves, his bushy hair, or some other place, without their being aware of it. Magicians do their tricks in this way, usually skillfully enough to baffle their audiences.

Does he take the objects out of his hair? I have taken a few hours of films and videotapes of Sai Baba during darshan, when he often produces vibuti. In these films he rarely touched or reached to his hair. On other occasions, during darshan as well as in interviews, I also noted that he seldom reaches for his hair.

Sai Baba's clothing is unusual and not generally worn in India: a one-piece robe that falls to his ankles, has a slit up to the middle of the calf on both sides, and has sleeves that reach his wrists. Two loose golden buttons close the top at the neck, but no other buttons or openings can be seen. He has several such robes, all of the same design. They are made of thin synthetic material and, apparently, have no pockets or folds. Underneath, I have been told by his former attendants, he wears only briefs or a dhoti. The climate is hot in India, people wear thin simple clothes, and so does Sai Baba

A tailor in Whitefield makes Sai Baba's robes, usually several at a time, since Baba frequently gives them away to devotees after he has worn them for some time. I have visited the tailor and seen the robes he was sewing. I have also seen some that Baba has given to devotees. None of them had pockets or folds or potential hiding places. One may ask whether these pieces are just for show and differ from the ones that he actually wears, but we have no evidence to support such a conjecture. In his younger days his devotees would often bring him new robes or clothes which he would put on. Apparently he produced objects just as easily wearing those robes as when he was wearing his own.

I never had the opportunity to examine clothing that Sai Baba actually had on, but some people I have met have done so. I described earlier an incident, reported by Dr and Mrs D.K. Banerjee and Dr Bhattacharya, that occurred when Sai Baba unexpectedly visited the Banerjee home and produced some objects. Sai Baba asked Mrs Banerjee to wash his robe so that he could put it on again the next morning, and Dr Bhattacharya and the Banerjees took the opportunity to examine the robe carefully. They found that it contained no pockets or hiding places.

Baba's robes are thin, like the material in men's shirts, and sunlight shines through them easily. Neither when the sun shines through the window in Baba's interview room nor out

in the open have I, even at close range, been able to see any
shadows that might indicate the presence of a hidden object.
When Baba is outside and the wind blows, the robe may cling
to his body; but on such occasions neither I nor anyone I
have spoken to has seen any protrusion indicating a hidden
object.

For sceptical observers Baba sometimes pushes his sleeves
high up his arms when producing objects. Also, I have sat
quite close to him and been able to see up into his rather wide
buttonless sleeves, and I have never observed anything
suspicious.

In brief, I have found no evidence that his clothing contains
pockets or any magicians' paraphernalia that could be used as
hiding places for objects and that would probably be necessary
to exercise sleight of hand.

I have made eight trips to India during which I have
interviewed in depth dozens of people, spoken more casually
to many more people, and listened to and checked up on
numerous rumours; but I have never found any solid evidence
to support the sleigh of hand hypothesis.

Since Baba's colleges were founded in Whitefield and
Puttaparti, Baba is mostly attended by students. A few of them
have left him, usually after losing faith in his claim to be an
avatar. When that happens they also tend to lose faith in the
genuineness of the phenomena; for the two seem for many to
be two sides of the same coin. Some of these apostate students
(such as Mr Satish Kumar, whom I met in Hyderabad in the
summer of 1983) believe that Baba makes pellets of solid vibuti
in his bathroom by wetting it slightly and then letting it dry;
these pellets he then supposedly keeps between his fingers.
When he gives darshan outside, they conjecture, he has three,
four or five of those pellets and crushes them between his
fingers as the need arises. It should be added that none of these
students claim to have witnessed Baba make any of the
presumed pellets. This may explain some of the vibuti
phenomena. For those instances when Baba produces large
amounts, such as when he produced on demand many
handfuls during his visit to the Roerichs, the students have no
plausible explanation.

The evidence offered by these students seems slight. To me it
seems that they have made conjectures based on a

psychological need to explain away the miracles after they lost faith in Baba's godliness. Be that as it may, these observations, weak as they are, should keep up our vigilance as long as Sai Baba has not given any experimental evidence of the paranormality of his physical productions.

Allow me to describe one more such incident. It occurred only three months before Captain Hartmanprit Singh Sidhu, aide to the Governor of Karnataka and his wife reported it to Dr. Thalbourne, who interviewed them for me in Bangalore in October 1981. Captain Sidhu and his wife, came to know Sai Baba in 1978. Three years later they had a child who Baba offered to name. The Sidhus and a few relatives went to Puttaparti in July 1981 to receive Baba's blessings for the baby, and without the usual prior notice for such occasions Baba performed the name-giving ceremony (*namkaran*).

> Usually, after a namkaran, it is auspicious to distribute some sweets. After producing the pendant (a golden medallion with a chain given to the baby), Baba called my wife over, saying: 'Let's have some sweets'. He asked her to spread her palms to form a cup. Baba rubbed his palms together above hers and filled up both her hands with a powderlike sweet that we call crushed ladus. It took only a few seconds, and there was so much of it that it was pouring out of his hands like rain, making a mound perhaps half an inch higher than the upper part of her palms. Baba went around and distributed the sweet to the five or six people who were also present. There was enough for everyone, and a little more besides, so when he came to my wife, he told her: 'See, a double share for you.' It tasted very good.

Apart from Sai Baba I have investigated three other purported psychics in India, two of whom were also swamis, who have developed some reputation for materializing objects. In spite of minimal cooperation on their part, I have found clear evidence of sleight of hand in the two swamis. The third case concerned an interesting woman in Calcutta who purportedly produces vibuti and occasionally small statues when in trance. I was not able to find fraud, and vibuti and a statuette were produced in the only session in which some controls could be enforced. Since then I have not been able to obtain her cooperation to continue this investigation. Recently I was informed by a close associate of hers that she is no longer able to perform these feats.[2]

In the literature on psychical research we find almost nothing on Sai Baba apart from what Dr Osis, Dr Chari and I have written. It was therefore of much interest to read the following sentences in a recent book by a well-known writer on psychic phenomena (Rogo 1982):

> There is ... some indication that Sai Baba often deliberately fakes his purported miracles. (When films taken of some of his exhibitions are slowed down, it is clear that he is quite an expert at sleight of hand.) (p.90)

In a letter to Rogo I asked for further details, particularly which films he was referring to. He answered in a letter that he had had several conversations in 1975 with Dr Edwin C. May, a physicist at the prestigious SRI Institute near San Francisco, and that Dr May had told him that he had filmed Sai Baba producing objects. According to Rogo, Dr May had told him that when the films were slowed down and examined frame by frame, sleight of hand was evident. Rogo himself, however, had never seen Dr May's films but had taken his word for this. He suggested that I write to Dr May.

Furthermore, Rogo said that he had seen some films at Sai Baba's headquarters in Los Angeles which to him had shown clear evidence of fraud. Rogo concluded that some of Baba's materializations had been hidden in his Afro-style hair, since it seemed to Rogo that Baba had 'touched his hair with passing motions on several occasions before producing his little objects.'

I wrote to Dr May, who rang me up a few days later and told me that he had never met Sai Baba; hence he had never taken films of him and had never even seen any film of Baba. He had filmed a woman in Bombay, alleged by a small flock of followers to produce kumkum paranormally, and he had found her clearly engaged in fraud. Rogo might have been referring to this film. I remembered that film; Dr May had shown it at the 1975 convention of the Parapsychological Association at the University of California at Santa Barbara, which I had attended, when he reported on this investigation (May and Jahagirdar 1976).

Mr Doug Henning, the famous American magician, is undoubtedly considered one of the most knowledgeable magicians in the world today. He has given sophisticated performances on Broadway and in many large cities in the United States and elsewhere. In New York he and Dr Osis viewed together the available films on Sai Baba (probably the same films Rogo had seen, since both Rogo and Dr Osis had obtained the films from Sai Baba centres). They came to a different conclusion from Rogo's. They thought that the films were too unclear to provide any evidence either for or against the sleight of hand hypothesis. This accords with the conclusion I reached after carefully viewing my own films as well as those of other people. Furthermore, neither Mr Henning, Dr Osis, nor I observed in these films that Baba 'touched his hair with passing motions on several occasions before producing his little objects.' In the end Rogo's statements proved to be mere conjectures.

Following up Rogo's claim did not bring us far. His main evidence evaporated as an apparent case of faulty memory; and his second piece of evidence seemed only conjectural, namely that since Baba was seen touching his hair before producing objects, they must have been hidden in his hair.

I am not alone in not being able to find evidence of fraud in Sai Baba. His Indian critics, such as Dr Narasimhaiah and the Miracle Committee (see 'The Critics'), have also not come across anything that can be clearly interpreted as evidence of fraud. And they certainly have not lacked the will to seek and find such evidence.

On the other hand, we also have no direct, experimental evidence that the physical phenomena are genuine. Only a carefully conducted investigation with a thorough examination of Sai Baba's body and other necessary controls could produce such evidence. A large amount of indirect evidence might be compelling, but it may never provide the same certainty as a carefully conducted experiment, especially if the experiment were successfully repeated by several qualified experimenters. Sai Baba has unfortunately and regrettably refused so far to allow such an investigation.

It is, however, not only the lack of evidence of fraud that keeps the question open. Some years ago Dr Osis discussed our observations with Doug Henning. Mr Henning said that he could, with advance preparation, duplicate all the phenomena he saw on the film. But when Dr. Osis described the incident in which the enamel stone with Sai Baba's picture disappeared from Dr Osis's ring, Mr Henning commented that this was beyond the skills of magicians. He stated further that if Sai Baba produces objects on demand, then he is performing feats that no magician can duplicate.

After all the interviews and inquiries, what evidence do we have that Baba does actually produce objects on demand? It seems not to be uncommon for Baba to produce objects in response to a specific situation, but one can perhaps argue that the situation was in some way foreseen or staged by him. Such might have been the case when he produced a double rudraksha for me (described in 'Face-to-Face with the Miracle Worker'), though it did not look that way to Dr Osis or myself. When Baba and the interpreter could not explain the meaning of a double rudraksha, he produced one on the spot. To possibly eliminate advance preparation as an explanation, there is for example the case, described in the chapter on the Roerichs. Baba asked the pujari: 'Whom do you worship most?', and when he replied: 'Ganesh' Baba produced a silver ring on which was chiselled a picture of Ganesh. Many similar examples could be cited.

There are also some instances when Baba produced something and distributed apparently all of it to a group of people; however, when someone arriving later, or accidently left out, asked for a share, Baba then produced more immediately. Dr Osis and I observed one such incident in the interview with the vice-president of India, and another is in the interview with the Roerichs; Baba produced a good deal of a hot, oily Indian sweet and gave to everyone present. Mrs Roerich happened to be in the kitchen at that time. When back, she brought it to Baba's attention and asked for the sweet, which he immediately produced, enough not only for her but also for several people to have a second helping.

Even Mr Krishna, who is highly critical of Baba, reports some such incidents. Once when they were travelling, he asked Baba for an apple. Baba walked up to a nearby tamarind tree and picked from it an apple. Mr Krishna also reported that he was fond of the Indian sweet kova, which was not available in Puttaparti, and that sometimes he would ask Baba for this sweet. Baba would always produce it for him. The Raja of Venkatagiri reports being present when Baba told some devotees to ask for any kind of fruit they wanted. They got what they had asked for, not from Baba's hand, but from a nearby tamarind tree. Mrs. Radhakrishna and her daughter Vijaya Hemchand report even more startling incidents, such as when Baba put leaves into their hands and asked them to think of something they wanted (such as chocolate, fruit, or small statues). When they opened their fists, they found what they had wished for on their palms.

It seems therefore that Baba has indeed produced objects on demand. It adds some strength to the evidence that there are two or more witnesses to some of these incidents. One may argue that some of these claims are exaggerations, are based on faulty memory or even are lies. The frequency of such claims reduces the value of such interpretations, though they in principle can never be absolutely ruled out.

There are other aspects of Baba's productions that may be difficult or impossible for a magician to produce, especially in India where sophisticated gadgetry would be impossible to obtain in a remote Indian village. Frequently he is said to have produced hot foods, sometimes steaming hot, even after he has been out of his quarters for an hour or longer. Such incidents, reported by Gopal Krishna, the Raja of Venkatagiri, Amarendra Kumar, Lakshmanan, and Dr Roerich, were described earlier. For example, Amarendra Kumar stated that some of the foods that Baba produced were 'as if fresh from the oven, and sometimes too damned hot – too hot, in fact – as if you had just taken them out of the frying pan.' Many more people have reported to me witnessing such phenomena. Most of these incidents occurred on the banks of the Chitravati River, where Baba was said to have taken some hot food out of the sand. If a trick was involved, a heater must have been placed with the foods in the sand before Sai Baba and his group arrived. That would have been difficult in the 1940s and 1950s, and have involved considerable preparation. Frequently it has been reported to me that he has produced hot food when he was travelling and the party stopped on the wayside for refreshment.

Other examples, even more difficult to explain, include the many reports of Baba producing fruits out of season. In a country where there are refrigerators and efficient transportation systems, and where many fruits are imported, such a feat might not cause a problem. In underdeveloped India, in a remote and poor village that did not in the 1940s and 1950s even have electricity or a motorable road, the case is quite different. Even today one cannot find imported fruits in Indian shops; fruit is grown locally. Several witnesses (Amarendra Kumar, Krishna Kumar, and many others who were informants in a survey to be reported in the following chapter) claim to have received from Baba fruits out of season and, according to them, not available anywhere in India.

Baba also produces liquids, such as oils and medicine, in his hands and gives it to someone or rubs it on the person. A moment later, however, his hands seem dry, even though he has not touched anything to dry his hands or fingers. On one occasion, I personally observed an incident of this kind at close range.

Finally Sai Baba is reported to produce objects never or rarely seen or unknown in nature. Firsthand observations of three such cases have been reported to me; but none of the objects concerned have been preserved, a loss that greatly reduces the value of these reports. One example is typical of the three:

Ms Leelamma a botanist in Guindy outside Madras, who has known Baba since the 1940s, related to me in an interview in November 1977 that Sai Baba once told her to pick an apple from a tamarind tree in Puttaparti. She found the apple on the tree and with Baba's permission cut off the part of the branch on which both the apple and tamarind leaves were attached. She preserved this specimen for some time in formaldehyde in the college at which she teaches. Eventually the apple was somehow detached from the branch. Later people would not believe that the two pieces had been joined and she finally threw the specimen away.

What then is our conclusion about the physical phenomena? For lack of experimental evidence it can only be somewhat tentative, though the testimony is extensive and consistent over four decades. Whether some of the physical productions, in some periods of Baba's life, may have been produced by sleight of hand, we cannot, of course, ascertain. What we can, however, squarely state is that in spite of a longlasting and painstaking effort, we found no direct evidence of fraud.

Notes

[1] Unfortunately I met this jeweller just before leaving Bangalore on my last trip and was therefore unable to meet this lady. Dr Osis and I had met her

and her husband several years earlier and they had reported to us a number of paranormal phenomena that they had associated with Sai Baba.

² Since these investigations cannot be described here in detail, it seems improper and premature to reveal the identity of these individuals more than I have already done.

22
Some Noteworthy Numbers

During my 1983 visit to India I administered a 104-item, multiple-choice questionnaire to a sample of 29 people with extensive observations of Sai Baba. 21 of them had known him over a period of 20 to 40 years, 4 for 10 to 19 years, and only 4 for less than ten years. Furthermore, all but two of them had had over 50 personal meetings with him ('over 50' being the highest response available on the questionnaire). The majority of these people had spent the equivalent of several years in Puttaparti; only 3 spent less than a year there. There were 24 males in the group; 20 were college-educated. The average age turned out to be that of Sai Baba, or 56; the oldest was 73 and the youngest 29, but most of them were in their 50s or 60s. All but three of them spoke Sai Baba's mother tongue, Telugu.

With three exceptions – Mrs Radhakrishna, Raja Reddy (whom I was not able to meet in 1983), and Dr Roerich (who has met Sai Baba only twice) – all the major interviewees in this book were included in the sample, in addition to other followers and ex-devotees. 7 former followers of Baba are included. I made an extra effort to find them, since they would seem less likely to exaggerate claims about Baba's purported powers than would those still following Baba (though they might tend to exhibit bias against him, mostly for religious reasons).

It must be remembered that we are dealing now only with what people report and claim, not with verified facts. With that reservation in mind, let us first consider a question concerning the physical productions ('materializations' or 'physical actualizations' as Dr Chari suggested that I term them). 'How often did you at close range observe Sai Baba produce any of the following objects?' The data from our sample are presented below:

	Never	Once	2-5	6-10	11-50	Over 50 times
Vibuti						29
Rings			3	1	6	19
Lockets			1	2	1	25
Sweets			3		2	24
Fruits	7	4	4	1	3	10

Many respondents replied that they had observed him produce the relevant item (particularly the first four on the list) not only over 50 times but innumerable times. It is of particular interest that 22 people claimed to have received from Baba sweets not available at that time in Puttaparti or the surrounding areas; 19 of these people claimed to have received such a sweet over 50 times. 14 people claimed to have received from Baba fruits out of season; this figure includes 4 of the 7 ex-devotees (57%, as opposed to 45% of the devotees). 10 informants claimed to have received fruits out of season over 50 times.

What about the production of hot foods? 25 people (including 4 ex-devotees) claimed to have observed this, and 3 people claimed to have observed it over 50 times. Mysore Pak and ladu were most commonly produced, but 9 other sweets and dishes were also mentioned, among them dosas (a kind of pancake). Many informants stressed that the food was so hot that it was difficult to hold, but others considered it only warm or lukewarm. In nearly all cases the observers had eaten the food that was produced.

Baba produces a great variety of solid objects, not only jewellery and ornaments of various kinds, sometimes even banknotes (rupees or US dollars, fresh as from the printer's office) and on a few occasions he has given watches to people. One such incident was related to Dr Thalbourne by Capt Harmanprit Singh Sidhu, aide-de-camp to the Governor of Karnataka, and his wife. This occurred shortly before we recorded the case. Present on this occasion was a friend of the Sidhus, Mrs Beri, a Colonel's wife who lives in Delhi, and their 11 or 12 year old son. Sometimes, as in this case, the gift serves some pedagogic purpose or as a future reminder:

Baba materialized and presented to this boy a nice watch for him – a Henry Sandoz brand jewellery watch. Swamiji told him,

'This watch is not just for wearing and for keeping the time. The word 'watch' has these five letters of the alphabet: W – A – T – C – H. These are for: Watch your Words, watch your Actions, watch your Thoughts, C for Character, and H for heart.' He said, 'That's the reason why I've given you this watch.'

Nearly all respondents (27, including 5 ex-devotees) reported having seen Baba produce oily, fluid foods. Again, 11 different varieties were mentioned, amrith and Mysore Pak being most common.

A question of much interest is how often Baba produces objects on demand. 17 people (including 4 from the critical ex-devotees group) reported seeing him produce objects on demand, some of them many times. 8 people had observed him produce food on demand.

Gopal Krishna of Venkatagiri was one of those. He added: 'Most of them (the devotees) did not have the guts to ask him for anything specific, when he asked them what they wanted. But I did, and he usually gave me what I asked for.'

6 people reported that they saw Baba produce whole meals for several people or even many people. The food was usually said to appear in empty vessels. A related phenomenon is the multiplication of food which has been reported in several interviews in earlier chapters.

I will narrate one such occasion that was reported independently by two ex-devotees, Mr Bharat Reddy – an investment banker – and his father, Mr Srinivasa Reddy, both living in Bangalore. They are no longer devotees of Baba as they could not accept his claim of avatarhood. This incident happened in the late 1950s or early 1960s. Bharat Reddy reports:

In those days as now Baba used to come to Bangalore. Whenever he returned to Puttaparti, some people used to accompany him in their cars outside the city where they would park and stop. One day when he left Bangalore it was already dusk. When he stopped outside the city, he suddenly said he was not going to Puttaparti now, not until a couple of days. We were about to turn back, but then he said: 'Why don't you sit down, and we will have some dinner.' But how could we have dinner when we had no food with us? Baba's host had only prepared a small meal in a tiffin carrier, which was only meant for him and one or two other people accompanying him to

Puttaparti. Baba said there was no problem, and we drove the cars into an abandoned airstrip at the roadside and sat on the ground. He asked us to pick some leaves to use as plates for our food.

To my memory we were 30 to 40 people, five to seven full cars. Baba started serving us from that small two-piece tiffin carrier. One part of it contained curry-rice, the other curd-rice. He kept on serving us, also a second and third time. All of us had a full stomach. Some people were keen on testing him; can he produce more? So we ate as we could, and everyone received as much as he wanted.

Srinivasa Reddy's account was more detailed. There was some inconsistency between his testimony and that of his son, but since this incident happened about twenty years ago, some discrepancy might be expected. The core phenomena were, however, the same in both accounts:

Sai Baba was here in Bangalore staying with one Mr Venkataramon, who had recently built a new house. When Swami came to Bangalore, he usually stayed with him and held bhajans, which were attended by around a hundred people, on a vacant lot in front of Venkataramon's house. After four or five days, he (Sai Baba) said he was leaving about 3.00 or 4.00 in the afternoon; but he was delayed till around 5.00. The host, expecting that he would go late, had fixed up a vegetarian meal for him in a medium size carrier, enough for all the three people in his car. He finally left at 5.30. As the custom was, we followed him in 5 or 6 cars up to 12 miles from the city where he would stop his car and say good-bye to everyone. We stopped near the abandoned airdrome of Yalanka that was close to the roadside.

Then he said: 'Let us do some bhajans and then we will part.' The bhajan went on up to 8.00 o'clock. The host then suggested that Swami should go back to Bangalore and go to Puttaparti the next morning. Then some of the old ladies asked him: 'Give us something to eat!' He said: 'Wait, wait' and started to sing another bhajan. After that song he said that they must all be feeling hungry, and they replied: 'Yes, Swami, we are all feeling hungry, let us go back to Bangalore.' He asked if there was a village nearby, and there was one. One man was sent to buy 30 leaves that we might eat on (use as plates). At nine the man came back, and Baba asked us to drive the cars on to the abandoned airstrip. We parked them in a circle, the front of the cars towards the middle of the circle, and put the parking lights on so that we had good light. Within that circle we sat down in circular formation. One man distributed the leaves, and Swami placed himself in the open space in the middle so that we might all see him clearly. With Swami, we were 27 or 28. I counted the people.

Sai Baba asked the host to bring the tiffin carrier[1]. Baba was alone in the circle that we formed and started to walk around from one person to another, serving the food to each of us with his bare hand, as is common in India. From the first container he gave each of us vegetable curry; not very much for each. Next he brought the sambar-rice and served a normal portion to everyone. He came and gave a second helping of the rice. The sambar-rice he gave us was at least ten times more than what could have been kept in the vessel. The normal portion to serve each person is about three-fourths of a full teacup. To those who wanted more he gave the same amount again. Next he served curd-rice (yogurt mixed with rice) of the same amount and served that also a second time. At the end, we all received about a teacup of a liquid sweet called payasam.

All this food he distributed from this tiffin-carrier. It had been meant for three and could not have contained much more. It was 10:30 when the meal was over and we parted company.

During the whole meal, Srinivasa Reddy told me, Baba stood in the circle in front of them and never left it till the meal was over. There was no question of anyone bringing him anything.

Srinivasa Reddy had not only witnessed Baba multiply food, but he also reported observing him change stones into food:

In full daylight at Horseley Hills, Baba gave me a rather flat stone of irregular size and asked me to throw it up in the air. I threw it high up, and he asked me to catch it when it came down. I was afraid the stone might hurt my hands. By the time I caught it, it was an apple.

I gave the apple to Swami, who took a knife and cut it into pieces, and everyone present got a piece of the size into which we normally cut apples. From this one apple he gave pieces to some 25 people. This was a medium-size apple; normally it might have sufficed for 8 to 10 people.

Bharat Reddy, who witnessed this incident, first mentioned to me the first half of this account, that of throwing the stone and catching it as an apple. Since I did not meet him again after the interview with his father, I wrote him a letter asking about this.

He replied that he had also witnessed the second part.

Srinivasa Reddy related another event that occurred during this stay (in the 1950s) at Horseley Hills (a resort in the mountains of South India). The morning after the above incident Baba went for a walk with a few people. Then Baba said: 'Look at that stone.' It was an irregular, hard granite stone about 5 to 6 inches long lying on the ground near them. He threw a towel over it and asked someone to pick up the towel. Under the towel they saw a sugar-candy of a different shape from the stone which had disappeared.

Apparent disappearances of objects are not uncommon with Baba if we can believe what observers report. One such case concerns a man who was particularly close to Baba in his early years. For reasons that will become evident to anyone who reads what follows, I will not reveal his name. It should be kept in mind that marriages in India are generally arranged by parents and the young usually barely know one another when they are married. Matters of caste, status and business connections are determining factors in arranging marriages.

Dr Osis and I learnt the whole story only gradually, so I will relate it in my own words. Baba had given a young man a most beautiful, exquisite ring. He had been married when he was quite young and was not happy in that marriage. He then met a girl and a passionate secret love affair developed. One day Baba described to him the girl, how they made love secretly, 'everything, as exactly as if he himself had been experiencing all this.' Baba warned him never to meet her again. Later, in spite of best intentions, the young man could not resist meeting his beloved. When he woke up at her side the next morning, the ring that Baba had presented to him and he always wore on his finger, had disappeared. In his view there was no doubt: Baba had taken away the ring. The young man never found the ring, Baba never gave it back to him, but the young man never met his beloved again.

Slightly more than half (16) of our respondents reported seeing Baba change an object into something else, such as leaves or pebbles into toffees or lockets, water into sweet liquid, coffee into milk, sand into ladu, a piece of granite into sugar-candy, or a stone into an apple. It was even more commonly reported that he changed objects he himself had first produced, such as by changing their size, or changing one metal into another. 23 people observed this phenomenon.

According to some respondents, Baba has sometimes used his alleged gifts for practical purposes. 5 people claim to have seen him change water into petrol for a car in which he was travelling. (See Amarendra's account of such an event). Krishna Kumar, Vijaya and Leelamma also claim to have been with Baba in a car whose petrol tank was filled with water only. Nagaratna Mudelier's brother, Parthasarathy (who died recently) also made that claim to us in 1975. All these instances occurred in the 1940s or the 1950s.

5 people in our survey (Krishna Kumar, Amarendra Kumar, Vijaya, the Raja of Venkatagiri, and Gopal Krishna) reported observing that Baba on some occasions suddenly changed the colour of his gown.

Some incidents concerned films and photographing, for which Baba seems to have had some aversion in his younger days. Nagaratna Mudelier (a now inactive devotee and a well-to-do Madras shipping contractor about 70 years old) reported that once, when he was photographing Baba and some other people (with Baba's permission), he ran out of film. Baba, who wanted more pictures taken, produced two rolls of film by a wave of his hand. The film was of the type used at that time: 12-exposure rolls used in box cameras. Varadu reported that he once saw Baba produce a roll of film (movie film, he thought) for either Nagaratna or his brother Parthasarathy, who were frequently together with Baba in Puttaparti and Madras. Whether this was the same incident I do not know. A third member of our sample, Krishnaswamy Ravel, also reported that Baba once produced for him by a wave of his hand a fresh roll of Agfafilm when he needed one.

22 of our sample reported having observed Baba producing photographs. In most instances they were of himself, but sometimes they were of Shirdi Baba or even of both of them, such as one of Puttaparti Baba with a small bust of Shirdi Baba on his chest. The sizes varied from that of a stamp to that of a postcard. Some photos were of a deity. I have heard no accounts from firsthand witnesses of Baba producing photographs that seemed to have been taken at the time they were produced. I have heard rumours that Baba has produced such photos, such as of a devotee smoking outside the ashram (a habit Baba opposes), but I have had no success in verifying these rumours.

One witness, Curdt Orefjaerd, a wholesale jeweller from

Stockholm who met Baba in the late 1970s and quickly became one of his favourites, has given me an interesting account for which there is unfortunately no second witness. During a short stay with Baba in Ooty (a summer resort in the mountains), he and Baba were sitting together on a sofa; no one else was in the room. Curdt thought how nice it would be to have a photo of himself and Baba sitting there together, but he did not reveal this thought to Baba. A month later they were flying from Bangalore to Bombay when Baba suddenly handed him an envelope saying: 'And no photographer was there.' As he opened the envelope, Curdt told me, he found in it a photo of himself and Baba sitting on that sofa in Ooty, just as they had been sitting when he wished for the photo. Curdt Orefjaerd is not in our sample.

I may add (though this question was not included in the questionnaire) that both Varadu and Eswar, son of Suseelamma, have reported to me obtaining either blanks or fully overexposed photos when trying to photograph Baba without his permission; Eswar to have taken about 40 or 50 photos of this kind on 10 to 15 rolls for the old box cameras.

2 respondents (Ramesh Kumar and Ms Leelamma) reported independently that they had seen Baba produce a photo of a deceased man for his widow, who had had no photo of him. According to Leelamma, the man had died before Baba was born.

Some of Baba's critics have claimed that he only produces objects that he can hide in his hand. What was the largest object that our subjects had witnessed him produce? Most reported the production of some idol. The sizes given varied from one foot high down to 4 inches. The tallest statue, purportedly produced by Baba, that I have seen, I measured to be 5 inches high. Photographs of Baba holding the Krishna statue he produced on the seashore of Gujarat indicate that it is perhaps 8 to 12 inches high.

How often did the interviewees estimate that Baba produced objects and vibuti on an average day when there were many people around him? Of the objects, 5 thought the figure was so variable that they did not even want to guess. 5 estimated 2 to 5 times a day, 8 thought 6 to 10 times, and 11 thought he would produce objects 11 to 20 times per day on the average. They estimated that vibuti was produced even more frequently: 12 said 11 to 20 times a day, 13 believed he would produce vibuti more than 20 times on the average day. Two-thirds of those of our sample who gave a definite answer estimated that Sai Baba produces vibuti or objects not less than 27 times during an average day.

The respondents were asked: 'What is the largest quantity of anything you have seen Baba produce on one occasion?' Most of them had seen Baba produce a greater quantity of vibuti than anything else. 7 people claimed to have observed him produce 5 to 10 kilograms of it on one occasion; one other person likened the amount to two full bags of cement. These instances took place at the Dasara festival when Baba would have someone hold a vessel upside down on a stage over a 2 to 3 feet high silver statue of Shirdi Baba. He would then place one hand into the vessel and move it in circles, and vibuti would start pouring down on the statue until it was partly or almost fully covered. 5 people said that the vessel was empty, but 2 people (Leelamma and Krishna) said that it had, at least sometimes, been partly filled by pressed, dry vibuti which Baba would loosen with his hand to allow it to fall on the statue or the floor. Leelamma claimed that the amount of vibuti falling out of the vessel was much more than the amount that could have been kept pressed in the vessel.

(Neither Krishna nor Leelamma considered this a case of fraud as it was known by those close to Baba and he made no effort to conceal it).

5 people said that food was the substance of which they had seen Baba produce the greatest amount on one occasion.

Baba's productions come not only from his hands. 27 respondents had seen him produce objects (lingams) out of his mouth, and 22 people had seen material appearing on his forehead. 5 people had seen something (usually vibuti, but sometimes amrith) appearing on or falling from his feet. One person reported that once when Baba placed his feet on a cloth and removed them, a yellow footprint was left on the cloth.

Inevitably, a matter of considerable discussion among those around Baba, as well as among those who have never met him, is how he produces the things that he brings forward. Does he produce them out of nothing, does he apport them from somewhere, does he sometimes create them out of nothing and sometimes apport them, or is he only exercising masterful sleight of hand?

2 people in our sample believe Baba used sleight of hand:

one of these was a former student of Baba's, and the other was a man who was for some time on the faculty of one of Baba's colleges. Both were young men who have had some but rather limited association with Baba and only in relatively recent years. The rest (27) believed that his productions were of a supernatural kind. Which kind? Four said they did not know. 22 respondents thought he created objects out of nothing; 7 of these thought that he also might sometimes apport things. One person believed that all his productions were apported (in other words, that they all existed somewhere and that through some paranormal power Baba was able to make them disappear at that place and suddenly appear in his hand or wherever he willed them to appear).

I asked some respondents if they had asked Baba how he explains his productions. His usual answer was a simple one: 'It comes from Sai Stores.' To one he said: 'Sometimes it is created, sometimes it is brought (apported from somewhere).' Some stories which might indicate that Baba apports things have come to my ears, but I have found none that could be verified by a second witness.

There is a saying among many of those around Baba that he is 'omnipotent, omniscient, omnipresent.' These truly extraordinary powers, I have been told in India, are considered divine attributes, just as they are in Christianity. We asked our respondents: 'Do you consider Sai Baba omnipotent?' To that question, 19 (65%) answered yes, 6 answered no, and 4 were not sure, did not know or were not willing to answer. Belief that he is omniscient and omnipresent was of a similar magnitude: 20 expressed such belief, 6 rejected it, and 3 were undecided.

We will close this chapter by discussing how respondents replied to the question: 'Do you consider Baba (a) an ordinary man; (b) a man with rare psychic gifts (siddhis); (c) a saint; or (d) an avatar?' Among the 7 ex-devotees, 2 (the youngest in our group) thought Baba was an ordinary man with no paranormal abilities, 3 viewed him as possessing rare psychic gifts, one viewed him as an avatar, and one ex-devotee was only satisfied by describing him as superhuman.

Of the respondents as a whole, 2 people viewed Baba as an ordinary man, 3 viewed him as a psychic but the great majority of the respondents (19) felt that Baba was an avatar, although 5 were not happy with any of the answers offered to them in the questionnaire and thought that he should be described as superhuman. No one found the classification of a saint sufficient or perhaps appropriate.

In later chapters we will deal with the results of some further items on our questionnaire.

Note

[1] Tiffin carriers are widely used in India and come in various sizes. They consist usually of 3 or 4 small pot-like containers, each of them containing about half a litre to a litre. They are held together by 2 iron rods that penetrate the ears that are found on each side of each of the containers; the iron rods end in a handle on the top to make the containers easy to carry. They can contain a meal for 2 to 4 people.

23
A Few Parallels

If we assume tentatively that Baba's materialization phenomena are paranormal, it would certainly be of interest to know if reliable reports of such phenomena can be found elsewhere in the history of psychical research. There are reports of sudden appearances of objects (apports) in connection with mediums, but the evidence for them is generally considered weak. On the other hand, short-lived materializations by mediums of parts of human figures were frequently reported during the heyday of Spiritualism.

Assuming for a moment that Sai Baba's physical phenomena are paranormal in nature, they resemble only slightly the phenomena attributed to the physical mediums of the 19th and early 20th centuries. The best known of the physical mediums, the Scottish-American medium D.D. Home, was investigated by numerous committees and scientists of his time but was never detected in fraud (Jenkins 1982). His seances often took place in full daylight and were characterized by raps, by movements of tables and other objects without any visible causes, and sometimes by levitations of Home himself. The Icelandic medium Indridi Indridason displayed similar phenomena (Hannesson 1924; Nielsson 1925). Materializations were often reported at the seances of these mediums, but they were usually of human forms, such as detached hands that were seen to move or manipulate objects.

There are other striking differences between these spiritualistic physical mediums and Sai Baba. In the case of the mediums, the materials generally vanished after a few seconds or minutes (if not, they were termed apports), whereas Baba's productions have remained as solid objects except on a few occasions when he has apparently caused them to disappear. Secondly, the mediums are reported to have produced living forms that would move and act for a short time whereas Baba produces objects of inorganic or plant matter. In the case of the spiritualistic mediums, it is sometimes reported that on occasion material called ectoplasm oozed out of their mouths, and created the short-lived forms that appeared at the seances. Perhaps the same or a related mechanism is behind both these phenomena and Baba's regurgitations of vibuti and other materials. Thirdly, Sai Baba's 'performances' almost invariably take place in full daylight or under normal lighting conditions; mediums, with the exception of D.D. Home, demanded darkness or subdued light.

Finally, the spiritualistic phenomena were interpreted by the mediums as coming from deceased human beings, and the mediums' purpose was to demonstrate the survival of the soul after death. Sai Baba's primary purpose seems to be to demonstrate the truth of religion and of Hinduism in particular, though he always stresses the universality of religion. The ostensibly psychic phenomena that he produces probably resemble more closely those of individuals who have displayed psychic gifts within the domain of an orthodox religion, although it is not easy to place Sai Baba in any category of individuals who are believed to have exhibited outstanding paranormal abilities.

From the 19th century there are several accounts of objects appearing at mediumistic seances (Fodor 1966, pp. 10-16). Among them are interesting observations by the celebrated British biologist Alfred Russell Wallace (1896, pp. 170-171) of sudden appearances of fresh flowers and fruits in the presence of the medium Mrs Guppy, even, it is reported, on demand, and while the medium was being closely observed and her hands were being held by the investigators (ibid. pp. 170-71). Reports of apports concerning mediums such as Charles Bailey (McCarthy 1904), Carlo Centurione Scotto (Hack 1929) and Eusapia Palladino (Lombroso 1909) can also be found.

Mr T. Lynn was an apport-producing medium who was investigated in England in the 1920s (McKenzie 1929). His seances were held in semidarkness. McKenzie and Major Mowbray, who conducted the experiments, imposed rather rigorous controls: the medium was fully stripped before and after the seance, dressed in fresh clothes, and placed in a bag made of black material that was sealed tightly at the neck. Sometimes the medium's hands were also firmly bound to his knees, and still some simple small objects appeared on a plate in front of him and were photographed by the light of a flash camera. No fraud was discovered during these experiments, but one wishes that modern techniques of continuous infrared photorecording in the dark had existed at that time.

When these experiments took place, Lynn had apparently been a physical medium for only about three years. Lynn was approached by Nandor Fodor in 1936 for another investigation but then he had become seriously sick and unable to perform as a medium. (From correspondence in the files of the Society for Psychial Research, London).

In Brazil Thomas Green Morton Souza Coutinho, a pharmacist in his thirties, has recently aroused national attention by various apparently paranormal abilities. Thomas, as he is generally called, has also been reported to produce out of nowhere objects, such as small metal statues (Pulos 1982), and so a veteran researcher and parapsychologist, William Roll of the Psychical Research Foundation in Chapel Hill, North Carolina, visited Thomas two years ago. Roll found a clear indication of fraud in his performances of extrasensory perception but observed no instances of alleged apports.

Fraudulent performances by a psychic do not necessarily exclude the possibility that genuine paranormal effects may have also occurred, as the great Italian medium Eusapia Palladino seemed to show (Carrington 1909). But fraud certainly does not boost a medium's credibility. Whatever genuine paranormal effects there may be in Thomas' phenomena remains for further research to reveal.

One recent report that may be relevant for our inquiry was published in a scientific journal, *Zitran Zazhi* (Nature Journal), of the People's Republic of China (Shuhuang et al. 1983). In this article 'several different types of experiments are described in which youthful subjects succeeded in moving a material object from one location to another without apparent use of direct physical means' (Haft 1982, p. 399). The thirteen authors of this article are associated with several scientific and educational institutions in China, among them the National Defence Science Commission.

In some of the experiments a miniature radio transmitter was placed in the pocket or on the person of the subject (a girl), and the radio signals were continually monitored. In the presence of observers the girl caused the object to be removed to a different location.

In other experiments a light-sensitive film placed in a light-proof bag was 'apported' across the room into a second light-proof bag; subsequent developing showed that the film had not been affected by light. Objects such as a metal nut placed inside a sealed film cassette case or a small piece of aluminium inside a sealed cloth bag were successfully apported (or 'transferred', as it is translated in the English version of this article).

According to the article, there were several observers whose sole function was to keep close watch on the one or two girls, apparently teenagers, who were the subjects in these extraordinary experiments.

What did these daring Chinese scientists conclude? 'Some "exceptional function" people', as the Chinese call them, 'can cause substances to enter into an extraordinary state, called the "exceptional state". These substances, when they are in the "exceptional state" cannot be detected by ordinary people or common detectors', and they 'can transcend physical obstacles in space' (Shuhuang et al. 1983, pp. 18-19). The scientists also 'think that it is still quite difficult to explain this process with present scientific theories' (ibid. p. 19). Lastly they, in a good scientific manner, 'want to emphasize that our results are preliminary. The reproducibility and accuracy of the experiments have not been perfect and the experimental procedures also need to be improved' (ibid. p. 19).

This highly interesting Chinese report is certainly open to many questions, but it is impressive that 13 authors, presumably all scientists, have written and published a report of this kind in a scientific journal with a wide distribution in China. One would expect them to have checked their experimental procedures well and to have good faith in the validity of their results before publishing a paper of that kind.

On the whole, it seems, the century-old effort of psychical research has been unable to bring forward solid, acceptable evidence that material objects can appear 'out of nowhere' and remain existing. Claims of apports and materializations have frequently been found ridden with fraud. There may, however, be isolated instances, such as those I have reported above, that may tentatively be considered genuine. Hasted (1981) mentions such instances, but again the evidence seems poor.

Do we find there are any references to physical phenomena

of the kind that is characteristic of Sai Baba? Probably no major religious scripture describes more miracles than the New Testament. How many miracles are reported there is debatable, since the definition of a miracle may vary. In his classic book on Jesus' miracles, Trench (1949) lists 33, about half of them reported in more than one canonical gospel. The apocryphal gospels of Jesus' infancy and youth, which are not contained in the New Testament, relate an even greater number of miracles: 'To say that the miracles occupy in them the foremost place would very inadequately express the facts of the case. They are everything.' (ibid. p. 27)

Even historical studies of Biblical writings have failed to reach consensus on the miraculous phenomena and have left us with many uncertainties. Still, it is tempting to indulge in some speculation by comparing miracles attributed to historical Jesus and the miracle-maker of modern times, Sai Baba, without, for the moment, worrying about their authenticity. As Dr Chari once wisely stated: 'With our abysmal ignorance of these phenomena, speculative and imaginative flights are harmless, provided we always come back to terra firma.' (1982, p. 258)

Two-thirds of the 33 miracles attributed to Jesus in the New Testament concern healing. Healing certainly figures in Sai Baba's reputation, but my impression is that it does not play such a prominent part in his activities as in those of Jesus.

One miracle attributed to Jesus, the stilling of the tempest (Matt. 8:23-27, Mark 4:35-41, Luke 8:22-25), shows exceptional control of the environment; his walking on the sea could perhaps also be included in this category (Matt. 14:22-33, Mark 6:45-52, John 6:14-21) although it is open to other interpretations, such as that Jesus controlled his body weight. Twice (Luke 5:1-11, John 21:1-23) he is credited with a miraculous haul (or draft) of fishes. None of these feats are reported for Sai Baba, although some accounts resemble them, such as controlling the rain, the levitation reported by Varadu, and perhaps his sudden disappearance at one place and reappearance almost instantaneously at another. The haul of fishes might also be comparable to Baba's multiplications of food.

Then we have the odd and, to some, somewhat embarrassing miracle of Jesus cursing the barren fig-tree. One morning he passed a fig-tree, and, being hungry but finding no fruit on it, he 'said unto it, Let no fruit grow on thee henceforward for ever. And presently the fig-tree withered away' (Matt. 21:18-22. See also Mark 11:12-14, 20-24). Reports in the apocryphal gospels of several miracles in Jesus' early years also show him to be primarily a miracle-maker, sometimes capricious and showing human weaknesses.

Finally we come to those miracles performed by Jesus that are also commonly reported about Sai Baba. The first miracle mentioned in the New Testament is the changing of water into wine at the marriage in Cana (John 2:1-11). Earlier in this book is reported the testimony of several witnesses who said that Baba had changed water into another drink or even water into petrol.

Twice it is written that Jesus multiplied food and fed large groups of people with only a few fishes or a few loaves of bread (the miraculous feeding of the five thousand (Matt. 14:15-21, Mark 6:34-44, Luke 9:12-17, John 6:5-14) and the miraculous feeding of the four thousand (Matt. 15:32-39, Mark 8:1-9)). There are several similar accounts about Sai Baba. He is said to have on several occasions paranormally produced a full meal for large groups of people, as we have already reported. We also have instances when he is said to have produced one kind of food, such as some sweet or amrith, which he then distributes to several or many people. Accounts of this phenomenon are reported by several eyewitnesses in earlier chapters. Other witnesses whose interviews are not reported at length in this book have also reported such observations.

At the time of the Dasara festival Sai Baba used to distribute amrith to all present. Several witnesses claim that on some occasions either there was no amrith in the small vessel used for the distribution or the amrith continually grew as Baba gave a spoonful away to each of hundreds of waiting people.

The instances on which Sai Baba has produced a mouthful of sweets or other eatables – both hot and cold, solid and fluid, homemade and even factory-produced – for one or more people at a time, are innumerable. Such incidents are reported by practically all who have spent even a few days with him or have had some personal encounters with him. I have observed such production of food several times and have enjoyed a few mouthfuls. Although the accounts about Jesus and Sai Baba concerning the production or multiplication of food are similar, they are much more commonly reported for Baba than for Jesus.

In the history of Christianity, ancient as well as relatively recent, there are several reports of alleged multiplications of food by people other than Jesus. Thurston (1952) reviews several reports of such phenomena among Catholic saints and clergy, and the pope Saint Gregory the Great (540-604) describes in his 'Dialogues' (1959) several instances of multiplication of food.

I will not attempt to evaluate the evidential value of these reports, some of which were collected and scrutinized in processes of canonization; but they are interesting parallels to the claims made about Sai Baba. I have not searched for reports of these phenomena in other major religions. An Indian scholar of Sanskrit literature has told me that there are several miraculous accounts in scriptures on the life of Lord Krishna. According to him, however, they are generally of quite a different nature since they tend to be of a type more fantastic than the reports on Sai Baba or Jesus. For example, there is a report that once when Krishna was in his chariot, an enemy threw a missile at him; the ground under the chariot is then said to have sunk enough for the chariot to escape the well-aimed missile.

24
Manifestations Of Religious Myths And Symbols

According to long-time observers of Sai Baba, objects or materials inexplicably appear not only in his hands; they also – vibuti, the sacramental ash in particular – emanate in some mysterious manner from his forehead, mouth and feet. Frequently such phenomena have been observed by multiple observers. Furthermore, there is some evidence that objects appear at some distance from him (for example, when he has told someone to pick an apple from a nearby tamarind tree and that person allegedly finds an apple on a branch of that tree).

There are numerous reports that vibuti has appeared in distant places, such as on photographs in private homes. Some people associated the vibuti's appearance with Sai Baba, though he himself in some instances, but not all, has denied producing it. I have visited about 20 such places in various parts of India, as well as one in London and one in New York, and been told of many, many more, but I have not had the opportunity to investigate the vibuti's actual appearance nor witnessed it myself. The appearance of vibuti seemed to reach epidemic proportions in the 1970s when such phenomena could be seen in several houses in practically every town and city in India that I visited at that time, and they were several.

In the survey I asked if vibuti (or amrith) had appeared in the respondents' homes; 12 of them, or 41%, related that vibuti had mysteriously appeared in their homes, some of them reporting that amrith had also appeared. How many had seen this phenomenon in other places? Seventy-nine percent of the sample (23 people) had seen it somewhere outside their own home. It is unfortunate that this phenomenon has not been properly investigated. Since it can be easily faked, the reports of it must be considered inconclusive until vibuti has appeared on objects under the direct control and observation of investigators.

In most cases the vibuti appears on photos that are hung on walls or that stand on tables. In one case Dr Osis and I observed vibuti between a photo of Sai Baba and the glass covering it. Vibuti was reported to have oozed out of the photograph on and off for several months. It was hung on the wall high above a door into the waiting-room of Dr P.B. Menon in Calicut in Kerala.

In Bangalore Dr Osis and I visited the home of Mr Kupanna, a retired civil servant who has since died. In his room (where bhajans were conducted every Thursday night), we saw many photos of Sai Baba, large and small, hanging on the walls and large amounts of vibuti on the photos and on the floor below. Every few weeks Mr Kupanna wiped off all the vibuti, but it would gradually appear again we were told. Dr Bhattacharya, whom we have mentioned earlier, was a friend of Mr Kupanna's and was impressed by the phenomena as well as by Mr Kupanna himself, who seems to have been highly regarded by all around him.

On one occasion Dr Bhattacharya had a visit from a colleague, Prof Kundu, director of the Saha Institute of Nuclear Physics in Calcutta, who was attending a scientific conference in Bangalore. One evening Dr Bhattacharya took Dr Kundu over to Mr Kupanna's room which was in a house nearby. Dr Bhattacharya had heard that vibuti would sometimes appear on photos brought by guests to the room, while they were present. The two scientists brought a photo and placed it flat on the floor in front of them. A puja took place, and they participated. When it was over, they saw that a small speck, apparently of vibuti, had appeared on the photo, which had been right in front of them the whole time. The speck was small, however, and they could not rule out the possibility that it had fallen from the air, though that did not seem likely.

I, along with Dr Joop Houtkooper, interviewed Dr Kundu about this incident in Calcutta in January 1980. He then told us of a related phenomenon that had occurred in 1975 or 1976, one that he was at a loss to explain. In the small diary that he kept in his wallet he had a few photos of Indian saints and philosophers, such as Ramakrishna, for whom he had regard and respect. Once he placed among these a photo of Sai Baba though he had never had a personal encounter with him. When he later took the picture of Sai Baba out he found a powdery substance on it, greyish-white dust that had also been smeared on the back of the photo next to it. It looked more like vibuti than ordinary dust. Why did it appear only on that particular photo and not elsewhere in his diary? This phenomena lasted for some time and remained a puzzle to Dr Kundu.

Let us look at some of Baba's physical phenomena again in more detail. Among those I have interviewed, everyone who attended the Dasara festivals in Puttaparti in the 1940s and 1950s described seeing vibuti, kumkum, and sandalpaste appear on Sai Baba's forehead during processions, even though he had had nothing on his forehead at the beginning of the processions. The processions usually took place at night, and the palanquin on which Baba sat was lit by strong lamps. 22 of the 29 respondents in our survey had observed vibuti and/or other material appear on Baba's forehead primarily during processions and festivals but also on a few other occasions, such as during bhajans and in trances. The Raja of Venkatagiri, his brother Gopal Krishna, the Hemchands, Amarendra Kumar, Krishna Kumar, Krishnamurti, the singers Lakshmanan and Raman, Varadu, Krishna and many others not mentioned in this book gave me basically the same account regarding this phenomenon. Much of this testimony has appeared elsewhere in this book. Let us read a part of what Mr Hemchand, who was not in our sample, reported about this phenomenon:

> We will see appear on his forehead the three wide stripes of vibuti that are characteristic of Shiva. First, there was nothing, and then suddenly we see these three bright stripes of vibuti. And after a few minutes it will disappear, and then we will see on his forehead the sandalwood paste (chandan) and a round spot of kumkum that is characteristic of Parvati.

Orthodox Hindus in India may be seen carrying three greyish-white stripes of vibuti across their foreheads; this shows that they are worshippers of Shiva. A different form made of kumkum and sandalwood paste, indicates that the person is a worshipper of Vishnu. These are the most visible signs of religion that a man can display on his body in Hinduism. The three stripes of vibuti that Baba displayed were of the kind shown on traditional pictures of Shiva, the figure in Hinduism with whom Baba perhaps identifies most. Frequently, however, witnesses report vibuti appearing on Baba's forehead as taking no particular form, but simply covering the forehead.

The religious imagery, symbols, myths, and writings that Sai Baba seems most familiar with are those of Hinduism. They provide him with the form for his religious expression. This imagery seems to have taken a physical, almost somatic form in these religious festivals if one may assume for a moment that these appearances on his forehead are genuine.

In the Christian tradition people are known to have taken on themselves the wound marks of Christ, in the form of stigmata (Thurston, 1952). There are many reports of religious stigmata, among both Christian saints and laymen. Francis of Assisi was the first Christian saint reported to have displayed such wounds, and other cases have been observed and reported sporadically up to the present time. The best-known stigmatizations in the modern era are those of Therese Neumann of Austria and the Italian saint Padre Pio (who, by the way, was also said to have possessed some remarkable paranormal abilities that in some ways resemble those of Sai Baba, though a proper assessment of his phenomena is still pending.) (Ruffin 1982)

The psychosomatic or psychophysical effects that can be observed in stigmatizations seem to be caused by the subject's identification with the image of Christ. In Sai Baba we may be observing a similar process at work but within a different religion and in a different form. In the Christian stigmatics the deep religious involvement causes visible changes in bodily tissues, whereas in Sai Baba's case foreign matter apparently forms the appropriate religious symbols on his body. Although the forms differ, in both the Christian stigmatics and Sai Baba the religious symbols have appeared at an appropriate location on the body.

There is another, perhaps related phenomenon. In our sample 27 respondents reported seeing Baba regurgitate objects from his mouth. For thirty years, at the height of the Shivaratri festival, and in front of a large crowd, there used to come out of Baba's mouth, usually with evident pain, an almost egg-sized, oblong, glass-like object (presumably made of a precious stone) that Hindus call lingam. Sometimes two or three lingams appeared on the same occasion. This production of the lingam from the mouth is an enactment of a well-known myth in Hinduism that concerns Shiva.[1]

On one occasion, several witnesses saw vibuti gush out of Baba's mouth along with small pieces of golden leaves on which were engraved one of the Indian names for God (for a fuller account see 'The Raja of Venkatagiri'). A few other people have reported seeing vibuti gush out of his mouth on other occasions while he was in a trance. Varadu reported, that once when Baba fell into trance, a large amount of vibuti fell from the sole of his right foot. A similar incident has been mentioned by the Raja of Venkatagiri. In these instances I, with my limited knowledge of Hinduism, am not aware of a religious interpretation for this phenomenon.

One phenomenon reported by several witnesses is the sudden manifestation of a beautiful fragrance that will be smelled by those near Baba. Krishna Kumar described it in this way:

> Suddenly it comes and stays for a few minutes and then disappears. It was mostly of sandalwood and musk. It was a common affair at the beginning of the bhajan. I used to help him with his bath. Sometimes after his bath in the morning he would smell of perfumes for a few minutes. At least at that time he never used any powders or perfumes but still he sometimes smelled of these beautiful perfumes.

I made no systematic inquiry about the fragrance phenomenon, but several people have described it to me. For example, Nagaratna Mudelier said that on three or four occasions, when he was sitting close to Baba, there suddenly came an odour of sandalwood, rose or jasmine. The singers Raman and Lakshmanan reported similar experiences, but added that they have also perceived this fine smell that they associate with Baba at bhajans when he is not present: 'The congregation will sense this smell. It will last for a few seconds, come suddenly and disappear suddenly. It is often a mild jasmine smell, but it may be of different kinds.' Gopal Krishna was another of those who had sensed this smell:

Suddenly there sometimes came from Swami a very beautiful aroma. Sometimes it faded away quickly, sometimes it lasted longer. We asked him: 'What is this, Swami?' He said: 'This is a divine perfume.'

We also sometimes felt this perfume when he was not present. We felt that it indicated his spiritual presence with us. I have never smelled such a beautiful perfume.

An engineer and industrialist in Madras, Mr V. Srinivasan (who was drawn closely into Baba's fold relatively recently), told me in 1983, that when he was on a business trip to Finland recently and was living in a guest house belonging to a Finnish firm, he suddenly smelled a perfume typical of the incense that Baba uses at some of his functions.

'The odour of sanctity' or the divine fragrance, is a phenomenon reported in the lives of many Catholic saints and mystics, and there seems to be much evidence to support it (Thurston, 1952). We will give only one example, which concerns St Maria Francesca delle Cinque Piaghe, a Franciscan nun who died in Naples in 1791. It is taken from her biography, which, according to Thurston, was based on a careful study of the material gathered in the course of her process of canonization. Thurston (ibid. p. 230) quotes the following passage:

There is hardly one of the numerous witnesses whose evidence is reported in the Summarium who does not speak in explicit terms of this perfume, and in order that there might be no doubt that the favour came to her from her Mother Mary and from her divine Spouse, it was regularly observed that this phenomenon manifested itself with special intensity on the great festivals of our Lady and on the Fridays in March on which she participated mysteriously in the sufferings of Christ's Passion.

Similar observations of the 'odour of sanctity' were frequently made in the presence of the famous Capuchin priest Padre Pio, who died in 1968.

A few instances of the sudden manifestation of fragrance are also found in accounts concerning 19th-century Spiritualism (Fodor, 1966). This was especially notable in the case of the mediumistic work of Stainton Moses who was a highly respected clergymen and university lecturer who, to quote

Thurston, '… is spoken of with the sincerest respect by all who knew him intimately' (ibid. 1952, p. 42).

Note

[1] Again, a phenomenon associated with Sai Baba has several parallels in Western sources, particularly religious ones. Dr C.T.K. Chari gives a short description of this phenomenon in his paper on 'Regurgitation, Mediumship and Yoga' (1973). A swami in Sri Lanka, Swami Premananda, has also performed this feat during the Shivaratri festival; but no investigation has been conducted of this phenomenon.

25
Raising The Dead?

Healing is not an outstanding feature in the psychic scenery around Sai Baba, but the number of claims is nevertheless considerable. In our survey 22 (76%) of the respondents, claimed to have personally known someone whom Sai Baba miraculously cured. 11 of these people reported themselves cured; 13 were referring to a healing of another person. In previous chapters we have presented some examples of reports of alleged miraculous cures.

Generally we speak of a miraculous cure when the healing in some striking way exceeds in speed and extent the normal processes of healing and seems inexplicable according to contemporary medical science. However, it is difficult for both laymen and physicians to determine with reasonable certainty what should be considered a miraculous healing and what should not. On rare occasions, so-called incurable diseases may have a spontaneous remission. Frequently it is difficult even for a specialist to predict the exact prognosis of a disease. Some patients may not know the correct diagnosis, or their disease may have been falsely diagnosed. Such factors may lead a patient to believe that he has experienced a miraculous cure, when in fact he has not (West 1957, Nolen 1974).

Since I am not medically trained and was aware of the many pitfalls in the investigation of miraculous healing, I made no attempt to examine the claims concerning Baba. Some of these claims, however, might warrant such an examination by a competent physician, such as a case reported to me by Dr Chari of the cure of a 'blue baby' (patent ductus arteriosus) who was given medicine produced by Baba (Chari 1978).

At darshan time in Puttaparti there is usually a line of people in wheelchairs. Baba sometimes stops to speak to one or more of these patients, but never have I observed among them any sign of a sudden healing.

Myths grow and spread fast around Indian swamis and holy men. Some of them may welcome such myths, or leave them uncorrected, since they may add to their fame and prestige. Often, however, the devotees may be more responsible for the creation and spread of rumours that come to be uncritically accepted as facts.

Resurrection of a dead person, if true, would certainly be an extreme case of healing. Two such claims have been made concerning Sai Baba. I tried to examine the evidence.

The first case concerns Mr Walter Cowan, a wealthy Californian and a devotee of Baba. This incident has been widely publicized in articles and books on Sai Baba (Cowan 1982, Sandweiss 1975, Fanibunda 1980), many of which allege that Baba raised Walter Cowan back to life, as Jesus is said to have raised Lazarus (John 11:1:54).

Walter Cowan's wife, Elsie, asked Dr Jack Hislop, an influential American fellow-devotee and a former professor of business administration and corporate executive, to write up an account of her husband's experience since he 'was there throughout almost the entire experience' (Cowan 1982, p. 236). Dr Hislop's account was written a few months after the incident occurred (Cowan, 1982). It has a brief introduction by Mrs Cowan and was published under her name. At the end of this article Walter Cowan gives a 'short account of his resurrection' (ibid. p. 244-45). I will first quote some paragraphs from Dr Hislop's account (pp. 237-39):

> On the morning of the 25th of December, 1971, news quickly spread that an elderly American had had a fatal attack of what was thought to be heart trouble, and had passed away. Upon hearing the rumor, my wife and I at once went to your (Mrs Cowan's) hotel. You, Elsie Cowan, confirmed the news, and told us how the attack had felled Walter in the hotel room. You had prayed to Sathya Baba for help ....
>
> Someone called an ambulance to take Walter to the hospital, but it was your experience that Walter had died in your arms, soon after having been lifted from the floor to the bed, and you were so exhausted that you could not accompany the then lifeless body into the ambulance. These events had taken place in the early morning hours of 25 December. But at 7.00 a.m. you had recovered sufficient strength to go with Mrs Ratan Lal to Baba's place of residence to tell him the news and ask for his advice and help. Baba said he would visit the hospital about 10.00 a.m.

At 10.00 a.m., Mrs Ratan Lal accompanied you to the hospital, but you were told that Baba had already been there, and had left just before you arrived. Upon entering the hospital, you found Walter alive. That Walter was alive at 10.00 a.m. on 25 December is certain. But how about his death? ....

To clarify this point, at my request, Judge Damodar Rao of Madras interviewed the doctor who had attended Walter when he arrived at the hospital .... The doctor told Judge Rao that Walter was indeed dead when he had examined Walter shortly after the ambulance had delivered him to the hospital .... But, medical testimony is not a factor of any importance to devotees of Baba. To his devotees, what He said about Mr Cowan was the truth of the matter.

I saw Baba at His place of residence after He had returned from the hospital. He told me and others within hearing that Walter Cowan had died, that the hospital had stuffed his ears and nose with cotton, and covered him with a sheet, and put the body in a closed room. Baba said that He had brought Walter back to life.

I have interviewed several witnesses to this incident, among them three doctors who attended Walter Cowan.

Dr O.G.C. Vaz, a general practitioner in Madras and house doctor for Connemara Hotel, which is one of the finest hotels in Madras, remembered Mr Cowan well; he had treated him for about two weeks six or seven years before my first interview with him in 1977. Dr Vaz said that he had been called to Connemara Hotel one night around midnight. Mr Cowan was very sick and had to be moved to a hospital (Lady Willingdon's Nursing Home, a private hospital in Madras). Dr Vaz no longer remembered clearly the nature of his sickness, but thought it had been a heart disease. He had brought in a consultant, Dr Rajagopalam, a cardiologist. Walter Cowan had been seriously ill, Dr Vaz reported, but it was not true that he had died. He was hospitalized for two weeks with high fever and other symptoms, but all the life signs were always present. He had stayed in the hospital until he recovered. He had been a little dazed at times but never lost consciousness while under treatment.

Dr Rajagopalam is a respected heart specialist in Madras. Yes, he had indeed been brought in as a consultant. He told me essentially the same story as Dr Vaz; as far as he knew, Walter Cowan had never 'died' during this particular illness.

According to the records of Lady Willingdon's Nursing

Home, Mr Cowan was admitted on December 25, 1971, and discharged on the 15th of January, 1972. The head nurse on duty when I visited the hospital told me that she remembered Mr Cowan quite well; he was a particularly pleasant and friendly patient. She also denied any knowledge of his having died or having been almost dead.

Dr Krishna Rao, the superintendent of Lady Willingdon's Nursing Home, checked the medical records for me; Walter Cowan had been alive when admitted into the hospital. Cowan would not have been admitted if he had been dead. The hospital has no mortuary, as Dr Vaz had told me earlier. Dr Krishna Rao also affirmed with the two other physicians that Cowan had not died while in the hospital.

None of the above informants revealed any antagonism toward Sai Baba; Dr Rajagopalam even showed definite interest in him. Dr Vaz, on the other hand, seemed somewhat irritated by the rumours of Mr Cowan's revival from death, as even television crews had wanted to interview him about this story. It may be added that Dr Rajagopalam became quite friendly with Walter Cowan and later visited the Cowans at their home in California.

Walter Cowan died two years after this incident, and I was not able to meet him. He did, however, very soon after the incident tape-record a statement about his encounter with death. Mr Richard Bock, a Sai devotee in Los Angeles, was kind enough to send me a copy of the tape. The Hislop-Cowan article ends with a statement by Walter Cowan which is essentially the same as the tape-recorded statement. I quote a part of it (ibid. pp. 244-45):

> While in Connemara Hotel in Madras, two days after I arrived, I was taken very sick with pneumonia and was in bed. As I gasped for breath, suddenly the body's struggle was over, and I died. I found myself very calm, in a state of wonderful bliss, and the Lord, Sai Baba, was by my side. Even though my body lay on the bed, dead, my mind kept working throughout until Baba brought me back. There was no anxiety or fear, but a tremendous sense of well-being, for I had lost all fear of death.

Walter continues by describing how Baba took him to a large hall where the records of his past lives were kept. There the 'Court of Justice' read the records, and Baba said that he (Walter) had not completed the work that he was born to do.

Baba asked the Judge to turn Walter over to him (Baba) and to return Walter's soul to his body. 'The Judge said, "So be it." The case was dismissed and I (Walter) left with Baba to return to my body' (ibid. pp. 244-45).

We have no firsthand report from Walter Cowan saying when he regained consciousness, whether in the hotel, in the car on the way to the hospital, or after arrival in the hospital. In the taped statement he describes only the subjective experience he had while unaware of his physical surroundings and that he 'talked it over with Baba, and He said it was not my imagination – it was a true experience' (ibid. p. 245).

In November 1980 I met his widow, Elsie Cowan, in India. She and Walter had been in their late seventies when the incident occurred at Christmas 1971. At about 11.00 in the evening, after they had gone to bed, she had heard her husband walking towards the bathroom, when he suddenly collapsed on the floor. She called the servants, and they brought him back to bed where he recovered. As he got up for the second time about an hour later, he collapsed and lost consciousness again. A doctor was called. When he (Dr Vaz) arrived about 20 minutes later, he examined Mr Cowan and pronounced him dead, Mrs Cowan told me. It is on this last point that Mrs Cowan and Dr Vaz radically disagree.

All four members of the medical staff report that Walter Cowan had been alive when he was admitted to the hospital and had not died while under their treatment. Dr Vaz and Dr Krishna Rao both told me that Sai Baba had visited Walter Cowan in the hospital in the late morning following Cowan's admission. Cowan had then been awake, according to Dr Vaz, who was in the hospital at that time. Sai Baba had talked to Cowan and had given him vibuti. 'This might have boosted his morale, but he would have recovered without Sai Baba's coming' Dr Vaz told me.

Earlier the same morning, prior to Sai Baba's visit to the hospital, Elsie Cowan told me, she went to see Sai Baba at his residence in Madras. When she and Mrs Ratan Lal, who accompanied her, entered the room, Baba said: 'Walter is alive.'

Mrs Ratan Lal, a Sai Baba devotee and a friend of the Cowans, was also staying at Connemara Hotel. I met Mrs Ratan Lal in India several years ago, but I have not been able to meet her since I began investigating this case; nor have I asked Sai Baba about it.

The incident occurred at a time when a conference of Sai Baba devotees (the Eighth All India Conference of the Sri Sathya Sai Seva Social Service Organizations) was being held in Madras. Sai Baba was staying in the home of the late Mr Venkatamuni and his wife Suseelamma. Their son Mr Eswar told me that Mrs Ratan Lal came to their house alone quite early the morning after Mr Cowan was stricken and met with Baba. Almost certainly she would have brought him the news of Walter Cowan's sickness. Apparently it was later that same morning that Mrs Cowan came to see Baba and still later that Sai Baba went to the hospital.

I have asked (over the phone) Judge Damodar Rao, a staunch devotee, about his involvement, since Dr Hislop's account reported that Judge Rao had interviewed Cowan's physician. He denied having made any investigation of this case. During our trip to India in 1975, Mr Eswar mentioned to Dr Osis that Sai Baba had told him 'to play the case down'. Furthermore, it is of interest that Kasturi refers only briefly to this incident in his official biography of Baba; he cites, without any comment, only a few sentences by Elsie and Walter Cowan (1982, p. 23). This may indicate that the case was primarily built up by Mrs Cowan and she may have received only a half-hearted consenting nod from others around her. (The Cowans were staunch American devotees and donated the most imposing college building in Whitefield.)

The report of Walter Cowan's experience resembles some 'near-death experiences'. According to Elsie Cowan, her husband had told her after the incident that he felt himself to be out of his body and looking at his body as he was being taken by car to the hospital. 'Every time the car came to a pothole or a stop, my body was slipping down and I was trying to reenter it.' This seems to indicate that he was, at times at least, semiconscious on the way to the hospital.

There is another case, less widely publicized, in which Sai Baba is said to have brought an apparently dead person back to life. It concerns Mr Radhakrishna. The case was reported to Dr Osis and me in 1975 by the widow of Mr Radhakrishna.

During a stay in Puttaparti in the early 1950s, Mr Radhakrishna had become seriously ill with gastric trouble so that he could not pass his urine and also had further complications. The next day he became semiconscious and his condition was very critical. The following morning around

11.00 he lost consciousness. According to Mrs Radhakrishna, no life signs, including breathing and pulse, could be detected, and the members of his family who were present (she and Mr and Mrs Hemchand), firmly believed that he had expired.

By the next morning the body had become cold and there had been no observable signs of life for over 20 hours. But Baba told them that they should not worry, that nothing had happened. When he at last came down from his room, he asked them all to leave the room where Mr Radhakrishna was lying; he then closed the door and was alone with him for a minute or two. When he opened the door, the group standing outside saw Mr Radhakrishna sitting up in his bed. 'People were so flabbergasted that everyone fell to his feet.' That was the oriental way in which Mrs Radhakrishna finished her account. Mr Radhakrishna recovered on this occasion, but died a few years later apparently of the same disease.

The present Raja of Venkatagiri was in Puttaparti at that time. When asked about this incident, he told me that he remembered it well. He had been with the swami when Mr Radhakrishna's relative came to tell Sai Baba that he was dying. About an hour after Mr Radhakrishna allegedly died, the swami came down from his room at last and said to them: 'Don't fear, nothing has happened.' They waited outside the room while the swami went in. When he opened the door and called them, they saw that Mr Radhakrishna was alive and talking slowly. The Raja did not see Mr Radhakrishna while he was allegedly dead.

No physician was present to examine Mr Radhakrishna, nor is there a clear diagnosis of his disease and over twenty years had passed when I started to enquire into the incident. There is, however, one contemporary record of it in the diary of Mr Radhakrishna's daughter, Vijaya Hemchand, who kindly allowed me to photograph the relevant passages and to reproduce them below in an English translation. They are written in the flowery style that is common in India:

> During the previous night all of us gave up hopes regarding our father. That was a very horrible and frightening night, like that of cosmic dissolution (death). Our father was uttering the names of departed people and was saying that he too would join them. Neither was his speech coherent nor was he conscious. He had (long since) stopped taking food. All of us started weeping. In the midst of our agony and even in the face

of this threat to his life, we took refuge in Lord Sai. We held his feet firmly in our minds and had strong faith in him. The moment we saw his beautiful enchanting face we forgot all our sufferings and became enthralled by bliss.

He came down and closed the doors to the room. He was inside for ten minutes. I could not control my grief. I was afraid of what others might think. All those in the shrine (Prashanti Nilayam) were staying there motionless and were anxiously waiting for the outcome. After ten minutes he opened the door ... came out brushing his hands together, saw my mother, and told her: 'I have given life to your husband. I have given it to him. The hurdle is over, there is no more fear.' As he was saying this, we held his feet and washed them with our tears. 'Alas, my innocent mother! She is frightened!' So saying he looked at our faces and said: 'None of you had faith that he was going to survive, did you? You go in and see.'

Our father, who had been lying unconscious for three days without speech and sight, looked at all of us and smiled.

In her diary, Vijaya did not clearly state how long Mr. Radhakrishna had been without the normal signs of life, or even whether he, in the view of those present, did in fact expire. Only Sai Baba's words 'I have given life to your husband' point in that direction.

26
The Dazzling Light

The incident when Sai Baba produced a dazzling light on a hill near Puttaparti is one of the more perplexing phenomena among the many inexplicable events connected with Sai Baba. I have found ten witnesses to this phenomenon of light, each of whom I have interviewed separately. They all agreed that these phenomena happened only in the late 1940s and only a few times.

The first people to mention the light phenomenon to Dr Osis and me were Mrs Radhakrishna and Vijaya Hemchand. Mrs Radhakrishna's descriptions are given in the chapter 'The Kuppam Family'. Let us read a part of them again:

> Just as we were looking at him on the top of the hill (from below the hill), we could see a brilliant light resembling the rising sun, and the rays of that light were unbearable. This brilliance of light started from his head and fell all over the place. There was suddenly a lot of light behind him as if the sun had risen.
>
> Before the light came to its full brilliance, people began to say they could not bear the light, and the women almost fainted. Because they started complaining and before they could think what might happen, he was with them again on the riverbank.

This incident occurred about six in the evening on an overcast day, and the darkness of the sky made the radiance more brilliant than it would have been otherwise, according to Mrs Radhakrishna.

Mrs Radhakrishna's son Krishna Kumar describes this event or another of the same kind as follows:

> In those days, at the time of Sivaratri, Baba used to tell us: 'I

251

will show you the divine light.' At about 8.00 p.m. we would all walk towards that faraway hill and we would go with Baba close to the hill. Then he would disappear – he was not to be found with us – and within seconds there would be seen a bright light shining from the top of the hill.

We did not actually see him appear on the hill, and in fact we could not see his form there at all because of the distance and the darkness. All we could see was this very powerful light. It was not lightning. Nor was it white. It was a yellow light, something like a huge candle flame. Baba would be up on the hill for two or three minutes, and then suddenly he would be with us again. He would ask people whether they had seen the light (jyoti), and some people, if they were not cautious enough, would say no, if they had not seen it because of some obstructions blocking the view. So Baba would say: 'Watch. I will now show you the light (jyoti) again', and he would immediately disappear again.

As soon as he disappeared, we could see the light shining on the hill. This phenomenon I have seen two or three times. We have seen him make light on both hills but more on the Chitravati River hill.

Amarendra, one of Krishna Kumar's brothers, was also present on two of these occasions (see 'Figs From Any Tree'):

There were some instances, when Baba was on the top of the hill near Chitravati, that he would create or produce light. I have seen this on two occasions. As we have been discussing earlier, Swami would sometimes disappear from us. We used to go to the riverside about 4.00 or 4.30 and return about the time of sunset, when it had not become quite dark. Then he would sometimes disappear from the crowd and suddenly call from somewhere, clap his hands, and shout like: 'Look, I am here.' On two occasions when I was there, something extraordinary happened. We looked into the direction where his call came from. We may not have been able to see Baba or see him in full. But you could see someone standing on the top of the hill, and from that figure would emanate a bright light ....

Suseelamma observed the light phenomenon with some other members of her family. I met her in Madras, where she lives at the home of her son Eswar. Unfortunately Suseelamma does not speak English. In the first interview in 1977 Gopal Krishna Yachendra interpreted for me, and her son Eswar was interpreter in the second interview, which took place in 1981.

As Suseelamma remembers it, the phenomenon occurred at dusk. The swami was with eight to ten devotees near the hill at the Chitravati River when he told them to concentrate their attention on the top of the hill. 'He just took two steps' away from them, and after that they heard him clap his hands from the top of the hill. They suddenly saw a great orange-coloured light on the hill: 'People felt it just like a flash, their eyes became blinded for a few seconds, and some people fainted.' By the time they opened their eyes Baba was with them. They were at a loss to explain how he produced this phenomenon.

From Suseelamma's descriptions it seems that Baba showed light from the hill (or 'visions', as Suseelamma termed it) on two occasions the same evening. First he had around him a halo of light that was not so bright. The second time, when the light was much brighter, is the occasion that has been described above. By that time the evening had grown darker.

A word may be appropriate here on how Sai Baba interpreted this vision of light. According to Suseelamma, Baba told them that he had shown them the form (*viswarupa*) that Lord Krishna had shown to Arjuna just before the latter went into battle (a story related in the Bhagavad Gita). On their way back to Puttaparti, some devotees expressed doubts as to whether they had really had a viswarupa darshan. Baba added that they would have been unable to tolerate even one-third of that vision seen by Arjuna; some people had already fainted. The difference between them and Arjuna, Baba told them, was that Arjuna had had the spiritual power to have that vision fully, whereas they had not.

Krishnamma, an elderly lady who lives now in Prashanti Nilayam, met the swami first in 1946. She also witnessed the light phenomenon. She does not speak English, and so Gopal Krishna Yachendra interpreted for me when I interviewed her in November 1977. One day at dusk, Krishnamma said, the swami was suddenly on the top of the hill while his group was sitting below. The next minute they saw a big halo of light around him. He shouted to them to ask whether they had seen him. After that they saw a bright dazzling light, which they could not look at directly because of its brightness. According to Krishnamma, Baba had shown the light three times that same evening; on the last occasion it had been a bright rotating light. Only during the first occasion had they been able to see him directly.

Lolitamma, wife of D.N. Krishnamurti in Bangalore and sister-in-law of R.V. Krishnamurti, was also a witness to the light phenomenon. According to her, Baba was suddenly up on the hill, calling loudly to them to look towards him. They saw a brilliant light around his head, but it was not difficult to look at or overpowering; nor did it light up the environment. Some inattentive people, she said, did not even see it. It had been a circling rotating light. Lolitamma recalled that Baba had demonstrated the same phenomenon to someone else on the previous day.

In photograph albums belonging to some devotees, I had noticed in photos from Puttaparti in the 1940s and 1950s a healthy-looking man, probably in his thirties, whom I had not yet met. His name was Nagaratna Mudelier, and he had not been with Baba for a number of years. Through one Mr Sivaram from Kuppam, a former admirer of Sai Baba, I was able to trace Nagaratna Mudelier, who is now a retired businessman living in Madras. It turned out that he had observed a number of the phenomena taking place in Puttaparti in these early days. I asked him if he had ever seen Baba go up to the hill in Puttaparti and make some kind of a light:

> Yes, indeed. We would be standing at the foot of the hill on the Chitravati riverbed. When we went to the hilltop, it would take some few minutes. But he would go just like that, in a flash, just in a blink of an eye and he was there. Just a few seconds. Before we had been sitting and chatting on the riverbank, and when it got dark he said he was going up the hill. We all stood up. The very second he said that he was going he was no longer there. We did not see him start running or anything like that. He would just disappear, and in the same moment we would hear him from the top, saying: 'I am here, look at me.'

When he was on the top of the hill, what happened?

> Just some light, a bright light. Not like a searchlight, like starlight maybe, round. Not very bright, not very dim either. It was a kind of yellowish.

When asked what people thought about this incident and how they reacted to it, Nagaratna Mudelier said that some devotees speculated that Baba was showing them a torchlight. Others thought it was magic, but they were all very puzzled about it.

It has now been about 35 years since the light phenomenon occurred. All the witnesses agree that this happened some time in the late 1940's, probably in 1947. Although the testimony of those who witnessed it varies, the basic phenomenon described is the same, and so there seems no reason to doubt that a light was clearly visible on that hill during the twilight hours. The question is, what was it? Since no one was present on the hill with him, we will never know for sure. The reports differ somewhat in such details as what events led up to the phenomenon, how bright the light was, and whether the light was so bright that people were blinded. Some of these differences might be explained by supposing that there were at least two different occasions and that some of the observers had been present on only one occasion. Other differences might be due to changes in memory with the passage of time. Finally, we know from studies of memory and eyewitness psychology that when several people are asked to describe an event, even one that they have just observed, there will always be some differences in their reports.

One of the reports, however, is contemporary: Vijaya Hemchand described the event in her diary, probably either on the same or the following day. She allowed me to photograph this passage and I had it translated:

All devotees had gathered at the bottom of the hill and were watching him. Already it was sunset. Sri Baba could be seen by all from there. Behind his head bright red rays, which resemble the rays of sunset, were shining. After some time, they disappeared and were replaced by a bright powerful light that was emanating *crores* (tens of millions) of blinding sunrays and that was glistening like a diamond on the head of a snake. Looking at it and unable to tolerate the brightness, 2 people collapsed to the ground. All the people were staring with wide open eyes, overwhelmed with joy. Immediately the light disappeared and there was pitch darkness. Suddenly going from very bright light to darkness, our eyes were blinded, but we recovered our sight in a little while. Before we could open our eyes, Sri Baba stood amidst us and was laughing aloud. All our hearts were filled with joy. He went to the people who had collapsed and applied vibuti, which he had materialized in his hand, to their foreheads. They regained consciousness and offered salutations to him.

I would estimate the distance from the top of the hill to the banks of the Chitravati River to be about 200 yards. At dusk no torchlight will blind anyone from such a distance, least of all to the extent that they faint! This phenomenon remains therefore as one of Sai Baba's enigmas.

In the literature of psychical research, I have not been able to find accounts of light phenomena of similar magnitude. Some luminous phenomena are reported in investigations of mediums. Generally speaking, these reports describe lights or a glow around objects (either apports or materialized parts of human bodies, such as a hand or a head) that appeared during a seance and vanished again during the same seance (Zimmer 1923). The renowned French psychical researcher, Gustav Geley, reported various luminous phenomena in his experiments with the Polish medium Franek-Kluski (Geley 1922). Sometimes, in the case of D.D. Home, luminous sparks or mist were reported around the medium's body, head or hands (Dunraven 1924, p. 195, 161), also around Indridi Indridason (Nielsson 1922).

In religious literature there are many accounts of light shining from saints or other religious figures. A famous one is in the New Testament (Matthew 17:1-2):

> And after six days Jesus taketh Peter, James, and John his brother, and bringeth them up into a high mountain apart, and was transfigured before them; and his face did shine as the sun, and his raiment was white as the light.

A similar account is given in the life of the Russian saint Seraphim of Sarov (1759-1833), who is considered by some to be the greatest of all saints of the Eastern Orthodox Church (Jones 1973).

In Herbert Thurston's (1952) classic book on the physical phenomena of mysticism, a full chapter is devoted to the evidence for luminous phenomena among Catholic saints. Some reports of luminous phenomena came under the scrutiny of the Church during the investigations involved in the process of beatification. Such was the case with St Bernardino Realino, who died in Lecce in Italy in 1616. Thurston is a Jesuit scholar of high repute who generally assumes a cautious and circumspect attitude in his writings. He sums up the evidence for this case:

> One may hesitate to regard the evidence as entirely satisfactory,

but it must not be overlooked that quite a number of people bore witness to the extraordinary radiance with which Father Bernardino's countenance was at times transformed ... some declared that they had seen sparks coming from all over his body like sparks from a fire ... and others asserted that the dazzling glow from his countenance on one or two occasions was such that they could not rightly distinguish his features, but had to turn their eyes away. (ibid. p. 165)

Thurston reports from another process of beatification, for 'the holy Franciscan Observant, Blessed Thomas da Cori', that witnesses stated that 'the whole church on a dark morning was lit up by the radiance, which glowed in the Father's countenance' (ibid. p. 169).

As reported by Thurston, the reports on lights around saints resemble more, in their intensity, some of the reports we have on Baba, such as that of Vijaya Hemchand. The lights of the mediums seem weaker in comparison. Apparently Baba's lights seem also to differ from those of saints in that Baba wilfully produced his light while those of Christian saints came in the course of prayer or religious ecstasy. (Seraphim of Sarov may be an exception.)

However, the records from the Christian sources quoted above may indicate that Sai Baba's luminous phenomena, if they are genuine, are not without parallel, however extraordinary they may seem.

27
Teleportation, Swift Movements
Or What?

One of the most stunning claims made about Sai Baba concerns his sudden or instantaneous movements from one place to another. Several devotees staying with him in his early days, especially in the late 1940s, claim to have seen him suddenly disappear at one location and reappear in a matter of seconds at a different location. So far I have reported four interviews with people who reported witnessing such 'disappearances' of Sai Baba – Mrs Radhakrishna, Vijaya Hemchand, Amarendra Kumar, and Krishna Kumar – in the late 1940s but not after Prashanti Nilayam was opened in 1951. Let me quote briefly from the interviews. First Mrs Radhakrishna:

> As we were approaching the river and passing a hill on our right-hand side, he (Baba) would sometimes suddenly disappear. He would, for example, snap his fingers and ask those around him to do the same. And hardly had we snapped our fingers when he had vanished from amongst us and we could see him on the top of the hill waiting for us.

Vijaya's report:

> On the way (to Chitravati River) he would be walking with us, ladies on one side and gents on the other. As we were passing the hill, and before we had crossed the river, he would suddenly vanish from our sight. He would then, in no time, appear on the top of the hill and call us.

Amarendra Kumar described this phenomenon in greatest detail. Let us re-read a few sentences:

On many occasions, especially when we were walking by the river, he would suddenly vanish from sight. As he vanished, he would be walking with us in a group and talking to us. We would not see him or find him. But then he would be calling me or someone by name, and when you looked for him you would find that he would be at the top of the mountain (hill). All this would happen within seconds.

Krishna Kumar describes these incidents somewhat differently:

I have seen him say that he will go up to the hill, and suddenly he would be up there …. When I say he 'disappeared', I do not mean that he disappeared into thin air. Rather we observed him climbing the hill very fast …. Whether he got there by flying or walking, we do not know. But it must be miraculous how he got there so quickly. He is on the top of the hill within seconds.

Only Krishna Kumar describes Sai Baba as 'climbing the hill very fast', but still in a miraculous manner. Were his memories of these events different from those of the other three informants? Did he lack knowledge of the exact meaning of the English word 'climb'? Krishna Kumar seems in later years to have been exposed to English less than Vijaya and Amarendra have. Was Krishna Kumar trying to accommodate a view he attributed to a sceptical enquirer? Or is his description of these events closer to the facts than are those of the other members of his family? In any event, all of them described the events as miraculous, differing only on whether he moved with extreme, even superhuman, rapidity through the air, or whether he vanished at one place and reappeared at another almost immediately.

So far I have reported interviews with only four people who were with Baba in the late 1940s, namely those four quoted above but I have interviewed several other people who stayed with the swami in the 1940s. After that, all agree, these phenomena, whatever their nature, stopped. What do they say? Do they support these extraordinary claims?

The additional information was not easy to find. First of all, relatively few people were around Baba in the 1940s. Secondly, many of them have died or have been impossible to trace. Mr Nagaratna Mudelier is one of the old devotees, whom I finally succeeded in tracing. He described what he witnessed:

We would be standing at the foot of the hill on the Chitravati riverbed. For me to get up to the hilltop takes some few minutes. But for him (Baba), he will just go like that, just like a flash. Just in a blink of an eye he is there, just a few seconds. We will be sitting and chatting.

In 1975 Dr Osis and I interviewed Mr Parthasarathy, (whom I much later discovered to be Nagaratna Mudelier's brother); he has since died. He told us that on one occasion, when they were down at the riverside, Baba said he would go up to the hill. Mr Parthasarathy was wearing a wristwatch, and Baba asked him to note the time it took him to get to the top of the hill. They were standing close together. Mr Parthasarathy looked at the watch, and Baba vanished immediately. According to Mr Parthasarathy, he had barely fixed his eyes on the watch when he heard Baba calling from the hill and, looking up, saw Baba on the top of the hill. 'The watch did not move even a second', he reported. When Mr Parthasarathy was asked if anyone saw Baba climb or fly fast up the hill, he answered: 'Nobody would see him, but in a fraction of a second he would be there (on the hilltop).' Mr Parthasarathy apparently observed this phenomenon only once.

Another witness, Miss M.L. Leelamma of Guindy, spent much time in Puttaparti in the 1940s, and she described this phenomenon as the majority of those quoted above did; she said that he would go up the hill 'like lightning'. She also reported that they had played a game: those around him would try to touch him, but just as someone was about to do so, he would disappear and then appear somewhere else close by.

Mrs V.S. Sundaramma in Bangalore related to me that Baba used to go up and down the hill 'like lightning', 'too fast for us to count.'

There is a particularly puzzling side to these accounts of Baba's mysterious swift movements from place to place. Venkamma, Baba's sister, who was apparently frequently with him, did not recall ever witnessing this phenomenon when I interviewed her.

In this case it may be worthwhile making an exception, and mentioning some secondhand testimony. According to Varadu, his mother had witnessed Baba's disappearances/appearances in the 1940s. The Raja of Venkatagiri has told me that several of the old devotees who have now died (such as Mrs Chandran, Mrs Purniya and Seshagiri Rao) used to talk about seeing Baba suddenly vanish from sight and then appear almost instantaneously at a different location.

How shall we evaluate these reports of Baba's apparent teleportation? Several witnesses seem thoroughly convinced that they were experiencing real events. It is hard to imagine how Baba might have slipped away from those around him in some normal way; in those days, as now, he was always the centre of attention. Could faulty memory and later exaggerations be responsible for the accounts? This explanation also seems unsatisfactory. It would be worthwhile for Indian psychologists to study the development of stories and myths in groups that develop around influential gurus. Such background information is sorely needed when we attempt to evaluate the veridicality of accounts such as those reported in this book.

Are there any reports of such swift transports of human bodies in the journals of psychical research? As for those with good evidence, the answer is certainly no, though Fodor (1966) states in his review of the subject that: 'Teleportation of human bodies through closed doors and over a distance is a comparatively rare but fairly well authenticated occurrence' (p. 392). Isolated instances with few mediums, such as Mrs Guppy (Podmore 1963, pp. 81-3) have been reported. The outstanding physical medium Indridi Indridason once reportedly disappeared from one room and immediately reappeared in another locked room (Nielsson 1919, p. 350).

Teleportation phenomena, if they are genuine, are a composite of apports and levitations, and for the latter there is a fair amount of evidence. The famous D.D. Home was reported to have risen in the air on a few occasions, once gliding in midair out through a window on a second floor and back again in through another window (Dunraven 1922). Indridason apparently arose in midair on several occasions, once in the presence of about sixty people (Nielsson 1919).

The phenomenon of teleportation seems to consist of both levitation and apporting of objects (in this case the human body). Apports have been discussed in an earlier chapter. The most authentic reports of levitations, however, are found in literature on a Catholic saint, St Joseph of Copertino (1603-1663), who was frequently seen to levitate, such as high above the altar of his church. In the processes of his beatification and canonization much of firsthand testimony was collected. His levitations were not only known by his community; there exists also an eyewitness account of one of his levitations written by a Lutheran German nobleman who was the patron and employer of the famous German philosopher Leibnitz (Dingwall 1947, Thurston 1952).

But the phenomenon of levitation differs from the swift movements attributed to Sai Baba. Baba's movements are described as instantaneous; he was never – as was frequently the case with St Joseph – seen for several minutes suspended in midair, (Varadu's account of Baba lying in midair may be an exception). Also, Baba seems to have directed his movements at will, whereas the levitations of St Joseph were reported, at least in most cases, to be involuntary.

28
Bilocation?

The wonders of Puttaparti do not stop at claims of Sai Baba disappearing from one place and then instantaneously reappearing at another. There are even people who believe, for what they consider good reasons, that he can be in two places at the same time. This is described as bilocation. These cases are few but should be given some attention and scrutiny.

First there is a group of cases in which Baba has supposedly appeared to one or more people in a distant place for a few seconds or minutes. Secondly, we learnt of two cases in which several people report having apparently seen, heard and interacted with Baba in a normal physical way for an hour or longer, while allegedly he was physically present elsewhere.[1]

When a person appears briefly at a distant place, be they of the living or the dead, such cases in psychical research are termed apparitions. Someone believes he has physically perceived a person near him, but soon that person disappears. The perceiver then realizes that this person could not have been physically present. Surveys of the general population reveal that perhaps 10 to 20% of people have such experiences at least once in their lifetimes (Gurney, Myers and Podmore 1886, Tyrrell 1953, Haraldsson 1985, Emmons 1982).

The cases concerning Baba vary in richness of detail. Some are quite meagre, like the experience of Mr Gupta in Meerut. Mr Gupta, who was living in the north of India, believes that Sai Baba, presumably in the south of India at that time, once spoke to him and gave him what became life-changing advice; Mr Gupta, however, did not see Baba or even think, as the incident occurred, that it was Baba addressing him.

Vijaya Hemchand and her husband related a similar case that was much richer perceptually, as reported earlier. A thief who broke into their yard and house was scared away by someone; they claimed that the thief's description of this person closely resembled Sai Baba, and so they were convinced that the thief had seen Sai Baba. By almost any standard the evidence for both of these cases is poor, for reasons that should be evident. Other cases are more puzzling. Almost accidentally we learned of the following when investigating a different case in Kerala.

The Calicut Case: Sai Baba Appears in an Eye Clinic

This incident occurred on 30 August 1970, in the Gitta Eye Clinic in Calicut, Kerala State, about 340 miles southeast of Baba's ashram in Puttaparti. This small clinic is owned and operated by Dr P.B. Menon, an eye surgeon, who is the only medical doctor on the staff. Both Dr Osis and I interviewed Dr Menon and one witness of the apparition, M. P. Moosad, a paramedical assistant to Dr Menon during surgery. The hospital journal with names of patients and dates of treatments was shown to both of us. Dr Osis alone interviewed the second witness to Sai Baba's purported appearance, Mutu Lakshmi Ammal, the patient, a woman in her seventies who resides in Alleppey, 130 miles south of Calicut.

The patient, a widow, specialized in singing bhajans during religious services. Her performances, we were told, are in demand in Alleppey and neighbouring cities, and she is an ardent devotee of Sai Baba. According to Mutu Lakshmi Ammal, prior to the operation she went on a pilgrimage to Puttaparti, where she sat on the ground with hundreds of others awaiting Baba. When she pleaded: 'Swami' he stopped and said: 'I know. There is a cataract on one eye and some problem with the other. There is pressure also …. Don't worry, I will be with you for the operation, so carry on (with it).' Mutu Lakshmi Ammal said that she arrived at the clinic at 8.00 a.m. on 30 August and met with Dr Menon. She told him that Baba had promised to be 'present'. At that time he did not believe in such apparitions, but did not dispute it and thought: 'When it is all over, I will ask: "Where was your Baba?" ' Then M.P. Moosad took over, washing her in preparation for the operation and administering medicine to her eyes. According to both Moosad and Dr Menon, Moosad had not been informed that Baba had promised to be 'present' at the operation.

Apparently Moosad had a hard time managing Ammal.

Ammal informed us that she was expected to be at complete rest, but she told Dr Osis that instead she sang a Sai Baba bhajan song full of 'sympathy and longing'. Later she chanted continuously, saying the name of her lord: 'Sai Ram, Sai Ram, Sai Ram ....' She said that Moosad scolded her, telling her that she must not make that noise; he also told her that he would administer medicine for the second time at 9.30. Moosad left the patient lying on a cot and went for the medicine.

A little while later Ammal heard footsteps, felt a touch, opened her eyes suddenly, and, seeing Baba standing near her, stood up. Then the door opened and Moosad entered the room in an angry mood, scolding her for standing. According to Ammal's testimony, Moosad was taken aback when he discovered Baba's presence, and stood there stunned. She remembered that Baba was dressed in his usual robe, red in color, and he stood holding his hand in a gesture of blessing, which she demonstrated. He remained there for a 'very short time'. She did not see him enter the room because her eyes were closed. He did not go away; he simply disappeared from her sight after 'about one minute.' She felt that she had received a 'great blessing' from Baba.

The operation went very well. 'The next morning', she said, 'there was not even a trace of the operation having taken place, no discolouration', and her eyes were clear. When pressed to explain why she thought the apparition was of Baba and not of someone else, she emphasized that she had him in person on many occasions. He had looked the same as when she had seen him in Puttaparti; he had the same face, height, hair and garment. He had not appeared transparent in any way.

Moosad stated that on entering the room he saw Baba silently standing by the cot. His appearance was the same as when he later saw him in Puttaparti. He did not observe Baba's disappearance. Not having expected to see him there in the preparation room, Moosad became frightened and fainted. When he came to, Baba was no longer there. Moosad did not know just how long he had been unconscious, but thought it was perhaps a few minutes. When we interviewed him in 1973, he still seemed to be embarrassed about his fainting spell. Prior to this event Moosad had not seen Sai Baba in person; he had seen only photos of him.

Dr Menon was not present when the apparition appeared. He remembered Ammal as a widow of the Brahmin caste. She had told him of Baba's promise to be with her during the cataract operation. 'I did not believe it', Dr Menon related, 'but she had absolute faith. When I was just starting the surgery, I asked her if the swami had come. She said: "Yes, I got darshan." '

Two or three hours later, Dr Menon overheard his assistants whispering and, noticing that Moosad was distressed, demanded an explanation. Moosad then told him about the incident. As Dr Menon remembers it, the paramedical assistant had gone into the room carrying medicine in his hands and had seen Baba standing near the patient's cot. She (the patient) was sitting up with her hands folded; Baba was standing facing her. Moosad was flabbergasted. 'He just dropped the bottle and everything, got frightened, and fainted.' Moosad still works for Dr Menon, who told us that he prizes him as a very good assistant, and added: 'He is now a devotee of Baba's, but he is terribly afraid to go near him. Even when he goes to Puttaparti, he stands far away. But he likes to see him. For him this incident had been something of a traumatic experience.'

Mutu Lakshmi Ammal was consistent in her statements and seemed to recall the incident clearly. Moosad struck us as being an unassuming man and gave straightforward answers to our questions. These witnesses were interviewed independently, Ammal in Alleppey and Moosad in Calicut.

Dr Menon, a prominent physician in Kerala, appeared to us as an intelligent, honest, well-educated man. He is now a follower of Sai Baba.

We also questioned Baba about this incident. He flashed a bright smile, said he remembered Ammal warmly, and affirmed that he had projected himself to her at the eye clinic.

Both witnesses agreed on the location and time of the incident. Both were convinced that the apparition was unmistakably Baba on the grounds that they had on this occasion seen him in person and recognized him. Moreover, Ammal described his robe, bushy hair, stature and tone of voice. Ammal did not remember Moosad's having fainted, but she may have been too absorbed in Baba's presence to notice anything else. We are inclined to accept Moosad's version not only because two hours later he reported to Dr Menon what had happened, but also because, even when talking with us, he seemed to be embarrassed about having fainted and fallen down.

Could the two witnesses have been in collusion? The distance of 130 miles between their cities is a forbidding one in India and they seem to have had no social contact. Furthermore, Ammal still seemed to harbour a grudge because Moosad had called her chanting of the lord's name 'that noise'.

We explored the possibility that someone (for example, Baba) could have intruded the clinic physically. The clinic is located inside a house behind high stone walls, and according to Dr Menon no one could enter its premises unnoticed. The sudden disappearance of a presumed intruder is difficult to explain.

Baba is a colourful personality. Because of his dress, bushy hair, and unusual facial characteristics, he is unlikely to go unnoticed when travelling. A statement made to us in 1973 by one of the top police officials in Delhi illustrates the popularity of Baba: 'His appearance creates traffic jams which last for two hours and are second only to Indira Gandhi.'

The characteristics of this appearance of Sai Baba in Calicut resemble Western reports of apparitions: the apparition was seen briefly, perhaps for about one minute; it was primarily visual (it did not speak, and it produced only sounds of walking and a sensation of touch); and it did not walk away but disappeared, leaving no physical trace.

The Manjeri Case: Sai Baba Appears to Several People
Manjeri is a small town in Kerala State about 25 miles southeast of Calicut. It has a mixed Hindu, Muslim, and Christian population. On 13 December and again on 24 December 1964, Sai Baba reportedly appeared at the home of Mr Ram Mohan Rao, principal of a junior technical school and a trained engineer.

Dr Osis and I visited the Rao family and their former neighbours in December 1973 and again in January 1975, nine and ten years after the events took place. By that time the ten witnesses seemed to remember the main events but were confused on minor details. Fortunately, however, we found some contemporary documentation. Ram Mohan Rao showed us a copy of the letter he wrote to Prof Kasturi about a month after the second occasion on which Baba appeared. We also interviewed two local investigators who came on the scene a few months after the incident. These investigators corroborated to some extent the story of the principal witnesses, the Rao family.

In contrast to the Calicut incident, the Manjeri case has many characteristics atypical of Western cases of apparitions, including its long duration and the lifelike behaviour (such as speaking, singing, eating, handling objects, bringing gifts, and healing) of the apparition.

This case is presented without prejudging its possible interpretation; for example, I will call the visitor Baba while keeping in mind the possibility that it could have been someone else.

The following narration relates what seems to have happened during the two ostensibly apparitional appearances of Sai Baba. Our analysis of the interview material will follow.

The family of Ram Mohan Rao at that time consisted of Mr and Mrs Rao and their daughter, Sailaja, who was about eight years old. On 12 December, Mr Rao was hospitalized, having suffered a severe electrical shock in the workshop of his school. He was released the same evening but was still not feeling well. Sailaja, his daughter, was at home ill. According to all three members of the Rao family, her leg was swollen by a kind of a growth from ankle to knee and was covered with eczema. The condition was very painful, and her temperature was elevated. She had been treated by a local doctor and had been taken to a Christian hospital in a different town. Neither treatment was successful. An Ayurveda doctor[2] also was consulted. He applied Indian folk remedies to the afflicted leg, but with no improvement. Sailaja had been excluded from school because of this malady. Neighbours offered to take Sailaja to Puttaparti for healing, but Mr Rao declined. The neighbours however, did bring back some vibuti which had been given by Baba. It was applied to the leg with no noticeable effect.

On the night of 12 December Sailaja told us that she was in pain and had a fever. Her parents were preoccupied with Mr Rao's injury and she was very depressed. Not being able to sleep, she went to their puja room, wept in front of Baba's picture, and prayed for his help. Mr and Mrs Rao did not report having made any special plea to Baba for help on that day.

Early the next morning, 13 December, a stranger wearing a yellow robe appeared at the Rao's door, chanting: 'OM'. According to Mrs Rao, who admitted him, he said: 'Don't get panicky. I am here to protect you, your husband, and your child.' He then asked for Sailaja and went to the corner of the veranda where she was lying. Sailaja told us he spoke to her in Malayalam (the national language of Kerala) saying: 'You called me last night and now I have come in the morning and will cure you.' Then the visitor demanded that he be seated in the puja room rather than in the waiting room where he had been invited to sit. He went there and sat beneath a portrait of Baba that hung among the pictures of several other deities and saints. Mrs Rao compared the visitor's appearance with Baba's picture and found them to be similar. Mr Rao and Sailaja joined them. Baba waved his hand in his characteristic manner, produced vibuti, and applied it to the girl's disfigured leg, saying that she would be well in three days' time. He was very warm and reassuring about the problems of all three of the Raos, held little Sailaja on his lap and asked her to sing some Sai Baba songs. Since she knew none, he taught her songs of the kind that are sung at his ashram. With the distinctive wave of his hand, he produced a song book which was printed in the Malayalam language by a Sai Baba organization but which, we were told, had not yet been distributed in that area. Sai Baba asked them to invite their neighbours. Some came and they all joined him in bhajans.

Some of the witnesses we met said that the invitation was given at the time of Baba's second visit; still others claimed to have attended on both occasions. Regardless of which of the two dates is correct, the neighbours did remember having participated in a service conducted by Baba at which time he attempted to heal two of those present. One of them was Mrs Madhavan Nair, the wife of a landowner and local newspaper publisher, who suffered from diabetes. According to her daughter, Mrs Janaki B. Nair, she complained: 'I own all these rice fields and cannot eat one grain.' It appears that Baba again waved his hand, materialized some medicine in a glass, and instructed her how to take it. According to the daughter, Mrs Nair's condition improved temporarily, as was proven by urinalysis and her tolerance of rice. However, she had a relapse and died from diabetes eight years later. The other patient was Thalayur B. Moosad, a landowner and the Raos' landlord. His leg was disfigured by whitish growths, which Mrs Moosad told us were cancer but which the Raos described as leprosy. According to the Raos, it seems that Baba had told Mr Moosad he could not do much for him because of his karma (past deeds), but he gave him vibuti, which Mr Moosad took home with him and showed to his wife. The following week Mr Moosad was hospitalized to undergo surgery and died after the operation.

In private after the bhajan Baba gave a shell necklace to Mr Rao and his wife, and a silken cloth and a tumbler to Sailaja. He told them about his own life, predicted the arrival of Mr Rao's father within a week to perform a certain Hindu ceremony for the cleansing of sins, and discussed spiritual matters with them. He spoke to each in his mother tongue: Tamil to Mr Rao, Canarese (of the Mysore region) to Mrs Rao, and broken Malayalam (the local language of Kerala) to Sailaja and the neighbors. He ate lunch with the Raos, insisting on simple foods. After three hours, the visit was terminated. Baba asked Sailaja if she knew her geography, and he explained that people were awaiting him far away in Kalahasti (a town 80 miles northwest of Madras on the other side of the Indian peninsula). Sailaja implored Baba to come again, and he promised to do so once more. He requested them not to follow him, and he went out of the gate and out of sight behind the stone courtyard wall.

No one seemed to doubt that the visitor had come, but there was a local controversy concerning his identity. Some believed and others doubted that the visitor was indeed Sai Baba, who in 1964 was already famous. Two witnesses told us that he had come by bus, something which no famous man in India would do. As predicted by Baba, Mr Rao's father made an unplanned visit to them and did perform the particular cleansing rite foretold by Baba. Despite the apparently correct predictions, however, the old Hindu gentleman could not believe that Baba, a famous religious leader, would simply drop in to answer a little girl's prayers. He suspected someone of planning a burglary and warned his daughter-in-law to lock the door if he came again. To clear up the matter, he took Sailaja with him and went to Mangalore (some 160 miles north of Manjeri) to consult a certain Mr Dixit, who knew Baba personally.

Eleven days later the second incident occurred. Feeling lonely without Sailaja, on 24 December at about 5.30 p.m. Mr and Mrs Rao went out for a stroll. It was still daylight, and the house lights had not yet been turned on. When they returned about an hour later, they found the lights on and feared there was a burglar inside. First they tried the back door and found that it was bolted from inside. Then, on unlocking the front door and entering the house, they found Baba inside making preparations for bhajan and arathi, the Hindu custom of worshipping a deity with a light offering of burning camphor.

After asking if they were afraid, the visitor displayed ostensibly paranormal knowledge of the Rao household. He said he knew of their loneliness and distress and had come to stay the night with them while Sailaja was away. He told them that since the preparations for bhajan, usually made by Sailaja on Thursday nights, had been neglected, he was doing it himself.

Then the bhajan took place. It is not clear if anyone other than the Raos and Baba took part, although one neighbour claimed to have been present. Mr Rao wanted the arathi ceremony directed to either Baba or his picture, but Baba did not like the idea. He took his portrait, walked out, and hung it in Sailaja's room. The Raos claim that at that time vibuti began forming on the picture, which had continued on and off to this day.

After partaking of a simple supper, the three of them discussed spiritual matters until they retired at about 1.00 a.m. Baba was up early, at 4.00 a.m., and took a cold bath. The Raos could hear him chanting. Later he asked for coffee and had breakfast with them.

Neighbours were invited to attend a bhajan, after which *prasad* (sacramental food) was served. Baba, whose conduct was incompatible with that of a burglar, again gave presents (a golden ring and a necklace) to Mr and Mrs Rao. These gifts, according to the Raos, were produced by a wave of his hand. He also produced a pendant and a gold leaf on which he drew a picture of Subramaniam, a deity popular in southern India. After a light lunch and a rest, Baba explained that devotees were waiting for him and, asking them not to follow him, left the house at 3.00 or 4.00 p.m.

This is how the Raos described the incidents. They became the centre of a stormy neighbourhood controversy. Some neighbours became devotees of Baba. Others said that Baba never travelled without an escort (usually a caravan of cars) and would 'never come like a thief' and enter a locked house. Some even questioned how a Hindu wife (Mrs Rao) could, with propriety, wear a necklace 'given by another man'. The Raos were upset to such an extent that ten years later they still felt badly about the incident. They were convinced that their visitor was Baba because of his likeness to Baba's photo, his paranormal powers, and his familiarity with Baba's life. Still, they wanted to clarify the matters. On 21 January 1965, a few weeks after the incidents, Mr Rao wrote to Prof Kasturi, who collaborates closely with Baba. In the letter, Mr Rao gave a brief report on the incident.

The only written record Mr Rao could find was the carbon copy of his letter to Prof Kasturi, which was not shown to us voluntarily but only after our repeated demands. Since we had dropped in unannounced, it could not have been prepared beforehand to impress us, and so we may probably assume that we saw the original carbon copy. The letter was composed with the assistance of Mr Rao's father (now deceased), and consequently undue emphasis was put on his activities, which were tangential to the case. It also leaves out some important details, such as the healing of Sailaja. Mrs Rao wrote an additional letter to Prof Kasturi, of which there are no records.

Prof Kasturi gives a detailed, seven-page description of the case in his 1973 book on Sai Baba (pp. 92-99), basing his account on Mr Rao's letter and the subsequent investigation he, Kasturi, initiated. We also discovered a one-page note by P. Appukutta Menon, a local osteopath who lived in Palghat in Kerala who Prof Kasturi had asked to investigate the case. Prof Kasturi was not satisfied with Dr Menon's first short report. For the sake of better documentation, he submitted a list of eighty questions to be answered and requested that a second investigator be included. P.K. Panikker then joined Dr Menon for further investigation. In the course of his inquiries, which were conducted in the spring of 1963, Panikker even performed a recognition test. Panikker told Dr Osis that he had approached the daughter of T.B. Moosad (the Raos' landlord), an eighth-grade student who was supposed to have been present at the Rao's bhajan, when she was returning home from school. He showed her Baba's photo and asked: 'Have you seen this man anywhere?' When she replied affirmatively, he asked her where she had seen him. 'In this house', she said, pointing to it. 'He was singing bhajan and we all participated.' Panikker said he did not disclose that it was a picture of Baba but simply showed it to her and asked if she had seen that man anywhere else.

Menon and Panikker sent a joint report to Prof Kasturi, but in spite of our repeated requests, the Menon-Panikker report could not be located. It may have been lost, since there seems to be no organized, systematic method of keeping records of Baba's paranormal cases. Menon and Panikker were interviewed individually by Dr Osis. They affirmed the correctness of Prof Kasturi's account but were unable to provide us with any written records.

We were successful in interviewing seven neighbours who professed to having seen the mysterious visitor: Mrs Thalayur B. Moosad, widow of the Raos' former landlord; Padmanabhan Nair, Moosad's servant; Mrs Sarojina Amma, a neighbour and the niece of Mrs Madhavan Nair (the widow who was purportedly cured of diabetes by the visitor); Venu Gopal, Sarojina Amma's son, nine years old as the incident occurred; Mrs Janaki B. Nair, a neighbour and the daughter of Mrs Madhavan Nair; K. Madhavan Kutty, Janaki Nair's son, then nine years of age; and K. Lakshmi Kutty Amma, Janaki Nair's cousin. The remainder of the people who were supposed to have witnessed the event could not be traced. Some had moved away and others had died.

We also interviewed the following people who were not personally present when the incident occurred: P. Appukutta Menon and P.K. Panikker, who investigated the case a few months after it occurred; Dr P.B. Menon, who treated Madhavan Nair; K. Bhaskaran, the relative with whom Madhavan Nair lived; Mrs Valsala Madhavan and Mrs Indira Patti, college teachers and the daughters of T.B. Moosad; Devada Moosad, a lawyer and the son of T.B. Moosad.

For our interviews, we used four interpreters: N.A.N. Nayar, R.R. Netar, P. Appukutta Menon, and Devada Moosad.

In Puttaparti, we also questioned Baba about the Manjeri case. He answered very briefly, asserting that he had been with the Raos, out of body, on two occasions.

The witnesses seemed to remember the main features of the case reasonably well, Baba's robe and Afro hairstyle, his singing of bhajan songs, and his attempts at healing. However, over the years their memories have become foggy about details, such as at what time of day and on which of the two visits they attended bhajans. Mr Rao repeatedly complained about his memory, saying that in his work he finds it increasingly necessary to rely on notes. At the time of our second interview, he was under obvious stress caused by the difficulties involved in handling a strike by his school employees.

In order to give an overview of witnessed events, we have summarized the major statements in Tables 1 and 2 at the end of the chapter. Such a presentation, we hope, will clarify how consistently the many witnesses reported each event.

The primary reason for Baba's ostensible visit to Manjeri was to call on the Rao family. However, he was seen outside the house by two neighbours, five others, who had come for healing and devotions, were in on a part of the visit. Therefore, while some of the events were witnessed by both the Rao family and their neighbours (Table 1), most of Baba's time was spent exclusively with the Rao family (Table 2). At the time of our investigations, the case was 9 and then 10 years old. Fortunately, some early documentation of the case was made within a few months of its incidence (Rao's letter to Kasturi, and Menon's and Panikker's interviews); this is included in Tables 1 and 2. That documentation, to a certain extent, helps to counteract the possibly confused memories of the eyewitnesses. But, as mentioned earlier, we were unable to find the Menon-Panikker report, so we had to rely on the informants' memories of it.

The focus of investigation: The identity of the visitor

In early 1965, the Raos reported to Kasturi, Menon, and Panikker that on 13 and 24 December they had received a visitor whom they identified as Sai Baba. We found in our interviews that every one of the ten witnesses agreed about the arrival of the mysterious man in monastic garb. There was not universal agreement about the identity of the visitor. The central question of our inquiry, then, is: How much evidence that the visitor was Sai Baba is available? If it was he, was it an out-of-body projection or was he personally present in body?

Table 1 summarizes the statements of the ten witnesses. There is a clearcut convergence of observations on the most distinctive features of Baba's appearance: his well-pressed silken robe in the colour he customarily wore. Nearly all the witnesses described the clothing as having been of the style characteristic of Sai Baba and unlike that of the traditionally shabby travelling sadhu.[3] Of the nine witnesses who commented on it, seven recalled that the hair was worn in the

Afro style typical of Baba but very uncommon in India. K.M. Kutty, nine years old at the time, remembered his having had short hair and said that he was not Sai Baba. His mother, Janaki Nair, thought his hair had been covered by a cloth, but her recollection was contradicted by all the other witnesses. At first she said the visitor was not Baba, and then she reversed herself and said that it was he. All of those who commented on it said that the visitor was of the same stature as Baba, that is, short. The little information we have about the voice and complexion is consistent with that of Sai Baba's. Allowing for some memory lapses, we can say that most witnesses specifically identified both the clothing and the physical appearance as having been typically like that of Baba. The early documentation of the case is supportive of this conclusion.

Because of the ostensible psychic powers and distinctive qualities as a spiritual leader displayed by the visitor, it would seem to have been difficult for a travelling sadhu to impersonate Baba. For example, in sharp contrast to the travelling monks, Sai Baba does not ask for alms or favours, but on the contrary is known for helping others and giving generous presents, usually produced 'by a wave of his hand'. We carefully examined the behavioural traits of the mysterious visitor for similarities to Baba. The visitor did not ask for alms, food, or favours. Instead, he engaged in spiritual discussions. Like Baba, he attempted to heal the sick, dealt with family problems, and made predictions of future events that, it is claimed, came true.

The most astonishing of the alleged paranormal events was his ostensibly immediate response to a child's appeal. Sailaja said that she wept in desperation before Baba's picture on the night of 12 December. Baba appeared early in the morning of the 13th and asked for her. Even if Baba had wanted to go to Sailaja in person in response to a telepathic request, there would not have been enough time for him to drive, over the poor Indian roads, from Puttaparti to Manjeri. Travelling by bus that far and on such short notice is totally impossible in India.

One possibility suggests itself. If Baba had been staying in the Calicut area, he might simply have made a short bus trip from there to Manjeri. Luckily, we were able to trace Baba's whereabouts at the time and learned that he was far away on the other side of the Indian peninsula, a guest at the Palace of

Venkatagiri in Andhra State (about 100 miles north of Madras). Dr Osis interviewed the Raja of Venkatagiri in Madras. The following day Gopal Krishna and his cousin, Madana Gopal, took Dr Osis to the palace. Madana Gopal kept a diary and, after consulting it, told us that Baba had been in Venkatagiri on the particular days in question. Furthermore, the palace manager showed us the palace records, which confirmed that Baba had arrived there on the 12th and departed for Kalahasti on 17 December 1964. He also showed us a printed announcement of a function, held at the palace, at which Baba had publicly spoken on 13 December. The records and announcements were written in Telugu, but we could read the dates, which were in English. (Kalahasti, 25 miles from Venkatagiri, is the closest larger town. When the Raos' visitor said he was expected in Kalahasti, he may have done so because it is a better-known locality than Venkatagiri.) The whereabouts of Sai Baba on 13 December can therefore be reasonably well accounted for. In addition, we talked with an American, Miss Hilda Charlton, who was with Baba in 1964. She told us that she had been in a group of devotees who accompanied Baba on a tour to Andhra State in December 1964. She remembers that the group returned to Brindavan, Baba's Bangalore residence, on 24 December, just in time to celebrate Christmas.

If the 13 December visit could not have been made by Baba in person, could he have appeared personally on 24 December? All the witnesses who saw the visitor on both occasions agree that it was definitely the same person.

Besides his having appeared in response to Sailaja's cry for help and subsequently healing her, many more indications of ostensibly paranormal powers were demonstrated. According to the Raos, Baba seems to have known all the family members and to have addressed each in his or her mother tongue, thus using three different languages. He presented them with eight gifts, produced in Sai Baba's customary manner. It is not clear if all or only some of the gifts were produced by a wave of his hand since we failed to ask that question in several of the interviews. However, the vibuti and the medicine for Mrs Nair were produced in this typical Sai Baba fashion. The gifts received by the Rao family were shown to the early investigators in 1965 and to us in 1973. The four predictions Baba made appear to have been correct: that Mr Rao's father would come to Manjeri; that while there he would perform a cleansing rite; that Dr Menon would bring to them from Palghat two more song books in the Malayalam language (Baba had already produced one by a wave of his hand); and that a son would be born to the Raos (although Mrs Rao had a history of miscarriages). Lastly, on the occasion of the second visit, we are told, Baba entered a locked house.

These signs of paranormal power seem to have convinced the Raos that their visitor was indeed Sai Baba. It was reassuring to them that Baba recognized them when they visited his ashram for the first time years later with their newborn son. Mr Rao told us: 'He (Baba) mentioned in Puttaparti what was talked about in Manjeri, and therefore (he) should be the same man.' The Raos and some of the witnesses were also impressed by the vibuti that, according to them, began to appear on Baba's picture after the second appearance. They seemed to interpret it as a sort of 'seal of approval' by the master.

Two of the people who told us they had seen vibuti appear on the picture were not Baba's devotees: Mr Bhaskaran, who was quite hostile to the whole matter and called the visitor a 'scoundrel', and Devada Moosad, who was not interested in the case.

Could this all have been a hoax, organized by Baba's devotees for publicity purposes? Neither the Raos nor their neighbours who testified were, they claim, followers of Baba at the time the events took place. The Rao family worshipped Hindu deities and gave special devotion to Shirdi Baba. Because Sathya Sai Baba claims to be a reincarnation of Shirdi Baba, the Raos had hung his picture beside others in their shrine room. They were, however, not then members of Sai Baba's organization and were not familiar with his songs. It was only after Baba's visits that they became his ardent devotees. It would have been risky to involve such people, mildly interested at best, in an elaborate fraud.

Another possible counter explanation is that witnesses at Venkatagiri falsely claimed that Baba was there on 13 December 1964. When we interviewed the Raja of Venkatagiri, he at first brushed us off, protesting that nine years was too far back for him to remember exact dates. He and his associates vaguely recollected Baba's having been there sometime in December, but he was correct in commenting that, for our purpose, an approximate date would not be helpful. Later, when the idea of checking palace records was brought up by his associates, he agreed to it. Prof Kasturi made no mention in his book of the existence of palace records. We assume that, had these records been 'doctored' for publicity purposes, they certainly would have been used before our visit.

When a person is said to have been physically in two places at the same time, the incident is described as bilocation. That this can in fact happen is certainly at the limit of what most people can believe. In ancient as well as modern literature, however, there are some claims of this kind. Iamblicus (died *c* AD 330), the Hellenic philosopher who wrote a book on the life of Pythagoras, states that Pythagoras' earlier biographers (whose writings no longer exist):

> confidently assert, that in one and the same day he was present in Metapontum in Italy and Tauromenium in Sicily, and discoursed in common with his disciples in both places, though these cities are separated from each other by many stadia both by land and sea, and cannot be passed through in a great number of days. (p. 72)

In modern times the most interesting claims of bilocation probably concern the Italian monk, Padre Pio, about whom there are numerous claims of other miracles as well; the case for his beatification was opened in 1969 (Carty, 1973). It would take too long to review these two cases here, but I mention them because they do show some similarities to the two Sai Baba cases. The nature of these cases remains a puzzle to those who study them.

Notes

[1] For much of the material in this chapter I am indebted to Dr Osis.

[2] An Ayurveda doctor is a practitioner of medicine who also has been trained in methods of Indian folk medicine as described in ancient Ayurvedas.

[3] Baba's special kind of robe is unique even in India. In all our extensive travels, we have never seen anyone wearing a similar one.

TABLE 1

Events witnessed by the Raos and their neighbours and documentation

Visitor	R.M. Rao	Mrs Rao	Sailaja	Mrs T.B. Mousad	Janaki Nair	Sarojina Amma	Venu Gopal	K.M. Kutty	K. Lakshmi Kutty	Padmanabhan Nair	Documentation P.A. Menon	P.K. Paniker	Letter
A: Similarities to Sai Baba's physical appearance.	√√	√√	√√	√	√	√	√	√	√√	√			
1. Observed him from outdoors (√) indoors at RMR's (√√).	√√	√√			√√		√√	√√		√√		√√	√√
2. Looked like SB (√√); some resemblance (√); none (-).	√√	√√	√√		√	√√	√√	-	√√	√√	√√	√√	√√
3. Bushy hair like SB's (√); different (-).	√	√	√		covered		√	-	√	√	√	√	
4. Robe like SB wears (√); different (-).	√	√	√	√		√	√	√	√	√	√	√	
5. Robe colour: red, yellow, orange, rose First visit: (R,Y,O,RO) second visit: (R,Y,O,RO).	Y RO	Y R	O	Y	Y		Y	O Y	O	O	R	R	
6. Robe fabric fine (√); coarse (-).	√	√	√							-		√	
7. Robe pressed (√); wrinkled (-).		√						√	√	√			
8. Stature like SB's (√); different (-).	√	√	√		√			√		√			

TABLE 1 (continued)

Events witnessed by the Raos and their neighbours and documentation

Visitor	R.M. Rao	Mrs Rao	Sailaja	Mrs T.B. Mousad	Janaki Nair	Sarojina Amma	Venu Gopal	K.M. Kutty	K. Lakshmi Kutty	Padmanabhan Nair	Documentation		
											P.A. Menon	P.K. Paniker	Letter
9. Complexion like SB's (√); different (-).	√	√											
10. Voice like SB's (√); unlike (-).	√	√	√										
11. SB photograph identified in a 'blind' test (√).												√	
B. Similarities to Sai Baba's behavioural characteristics													
1. Sat in bhajan room (√); under photo of SB (√√).	√√	√	√		√√				√		√√	√√	√√
2. Sang bhajan songs (√) typical SB songs (√√); taught songs (√√√).	√√ / √√√	√ / √√√	√√ / √√√					√√	√		√√ / √√√	√√	√ / √√√
3. Language spoken: Malayalam (M); Kanarese (K); Tamil (T).	T K M	T K			M			M		T K M	T K M	T K M	T K M
4. Blessed and distributed sacramental food (prasad) (√).	√	√		√						√		√	√
5. Tried to heal Nair (N); Sailaja (S); Moosad (M).	S M	S N M	S	M	N S		M					S	

TABLE 1 (continued)

Events witnessed by the Raos and their neighbours and documentation

Visitor	R.M. Rao	Mrs Rao	Sailaja	Mrs T.B. Mousad	Janaki Nair	Sarojina Amma	Venu Gopal	K.M. Kutty	K. Lakshmi Kutty	Padmanabhan Nair	P.A. Menon	P.K. Paniker	Letter
											Documentation		
6. Gave vibuti (V); medicine (M).	V	V M	V	V	V		V	V	V			V	V
7. 'Created' or materialized it by wave of hand (√).	√	√			√	√		√	√			√	
8. Gave presents to the Rao family (√).	√	√	√		√	√		√			√	√	√
9. Alms or favours: Requested (√); not mentioned (-).	-	-	-	-	-	-	-	-	-	-	-	-	-
C. Details of sequence and participation.													
1. First visit: Saw SB arrive (√); attended bhajan (√√); don't know which visit (-).	√√	√√	√√	√	√√	√	√ √√	√	√√	√ √√			√√
2. Second visit: a.m.; p.m.; saw SB (√); attended bhajan (√√).	√√ p.m.	√√ p.m. and a.m.			p.m. √√			√√(?) p.m.			p.m.	p.m. a.m.	√√ p.m. and a.m.
3. Only heard about the second visit from either Mr or Mrs Rao (√).			√										
4. Number of people present at bhajan.	50	150					many			40	40 25-30		

				Documentation		
	Mr R	Mrs R	Sailaja	Letter	Paniker	Menon
A. General Activities of Sai Baba 1. Talked, chanted, sang	√	√	√	√	√	√
2. Performed devotional ceremony	√	√	√	√	√	√
3. Hung picture		√				√
4. Ate	√	√	√	√	√	√
5. Bathed	√	√		√		
6. Rested	√	√		√	√	√
B. Presents which were given (G) or appeared (A). 1. Songbook in Malayalam	A	G	G		G	A
2. piece of fine clothing for Sailaja	G		G	A		G
3. Locket		G				A
4. Ring	A				Janaki	
5. Golden leaf	G	G				A
6. Tumbler	A					A
7. Rudraksha beads	A	G	G	A	G	A
8. Shell beads	A	G	G	G	G	
9. Vibuti	A	A	G		G	A

TABLE 2

Events witnessed only by the Rao family

TABLE 2 (continued)						
Events witnessed only by the Rao family						
				Documentation		
C. Activities indicative of the identity of Sai Baba or his powers	Mr R	Mrs R	Sailaja	Letter	Paniker	Menon
1. Immediately asked for Sailaja at the first appearance.	√		√			
2. Said he came in response to Sailaja's prayer, or bhakta.	√	√	√	√		√
3. Demanded to be received in puja room	√	√	√	√	√	√
4. Healed Sailaja of chronic illness in 3 days' time.	√	√	√		√	
5. Addressed each in his mother tongue: Tamil, Kanarese, Malayalam.	√	√		√	√	√
6. Predicted the visit of RMR's father.	√	√	√	√		
7. Predicted father's cleansing ceremony	√			√		
8. Predicted birth of son (history of miscarriages after Sailaja's birth).	√	√				√
9. Predicted (after producing a book by the wave of his hand) that A. Menon would bring two similar books.	√					
10. Second visit: Made his appearance in a locked house.	√	√		√	√	√
11. House was lighted (no secrecy).	√	√		√	√	√

TABLE 2 (continued)

Events witnessed only by the Rao family

	Mr R	Mrs R	Sailaja	Documentation		
				Letter	Paniker	Menon
12. Told where Sailaja had gone.	√			√	√	
13. Said he would substitute for Sailaja in preparing for bhajan.	√	√		√	√	
14. Correctly interpreted Rao's mood and identified his family's troubles.	√	√		√		√
15. Insisted on simple food.	√	√		√	√	
16. Showed thorough familiarity with Sai Baba's personal history.	√	√				
17. Discussed predominantly spiritual matters.	√	√		√		
18. Recognized the Raos when they visited·Puttaparti later on.	√					
19. Mentioned in Puttaparti what was talked about in Manjeri.	√					
20. Statement about going to Kalahasti verified later.	√		√	√	√	√
21. Observed vibuti falling from the photo of Sai Baba after his visit.	√	√		also	√ Janaki	√

29
Extrasensory Perception

One facet of Baba's life we have not dealt with specifically; his alleged extrasensory abilities which, for Indians are commonly taken as signs of his omniscience. Does he in fact read peoples' minds? Has he expressed knowledge of contemporary faraway events, or such that still lie in the future? Claims are abundant as can be seen in earlier chapters. Our small-sample survey revealed a comparable view of him.

The interviewees were asked: 'What miraculous phenomenon did you first observe in Sai Baba's presence?'. 20% of those who remembered their first observation reported mind reading whereas 75% claimed to have witnessed a materialization. These proportions seem to reflect the success Baba has in convincing the more sophisticated people of his two-sided paranormal gifts, 'mind-reading' and 'mind over matter' – ESP and PK as they are termed in parapsychology; the physical phenomena are prominent.

Unquestionably Sai Baba often exercises 'mind-reading' on those he meets. Several instances are given in earlier chapters, such as the case of Varadu. The question is how successful he is in doing his mind-reading paranormally. Is he using more than mere clever guessing and the sharp judgement of people that he undeniably possesses?

26 of 29 interviewees had observed Baba exercise mind-reading on themselves. 19 reported he had done so fully correctly, 5 only partially correctly whereas 2 ex-devotees considered his endeavours sheer clever guessing.

There is no reason to doubt that Baba sometimes goes wrong in his statements when exercising his mind-reading. I recall one Australian lady, probably in her late thirties, who I met in Puttaparti a few years ago. One day at darshan time Baba briefly spoke to her: 'You should get married', he said. In fact she was married, and as I met her just after that darshan she was walking towards the bus to Bangalore to receive her husband at the airport as he was flying in from Australia. Baba did not know this woman, and had only seen her a few times. She was not an attractive lady, careless about her looks and dress and perhaps from that Baba inferred that she was unmarried.

There are many instances when Baba fares better in his statements than he apparently did with the Australian woman. Once during crowded festival days in Puttaparti I shared a room for a few days with a New York businessman and manufacturer of expensive carpets, Mr. Harry Patterson. He impressed me then as a thoughtful, reliable man of an enquiring mind and several later meetings did not change that impression. He gave the following account:

> On 7 December 1977 I had an interview with Swami in Whitefield. After talking to me for a while he asked me if I had any questions. I explained to him that my daughter, living in Sydney, Australia, had been expecting a baby in November. My wife had left in November to stay with our daughter and since I had had no knowledge of just what had happened to our daughter as I had been travelling in India. I asked Swami about it and he said: 'Oh yes, baby girl two days ago, mother and baby fine'.
>
> Later that same day I left for Bombay and flew straight on to New York. There I learnt that a healthy baby girl had been born on 5th December, two days before my interview with Swami. I had absolutely no indication of when the baby had been born. Actually it had been due about the middle of November and I thought surely that she would have the baby around that time.

No contemporary written statements exist to document this case and when I met Harry Patterson's wife Hilda in New York in 1982 she – in no way devoted to Baba – did not recall that her husband had told her of this incident.

Another question in the survey: 'Has Sai Baba described to you an event occurring at the same time at a distant place?' 10 did not recall such an experience, two remembered instances they could then not verify, but 17 reported having observed him describe a distant event. In one case our respondent later learnt that Baba's description was wrong, but 16 claimed that he had done so fully correctly. Unfortunately for us none of these cases of alleged clairvoyance was of a kind that allowed us an independant verification from two or more witnesses.

Predictions are not a prominent feature with Sai Baba. Only to half of the 29 interviewees of our survey had he made predictions about their future. To 9 of these interviewees Baba's statements were reported as fully correct but with 4 of them he proved either partially or fully wrong. To one lady devotee hoping for a baby he had predicted that she would have one but she never did. He advised a close devotee to let his brother go to Delhi for a job interview. Contrary to Baba's predictions the brother did not get the job, only costly travel expenses.

On one item Baba was by any standard astoundingly successful. He had already made some very correct statements in his youth about his own future. Most of the people who spent some time with Swami before 1959 clearly remembered him telling that huge crowds ('hundreds of thousands of people') would come to see him and that the old devotees would only be able to see him from a distance. This is reported in several earlier chapters. He then also described the enormous growth of Prashanti Nilayam, now an independent township with many large and imposing buildings; at festival times it changes into a colourful buzzing city. Mr Eswar told me a related incident that he had witnessed. When the new mandir was being built in Puttaparti, Eswar's father asked Baba why he wanted the mandir so large. Baba replied that it would, in due time, become much too small. Now on a normal non-festival weekday only a part of the crowd gets into the mandir for bhajan. At festivals, even the huge Poorna Chandra hall, said to be one of the biggest assembly halls in Asia, takes only a part of the crowd that assembles.

Baba's early statements about his future life are attested by numerous witnesses and are remarkable, however we may interpret them. Are they genuine predictions or signs of visions of glory at an early age, that he was so strikingly successful in achieving? Did that poor, young boy in a remote Indian village far from anywhere foresee his own future, or did he make his future the way he already then envisioned it? It is not easy to get across to the reader the unusualness of that future; the image and popularity that Baba has attained in India, though he is certainly also disputed. Perhaps it helps to state that he is frequently visited by the highest officials of the land; ministers of the state and central governments, governors, members of the supreme court, generals and chiefs of the armed forces. Indian VIPs seem proud to be seen in Baba's company, or hold speeches at his festivals or at the inaugurations of his schools or colleges. He predicted this some 30-40 years ago as a youth. No wonder some fellow-villagers thought that he must be crazy and others that he must suffer from megalomania.

One of Baba's predictions I will leave with the readers to check in due time; he has frequently repeated that he will live to be 94 years of age; that is, that he will die in the year 2020 or 2021.

30
Closing Words

In the early chapters of this book we described some interviews and meetings that Dr Osis and I had with Sathya Sai Baba. The reader may ask, what since? There were several further interviews with Baba, especially two in 1976 when I went with my son Haraldur, and a long interview when I went alone to India in 1980. In spite of great and ever-increasing crowds around him, on all my visits he came over to me when he first saw me and briefly exchanged some pleasantries. He produced several objects in all these later interviews, and also on a few other occasions when we met briefly in the open. Once, very spontaneously, he handed me a good piece of rock candy when he unexpectedly learnt from me that I was leaving the country that very day.

Observations gathered in these interviews added nothing basically new to those earlier reported. It was more of the same thing. He was always cordial and friendly, but when the discussion turned to experiments there was a silent refusal. Religion was what he wanted to talk about. Sometimes he seemed to want to do something that I might find valuable, but then apparently he did not understand what constituted good evidence for me, or my colleagues for that matter.

Baba is a man of great and unpredictable spontaneity. In 1980 I decided in an interview, for a change, not to pester him with requests that he had earlier turned down nor to argue with him about the necessity for controlled research of his gifts as I was wont to do. Then he seemed irritated and reprimanded me for not doing so. In the interview room with me there were a few people that I had not previously met. Apparently in a move to show me something special he asked an elderly gentleman, who was sitting with us on the floor for a ring he had on one of his fingers. He took it in his hand, held it before our eyes and said to me: 'See scientist, within a minute I will change this into different size, style and shape'. He gave it to me to examine, took it back, closed it in his fist, blew on it three times and handed me a ring that was markedly different. Then he exclaimed to those around him in boyish naïvety and with a triumphant look on his face: 'How can science explain that?!'

Any magician might, when prepared, do this by exchanging rings in his hand. But the nagging question was, did he do it that way?

In a private interview that followed we had some arguments about the value of science and I listened to a long monologue on the importance of spirituality. When I told him that I was interviewing a number of his older devotees and was planning to write a book on him, he urged me to meet some of the students that had attended his schools or colleges and who were now active in his movement. (Later I found them more reluctant to talk freely than the older devotees who were at a greater distance from him). Finally he produced a locket to give to my son who already had two from our trip in 1976. There was always that steady stream of objects from him. My estimate is still about twenty to forty pieces a day.

The aim of this has not been to convince the reader about the genuineness or otherwise of the phenomena. Rather it has been primarily to present the testimony of several key witnesses who had been in a position for extensive or prolonged observation of Sai Baba, so that the reader can form a judgment of his or her own, and perhaps be reminded of some enormous potentialities that may lie dormant somewhere within all human beings.

The attentive reader may find discrepancies in the descriptions of the witnesses, and even within some of the testimonies. We have not tried to gloss over them. Each witness has his or her own biases, preconceptions and personal approach.

The question of 'proof' is generally a cumbersome one for psychical phenomena. One reason is that most scientists believe that psychic phenomena violate some of the most basic and best attested physical laws that science has established; hence for them a stronger proof is demanded than for most other occurrences in nature. The second reason is the apparent evasiveness of psychic phenomena and how often such instances may be open to various interpretations, all of which have to be excluded before we can be tolerably sure about the paranormal nature of the event. This is particularly the case with 'real-life' or spontaneous phenomena but less so with scientific experiments where the environment is under full control and observation by the scientist.

In science, experimentation is traditionally the ideal way to certainty about the nature of any phenomena. In our research on Sai Baba this approach was closed to us. By that criterion there is no evidence of genuine paranormal phenomena having been produced by Sathya Sai Baba.

Experimentation, however, is not the way most questions of truth or falseness, fact or fallacy are settled in daily life; nor indeed is it the only way in certain branches of science, such as in some of the social sciences that involve case studies and field work. *Experimental* science has one way of approaching truth; *descriptive* science another. Our judicial systems have evolved interrogation and corroboration of witnesses, investigating relevant contemporary documents and so on, as ways of accruing evidence.

Scientists are certainly not always free of biases in their observations and interpretations, but human testimony is based on perception that is always selective, on memory that is far from being computer-like and that also corrodes with time. Memories and perceptions can also be affected by expectations and preconceptions, both of our own and of those around us. Some psychologists may even argue that ethnic or cultural groups may vary in their reliability as witnesses; here I think of an Indian scholar-friend of mine who did not think too highly of his own ethnic group in this respect.

In dealing with these well-known weaknesses of human testimony our courts rely primarily on quantity of testimony or on the consensus of witnesses. This has been our approach. Numerous followers – and critics as well – with extensive observations of Sai Baba, arrive at a general consensus about the paranormality of the frequent appearance of objects in his presence or on his body on certain occasions.

Of course, any vigilant sceptic will certainly come up with the sleight of hand hypothesis. During a brief visit to Puttaparti an amateur magician viewed Baba from a distance as he produced vibuti by a wave of his hand. Such a poor observation sufficed him to conclude that Baba used sleight of hand, though another skilful amateur magician, Dr Fanibunda, with his plentiful experience of Baba, considers this hypothesis absurd. In my view such a meagre, poor observation does not prove anything either way, though he, I am told, felt no need to further examine the evidence. This example shows how easily one may come to quick superficial solutions pro or contra by a shallow weighing of only a tiny portion of available evidence.

Bibliography

Anand, B.K., Chhina, G.S., and Singh, B. Some Aspects of Electro-encephalographic Studies in Yogis. Electro-encephalography and Clinical Neurophysiology 13 (1961): 452-456.

Akhilananda, Swami. Hindu Psychology. London: Routledge and Kegan Paul, 1965. (First published in 1948).

Bender, H. New Developments in Poltergeist Research. Proceedings of the Parapsychological Association 6 (1969): 81-102.

Brooke, R.T. The Lord of the Air. Berkhamsted, Herts: Lion Publishing, 1976.

Brunton, P. A Search in Secret India. New York: E. P. Dutton, 1935.

Carrington, H. Eusapia Palladino and Her Phenomena. New York: B.W. Dodge, 1909.

Carrington, H. The Physical Phenomena of Spiritualism. (2nd ed.) New York: Dodd, Mead, 1920.

Carty, C. Padre Pio the Stigmatist. Rockford, Illinois: Tan, 1973.

Chari, C.T.K. Parapsychological Studies and Literature in India. International Journal of Parapsychology 2(1) (1960):24-36.

Chari, C.T.K. Regurgitation, Mediumship and Yoga. Journal of the Society for Psychical Research 47 (1973): 156-172.

Chari, C.T.K. Correspondence: On the Phenomena of Sai Baba. Journal of the American Society for Psychical Research 72 (1978):66-69.

Chari, C.T.K. Some Questions about 'Psi-Genetics.' (Letter to the Editor). Parapsychological Journal of South Africa 3(1) (1982):50-53.

Cowan, E. Sai Baba and the Resurrection of Walter Cowan. In Ruhela S.P. and Robinson D., Sai Baba and His Message. (6th Edition) Ghaziabad, U.P., India: Vikas Publishing House, 1982.

Cox, H. Turning East. New York: Simon and Schuster, 1977.

Crookes, W. Researches in the Phenomena of Spiritualism. London: J. Burns, 1874.

Dass, R. Miracle of Love. Stories about Neem Karoli Baba. New York: E.P. Dutton, 1979.

Dingwall, E.J. Some Human Oddities: Studies in the Uncanny and the Fanatical. London: Home and Van Thal, 1947.

Dunraven, Earl of. Experiences in Spiritualism with D.D. Home. Proceedings of the Society for Psychical Research, 35 (1924):1-285. (First published in 1870).

Emmons, C.F. Chinese Ghosts and ESP: A Study of Paranormal Beliefs and Experiences. Metuchen, N.J. : Scarecrow Press, 1982.

Fanibunda, E.B. Vision of the Divine. Bombay: E.B. Fanibunda, 1980. (First published in 1976.)

Fielding, E., Baggally, W. W., and Carrington, H. Report on a Series of Sittings with Eusapia Palladino. Proceedings of the Society for Psychical Research 23 (1909): 306-569.

Fodor, N. Encyclopaedia of Psychic Science. New York: University Books, 1966. (First published in 1933.)

Gauld, A. and Cornell, A.D. Poltergeists. London: Routledge and Kegan Paul, 1979.

Geley, G. La lumiere vivante metapsychique. Revue metapsychique. No. 4 (1922): 169-181.

Green, E.E., and Green, A.M. Beyond Biofeedback. New York: Dell, 1977.

Gregory, A. The Strange Case of Rudi Schneider. Metuchen, N.J. : The Scarecrow Press, 1985.

Gurney, E., Myers, F.W.H., and Podmore, F. Phantasms of the Living. (2 vols.) London: Trubner, 1886.

Hack, G. W. Modern Psychic Mysteries, Millesimo Castle, Italy. London: Rider, n.d. (1929)

Haft, L.L. Abstracts of Chinese Reports on Parapsychology. European Journal of Parapsychology 4 (1982): 399-402.

Hannesson, G. Remarkable Phenomena in Iceland. Journal of the American Society for Psychical Research 18 (1924):239-272.

Haraldsson, E. Representative National Surveys of Psychic Phenomena: Iceland, Great Britain, Sweden, USA and Gallup's Multinational Survey. Journal of the Society for Psychical Research 53 (1985): 145-158.

Haraldsson, E., and Osis, K. The Appearance and Disappearance of Objects in the Presence of Sri Sathya Sai Baba. Journal of the American Society for Psychical Research 71 (1977): 33-43.

Hasted, J. The Metal-Benders. London: Routledge and Kegan Paul, 1981.

Hilgard, E. Divided Consciousness: Multiple Controls in Human Thought and Action. New York: John Wiley & Sons, 1977.

Iamblichus. Life of Pythagoras. London: John M. Watkins, 1965.

Jacolliot, L. Occult Science in India. New York: The Metaphysical Publishing Company, 1901. (First published in French in 1884.)

Jenkins, E. The Shadow and the Light: A Defence of Daniel Dunglas Home, the Medium. London: Hamish Hamilton, 1982.

Jones, F. The Spiritual Instructions of Saint Seraphim of Sarov. Los Angeles: The Dawn Horse Press, 1973.

Kasturi, N. Sai Baba: The Life of Bhagavan Sri Sathya Sai Baba. Part 1. (2nd American ed.) Justin, California: Sai Baba Society, 1971.

Kasturi, N. Sathyam Sivam Sundaram. Part III. Bangalore: Sri Sathya Sai Publication and Education Foundation, n.d. (ca 1972)

Kasturi, N. Sathyam, Sivam, Sundaram: The Life of Bhagavan Sri Sathya Sai Baba. Part II. Bangalore: Sri Sathya Sai Publication and Education Foundation, n.d. (1973?)

Kasturi, N. Sathyam Sivam Sundaram. Part IV. Andhra Pradesh: Sri Sathya Sai Books and Publications, 1980.

Koestler, A. The Lotus and the Robot. London: Hutchinson, 1960.

Kolhari, C.K., Bordia, A., and Gupta, O.P. Studies on a Yogi During an Eight Day Confinement in a Sealed Underground Pit. Indian Journal of Medical Research 61 (1973): 1645-1651.

Lombroso, C. After Death – What? Boston: Small, Maynard, 1909.

McCarthy, C.W. Rigid Tests of the Occult. 1904.

McKenzie, B. An 'Apport' Medium, Mr T. Lynn. Psychic Science, 8 (1929):129-137.

May, E.C. and Jahagirdar, K.T. From Where Does the Kum-Kum Come? A Material-ization Attempt. In J.D. Morris, W.G. Roll, and R.L. Morris, (Eds.) Research in Parapsychology 1975. Metuchen, N.J. : Scarecrow Press, 1976.

Murphet, H. Sai Baba, Man of Miracles. London: Frederick Muller, 1971.

Murphet, H. Sai Baba Avatar: A New Journey into Power and Glory. San Diego: Birth Day Publishing Company, 1977.

Narasimhaiah, H. Letter to Sathya Sai Baba, 'Sunday', June 2, 1976, September 5, 1976.

Nielsson, H. Some of My Experiences with a Physical Medium in Reykjavik. In C. Vett (Ed.), Le Compte Rendu Officiel du Premier Congres International des Recherches Psychiques a Copenhague. Copenhagen, 1922.

Nielsson, H. Poltergeist Phenomena in Connection with a Medium, Observed for a Length of Time, Some of Them in Full Light. Psychic Science 4 (1925): 90-111.

Nolen, W.A. Healing: A Doctor in Search of a Miracle. New York: Random House, 1974.

Oman, J.C. The Mystics, Ascetics, and Saints of India. London: T. Fisher Unwin, 1903.

Organ, T.W. Hinduism: Its Historical Development. New York: Barron's Educational Series, 1974.

Osborne, A. The Incredible Sai Baba. London: Rider, 1958.

Osis, K., Bokert, E., and Carlson, M.L. Dimensions of the Meditative Experience. Journal of Transpersonal Psychology 5 (1973): 109-135.

Osis, K. and Haraldsson, E. OBEs in Indian Swamis: Sathya Sai Baba and Dadaji. In J.D. Morris, W.G. Roll and R.L. Morris, (Eds.) Research in Parapsychology 1975. Metuchen, N.J. : Scarecrow Press, 1976.

Osis, K. and Haraldsson, E. Parapsychological Phenomena Associated with Sri Sathya Sai Baba. The Christian Parapsychologist 3 (1979): 159-63.

Owen, A.R.G. Can We Explain the Poltergeist? New York: Garrett, 1964.

Philostratus. Life of Apollonius. (Translation by C.P. Jones. Edited by G. W. Bowersock.) London: Penguin Books, 1970.

Podmore, F. Mediums of the 19th Century. (2 vols.) New York: University Books, 1963. (First published in 1902.)

Polo, M. The Book of Ser Marco Polo. (Translation by Sir Henry Jule.) New York: Charles Scribner's Sons, 1929.

Pulos, L. Evidence of Macro-Psychokinetic Effects Produced by Thomas of Brazil. Psi Search, 1(3) (1982):27-40.

Richet, C. Thirty Years of Psychical Research. (Trans. by S. de Brath.) New York: Macmillan, 1923. (First published in French in 1922.)

Rogo, D.S. Miracles: A Parascientific Inquiry into Wondrous Phenomena. New York: Dial Press, 1982.

Roll, W.G. The Poltergeist. New York: New American Library, 1974. (First published in 1972.)

Ruffin, C.B. Padre Pio: The True Story. Huntington, Indiana: Our Sunday Visitor, 1982.

Saint Gregory the Great: Dialogues. (Translated by O.J. Zimmerman) Washington, D.C.: Catholic University of America Press/Consortium Books, 1959.

Sandweiss, S.H. Sai Baba: The Holy Man and the Psychiatrist. San Diego: Birth Day Publishing Company, 1975.

Schrenck-Notzing, (A.F.) Baron von. Phenomena of Materialisation. (2nd revised ed.) New York: Dutton, 1920. (First published in German in 1914.)

Shuhuang, L., Zhungchi, Z., Weiyi, L., Yuzung, H., Pinghuei, Z., Hanli, Z., Jia, S., Zenwu, D., Shiung, D., Yu, Z., Xuekai, Z., Fang, Z., and Zexiang, Z. Some Experiments with the Moving of Objects through 'Exceptional Functions of the Human Body'. Psi Research, 2(1) (1983):4-24. (Translation of a Chinese article in Zitran Zazhi, 4.9, 1981).

Sheehan, P.W. and Perry, C.W. Methodologies of Hypnosis. Hillsdale, N.J.: Lawrence Erlbaum Associates, 1976.

Schulman, A. Baba. New York: Viking Press, 1971.

Smart, N. The Religious Experience of Mankind. (2nd ed.) New York: Charles Scribners, 1976.

Thakur, J. Challenge to Sai Baba: Is he God? 'Sunday', 4(24) September 5, 1976, pp. 6-13.

Thurston, H. The Physical Phenomena of Mysticism. London: Burns Oates, 1952.

Trench, R.C. Notes on the Miracles of Our Lord. Grand Rapids, Michigan: Baker Book House, 1949. (First dated edition 1949).

Tyrrell, G.N.M. Apparitions. New York: Pantheon Books, 1953. (First published by the Society for Psychical Research in 1942.)

Wallace, A.R. Miracles and Modern Spiritualism. London: George Redway, 1896. (First published in 1874.)

Wenger, M.A., and Bagchi, B.K. Studies of Autonomic Functions in Practitioners of Yoga in India. Behavioral Science 6 (1961):312-323.

West, D.J. Eleven Lourdes Miracles. New York: Helix Press, 1957.

Zimmer, C. Biolumineñz: Leuchterscheinungen an Organismen und bei Medien. Psychische Studien 50 (1923):193-210.

Index

abisheikam, 115-16, 187
accomplices, explanation of materializations, 50-51, 207
Akkamma, 138
Aloyi Baba, 17
alteration of objects: 223; at a distance, 91; fruits, 114, 116, 188; iron beams, 87, 118; jasmine leaf, 109; Jesus Christ, 234; paper into ivory, 188; ring, 43-44, 45, 83, 91, 289-90; stamps, 84; stones into food, 187-88, 222, 223; water, 137-38, 162-63, 234; water into petrol, 138, 224, 234
altered states of consciousness, 46, 47
Amarendra Kumar, 96, 125-48, 215, 216, 224, 238, 252, 258, 258-59
Amba, Sai Baba, as, 93
American Society for Psychical Research, 14, 15, 34
Amist, 89
amrith: 19-20, 88, 109, 150, 152, 226; on photograph, 19-20
anand, 46
Angarika Munendra, 17
Antichrist, Sai Baba as, 61
anti-Sai Baba attitudes: sadhu, 116-17; sanyasin, 79; villagers, 81-82, 106-07, 127
Anupama Niranjana, 200
appearance of Sai Baba: 23-24; aura, 93; brilliant light, 97-98, 105-06, 115, 121; colors, 93; diferent form, 93, 107, 120, 134- 35, 169; incense smoke, 74
apparitions, 263-84
Appolonius of Tyana, 205
arati, 138
ardha chandra, 135
Ardha Nareeswar, Sai Baba as, 107
Arjuna, 130, 148, 165, 172, 253
attendants, 24, 131, 136, 156, 180, 207
automobile running on water, 91, 92, 138, 224
autosuggestion, 74
avatar: 60; Sai Baba as, 94-95, 129-30, 227

Bailey, Charles, 230
bakta, 114, 115
Balu, 163, 164
Balyogi Premvarni, 17
Banerjee, D.K., 35, 53, 65-75, 209
Banerjee, D.K., Mrs., 66, 209
Bangalore, University of, 199-204
Beri (Mrs.), 219

St. Bernardino Realino, 256-57
Bhagavan: 89; Sai Baba as, 89, 95, 96
Bhagavantam, S., 31, 35, 36, 38, 41, 53, 67-68, 202
Bharat Reddy, 209, 220-21, 223
Bhaskaran, K., 273, 277
Bhattacharya, P.K., 53, 65, 209, 237
bilocation: 263; Sai Baba, 31, 98-99, 103-04, 120, 263-78; compared with Western apparitions, 267, 268; healing, 269-70; Padre Pio, 278; Pythagoras, 278; trance, 120
Blitz, 205
Bock, Richard, 246
Brahman, Sai Baba as, 94
Brindavan, 35
Brooke, R.T., 61
Bukkapatnam, 55

Cape Comoron, 92
caste of Sai Baba, 55
Chakravarty, 66
chandan, 107, 238
Chandra Mohan, 17
Chandran (Mrs.), 261
changes in objects, see alteration of objects
Chari, C.T.K., 54, 149, 154, 160, 162, 167, 168, 169, 172, 173, 218, 233, 243
Charlton, Hilda, 276
Chidambara Iyer, 150
Chimnayananda, Swami, 178
Chinese investigation, 231-32
Chinjoli, Raja of, 144, 181
Chinjoli, Rani of, 144-45, 181
Chitravati river, 21
Christianity: healing, 233, 244; luminous phenomena, 255-57; miracles, 233-35; resuscitation of dead, 244; stigmatization, 239
clairvoyance of Sai Baba: 111, 142, 163-64, 168, 169; survey response, 287
Cowan, Elsie, 244, 247, 248
Cowan, Walter, 244-48
Craig, Wiley, 89
critics: Amarendra Kumar, 130, 147; Karanjia, R.K., 205; Narasimhaiah, 199-203; sadhu, 116-17; sanyasin, 79; see also ex-devotees
Crookes, William, 49

Dadaji, 17

296

KING ALFRED'S COLLEGE
LIBRARY